THE LANGUAGE-MAKERS

THE
LANGUAGE-MAKERS

ROY HARRIS

Professor of General Linguistics
in the University of Oxford

Cornell University Press

Ithaca, New York

© 1980 by Roy Harris

First published 1980 by Cornell University Press

Library of Congress Catalog Card Number 79-6029

International Standard Book Number 0-8014-1317-6

Printed in Great Britain by
Ebenezer Baylis and Son Limited
The Trinity Press, Worcester, and London

. . . lest even Knowledge should obstruct its own growth, and perform in some measure the part of ignorance and barbarity . . .

Preface

Harris's *Hermes*, from which come the various quotations prefaced to the following chapters, has an engraved frontispiece which depicts a statue of the god, in the form of a head wearing a winged helmet, placed upon a quadrilateral base bearing the letters of 'some old Alphabet'. The author explains why the god of language is represented as having no body: 'No other part of the human figure but the Head . . . was deemed requisite to rational Communication.'

The beheaded Hermes may be seen as symbolical of a fallacy which threatens to distort the perspective of much modern linguistic theorising. It is the idea that language is somehow separable from the rest of man's bodily activities and physical behaviour; the idea that a linguistic community is just a congregation of talking heads. It is to think of man primarily as a language-user, while forgetting that he is also, more importantly, a language-maker.

Languages do not come ready-made, any more than philosophies, religions, or forms of government. They are what men make them.

As language-makers, men need more than heads for talking. They need the physical and mental equipment to take part in the many social activities which alone provide the context for a relevant conceptualisation of what a language is.

For language-making involves much more than merely the construction of systems of signs. It is also the essential process by which men construct a cultural identity for themselves, and for the communities to which they see themselves as belonging.

I

Methinks I hear some Objector, demanding with an air of pleasantry, and ridicule 'Is there no speaking then without all this trouble? Do we not talk every one of us, as well unlearned, as learned; as well poor Peasants, as profound Philosophers?'

The concept of a language is one we take so much for granted that 'What is a language?' sounds a very odd question. It is certainly a question which is enough to put any right-minded person on his guard. It is too easily recognised as belonging to that class of bogus inquiries which are justified neither by a genuine desire for information nor by social obligation. Leaving aside children, mental defectives and linguistic theorists, what a language is is something already perfectly well understood by anyone who can ask what it is.

Accordingly, one who does ask 'What is a language?' must expect to be treated with the same suspicion as the traveller who inquires of the other passengers waiting on Platform 1 whether any of them can tell him the way to the station. Even Monsieur Jourdain did not manage to express himself in prose all his life without realising what he was doing. What he had failed to realise—and was absurdly delighted to discover—was that that was what prose was. But if for 'prose' we substitute 'a language', we shall not be able to find any plausible substitute for Monsieur Jourdain, at least among educated Europeans. Those of us who might feel generously inclined to give the benefit of the doubt to the engaging P. G. Wodehouse character who claimed not to know whether he could speak Spanish (on the ground that he had never tried) would stand no nonsense from one who claimed not to know whether he could speak a language at all (on the ground that he did not know what a language was).

1*

Not that the possibility of intelligent, rational beings to whom the concept of a language would be totally alien is to be rejected out of hand. It might be, for instance, that Martians communicate with each other solely by means of telepathy. If so, when the first Martian sets about learning English, 'What is a language?' is something he may at some point ask of his terrestrial teacher not as a bogus question but as a genuine one. Probably the best answer will be to tell him that a language is just the kind of thing he is engaged in learning. (That is all, in the final analysis, his teacher will know anyway.) But whatever his teacher replies, the Martian's concept of a language and his teacher's will never match, because language-using will always be integrated into the Martian's existence in an ineradicably different way. By teaching the telepathic Martian a language, we shall doubtless give him access to an insight into the human condition he did not have before. But that is a different matter from turning him into a human being.

Is, then, this apparently most fundamental of questions about languages to be dismissed in such a cavalier fashion? It would at least be honourable to try to read a subtlety or two into it. After all, is it not a question sometimes asked by persons who are in no position to plead ignorance, either of a Martian variety or any other? Yes, it is. Unfortunately, the difficulty often is understanding what it is the questioner wants for an answer. Or when that is clear, it is far from clear that his question was best put in that form in the first place. Not infrequently, it is a question put up by a linguistic theorist as a peg on which to hang his linguistic theorising. In such cases, the question takes its point from the answer immediately proposed. But it does not thereby become a *bona fide* question, any more than 'What is a free country?' becomes a *bona fide* question when it immediately emerges that the point of my asking it was to inflict on you my analysis of the restrictions imposed by current government policies.

It may be that 'What is a language?' is held to be a question to which some academic discipline, e.g. linguistics, is trying to give a definitive answer. But that would not automatically make it a genuine question either, since academic disciplines are not immune from making quite fundamental mistakes about the field of their inquiries. Furthermore, if we were to suppose that the existence of an academic discipline guaranteed the genuineness of the most general questions that could be formulated under its auspices, we should presumably have to grant that the existence of psychology was an academic warrant for the question 'What is mind?', and the existence of philosophy likewise for the question 'What is truth?' But it is far from clear that 'What is mind?' and 'What is truth?' are questions which have any academic warrant whatsoever.

In particular, there may be a layman's temptation to suppose that 'What is a language?' must be a question like 'What is electricity?' That is to say, although we may in practice know what it is – in the sense that we do not mistake it for anything else, or go manifestly wrong in our practical dealings with it—we may none the less legitimately ask 'What is it?' at some higher level of inquiry. So although as practical householders we know what electricity is when it comes to switching on lights, mending fuses, paying the electricity bill, and getting other electric shocks, we may claim that we none the less do not understand what electricity 'really' is. In such cases, the question 'What is electricity?' seems to call for a formulation of the concept in terms quite different from those drawn from the householder's banal experiences. It invites some kind of scientific or technical definition which will capture the 'essential nature' of electrical phenomena. Correspondingly it might be supposed that there is a higher level of inquiry at which the question 'What is a language?' may be raised, where the 'essential nature' of languages is scientifically defined, and where the ordinary language-user's mundane language-using is, if not quite irrelevant, at least left far behind.

If there is a temptation to suppose something like this, it is a temptation best resisted; at least until it has been shown that there is anything interesting to be gained by yielding to it. Languages are not like electricity. The language-user already has the only concept of a language worth having. Whereas the electricity-user does not automatically have the only concept of electricity worth having, or indeed any concept of electricity at all. Belief in some superior concept of a language, to which only the language expert has access, is probably the result of confusing the concept of a language with knowledge of what there is to know about languages.

A contributory cause may be the confusing fact that it is open to the linguistic theorist to introduce his own definition of terms like *language*. He may say, for example, 'By a language I shall mean an infinite set of fully grammatical sentences.' If he can get anyone else to understand such a definition, good luck to him. All that shows is the kind of difference there is between linguistics and, say, geometry. It is not open to a geometer to define *triangle*, and say 'By a triangle I shall mean a plane three-sided figure.' If, *qua* geometer, he uses the term *triangle* at all, what he shall mean by it is already defined for him in advance. Not so for the linguistic theorist and *language*. In linguistics, if we are to believe Saussure, it is the point of view that creates the object.[1] Whether or not one agrees, it would be foolish to object to the theorist's right to introduce stipulative definitions of the term *language*. Such definitions do not tell us what a language is (in case we did not know). But an essential condition of their being any use at all is that they should not be misconstrued as capturing some 'truer' concept of a language, of which the unenlightened ordinary language-user has but a blurred and inferior version.

* * *

To say that a language-user already has the only concept of a language worth having is not to claim that all language-users have the same concept of a language; nor that such a concept is simply a reflexion of man's intuitive awareness of his own linguistic capacities. We may properly ask where a concept of a language comes from, and what purpose it serves. Unfortunately, so familiar is our concept of a language and so easily taken for granted that such questions may at first sight appear just as idle or perverse as 'What is a language?' But they turn out not to be. To start off, it might be asked how far one's concept of a language is based on what one has been taught about languages.

A pointer here is provided by the apparent willingness of the educated European to entertain certain rather remarkable propositions concerning languages. For example, among the most remarkable is the proposition that languages are translatable. In no way is this something which could plausibly be said to be intuitively obvious. An isolated monoglot community having only the most tenuous contacts with its linguistically alien neighbours would have no reason for supposing that languages were in principle translatable. The European, on the other hand, has this assumption incorporated from the start into the basic framework of his education.

[1] *Cours de linguistique générale*, 2nd ed., p. 23.

He is brought up to regard the words of his native language as items which have their equivalents, more or less, in other languages. For him, the world would be an entirely different place were it the case that no one had yet discovered how to build the linguistic bridge of translation between different linguistic communities. His concept of a language is one which thus intrinsically accommodates the principle of translatability. He may not be brought up as a bilingual, but he is brought up, whether he likes it or not, as a potential bilingual; and this makes a fundamental difference to his grasp of what a language is. His native language may be English, and he may know no other, nor wish to; but however ingrained his chauvinism, he knows full well that but for the grace of God he might be speaking French. That this is so has a lot to do with the linguistic history and geography of Europe, which has been a more powerful and more pervasive force in the shaping of European culture than is commonly recognised.

No less remarkable are certain other propositions which the European finds no difficulty in taking in his stride. In 1580 Goropius Becanus of Amsterdam argued that the sacred language of the priests of ancient Egypt was in fact Dutch. In 1786 Sir William Jones suggested that Sanskrit, Greek and Latin were all derived from a common parent language. It makes little difference that posterity decided that Goropius Becanus was barking up entirely the wrong tree whereas Sir William Jones was not. The point is that in order to entertain such propositions at all one needs a considerably more sophisticated concept of what a language is than could plausibly be arrived at without certain quite specific forms of cultural conditioning. The concept of a language which is required has to be such as to admit the possibility in principle of the same language cropping up in two different civilisations widely separated in time and space, in such manifestly disparate guises as Egyptian hieroglyphs and the Dutch alphabet; or the possibility in principle of one language developing into several mutually incomprehensible languages. These are possibilities which do not readily suggest themselves on the basis of the everyday experience of the monoglot language-user, any more than the theories of Marxist or Keynsian economics readily suggest themselves on the basis of our everyday experience as workers and consumers. But just as the educated European's concept of money is considerably more sophisticated than it would be if he were living in a more primitive, economically naïve form of society, so it would seem there must be cultural factors to account for the ways in which his concept of a language goes beyond the crude notions which might derive merely from an intuitive grasp of the nature of man's linguistic capacities.

Some of the relevant cultural factors are not difficult to identify, such as acquaintance with the existence of different languages, and acquaintance with the practice of translation. Of these widespread forms of cultural conditioning, undoubtedly the most important is acquaintance with the practice of writing. Throughout by far the greater part of the language-using history of *homo sapiens*, man's concept of a language must have been inadequate even to articulate the kind of proposition that Goropius Becanus advanced in 1580, or—to choose a twentieth-century example—that Michael Ventris advanced in 1952 when he suggested that the language of the Linear B texts was in fact Greek. For writing is a cultural innovation of relatively recent date, and any civilisation in which writing was unknown was hardly likely to develop the concept of a language as words potentially expressible in other than vocal form. Hence even less likely in those circumstances would be the development of a concept of a language which allowed the possibility of distinguishing in general between language-using and speech.

The advent of writing was the cultural development which made the most radical alteration of all time to man's concept of what a language is. It opened up the possibility of regarding articulated sound as a dispensable rather than an essential medium of expression for languages; and even as being an intrinsically defective or imperfect medium. The consequences of this have been incalculable throughout the subsequent history of human thought.

For most of that time, writing has been the prerogative of relatively small and relatively privileged classes of people, and this is undoubtedly the social basis of the prestige widely accorded to it. But whatever the social distribution of reading and writing skills, the concept of a language in a literate society may always be expected to tend towards what, for want of any existing term, may be called 'scriptism': that is to say, the assumption that writing is a more ideal form of linguistic representation than speech. By comparison with the unsatisfactory transience of speech, writing is a relatively permanent form of expression. It can overcome the limitations of time, place and memory which inherently beset the spoken word. It is comparatively context-free, less tied to the particular circumstances of its production. Without the advantages conferred by writing in the conveyance and storage of information, the practical organisation of the world's major civilisations to date would have been impossible. To go as far as H. G. Wells and say that in the history of man it was the invention of writing that 'made a continuous historical consciousness possible'[1] is doubtless going too far: but it certainly made that consciousness immeasurably more authoritative, a more powerful psychological and social force to be reckoned with in the conduct of human affairs. It is hardly to be wondered at that script should come to be regarded as what utterance aims at, but falls short of.

One of the sophistries of modern linguistics is to treat scriptism, which has probably dominated the concept of a language in literate societies for at least several millennia, as some kind of theoretical heresy. Novice linguists are warned against it in the strictest terms, in case the corrupt example provided by the rest of the world might taint their linguistic souls. Writing, they are taught, is nothing but a representation of speech, merely a convenient ancillary notation. Saussure insisted on the primacy of the spoken word as an indispensable foundation of modern linguistics, and reproached nineteenth-century comparativists such as Bopp and Grimm with failure to distinguish clearly between sounds and letters.[2] Scriptism has been denounced as part of the 'classical fallacy'[3] allegedly propagated by the Greek scholars of Alexandria, in which form it is complemented by the equally grave misconception that the language of the current generation is always less 'correct' than that of previous generations.

The irony of all this resides in the fact that, these dire warnings notwithstanding, modern linguistics has itself remained consistently

---

[1] *A Short History of the World*, rev. ed., Harmondsworth 1946, p. 49.

[2] Reading Bopp, said Saussure, 'one would think that a language was inseparable from its alphabet' (Saussure, op. cit., p. 46).

[3] J. Lyons, *Introduction to Theoretical Linguistics*, Cambridge 1968, p. 9. The 'classical fallacy' was longer lived than the term perhaps suggests. In fact, it was simply one version of what might more appropriately be called the 'orthological dogma', which has persisted throughout the Western tradition, and is one of the most striking features of the Western concept of a language. The basic assumption is that some linguistic usages are 'right' and others 'wrong'. Different versions of this dogma vary in their characterization of 'right' and 'wrong'.

and irredeemably scriptist in orientation, or so it might appear to
the ghosts of some much criticised nineteenth-century philologists.

The scriptist bias of modern linguistics reveals itself most crudely
in the way in which, for all their insistence in principle on the
primacy of the spoken word, linguistic theorists in practice follow
the traditional assumption that standard orthographic representation
correctly identifies the main units of the spoken language. Thus, for
example, *Mary had a little lamb* will be treated for all practical purposes as unquestionably identifying a 'sentence' of English, and the
'sentence' will be cited thus on the printed page, and its construction
analysed, without any reference to how the given sequence of orthographic forms *Mary had a little lamb* is to be pronounced. The
appropriate pronunciation is taken to be already known to the
reader, or irrelevant, or both. Thus there is created *ab initio* the
myth that spoken English includes a unit called 'the sentence *Mary
had a little lamb*', which somehow exists independently of any precisely identified sequence of English sounds. What is the basis of
this myth? Simply the fact that *Mary had a little lamb* occurs as a
unit in written English, where its status is indeed guaranteed independently of pronunciation. But to take it for granted without further ado that there will turn out to be some uniquely corresponding
phonic unit is an assumption of quite remarkable temerity in the
context of what purports to be an autonomous, scientific and empirical analysis of the evidence relating to English speech. For it
does not take much acquaintance with English to realise that there
are various distinct English utterances which might possibly be
represented in standard orthography by *Mary had a little lamb* (e.g.
replies to the questions *What did Mary have?* and *Who had a little
lamb?*, replies which any learner of spoken English has to be taught
to distinguish, even though there is no equivalent distinction in
written English), but which would not be treated as interchangeable
in spoken usage. Furthermore, while paying lip-service to the
primacy of the spoken word, linguistic theorists are in practice all
too ready to assume that when a given written sequence, taken out of
context, is open to two possible interpretations (e.g. *John hit the man
with the umbrella*), this establishes the existence of an 'ambiguous
sentence', irrespective of the fact that in speech there need be no
'ambiguity' at all. Such assumptions, when made on page after
page, amount virtually to presupposing that the linguist's analytic

task has already been done for him in advance, and its results conveniently embodied in traditional orthographic practice. The pretence that one is being presented with a description strictly of spoken language begins to wear thin as soon as it occurs to the reader that the real 'discovery procedure' being employed is invariably: 'Assume that standard orthography identifies all the relevant distinctions, until you are forced to assume otherwise.' It is as if the two basic principles of geographical surveying were taken to be (i) that an existing map is always accurate until it is proved inaccurate, and (ii) that no existing map can be totally inaccurate. The consequence of these two principles would be that the surveyor should never start from scratch making a new map of an area already charted, but make only the minimum adjustments to the existing map. This corresponds roughly to the rule of thumb modern linguistics has adopted, whereby an existing orthographic map is made wherever possible to serve as a guide to the topography of speech.

Paradoxically, this is nowhere more apparent than in the branch of modern linguistics devoted specifically to the description of sound systems: phonology. The phoneme, as the unit on which the greater part of twentieth-century phonological analysis has been based, would not deceive the shades of Bopp or Grimm. They would recognise it immediately as the letter in disguise – and not a very convincing disguise at that. Phonemic analysis they would regard as an updated form of alphabetisation, with a few supplementary diacritics.[1] If the nineteenth century failed to break with established orthographic tradition, the twentieth century showed itself for a long time equally reluctant (or powerless) to do so. Thus there is a hollow ring to Jespersen's criticism of Grimm, whom he described as 'anything but a phonetician', and to prove it cited Grimm's statement that the word *schrift* uses seven signs to express eight sounds. This, said Jespersen patronisingly in 1922, 'nowadays cannot but produce a smile.'[2] But, as Grimm's ghost would not be slow to point out, Jespersen's smile was premature. Had he waited until 1933, there would have been Bloomfield's celebrated analysis of the phonemic composition of the English word *pin* to cap it. For bad as

---

[1] A well-known manual of phonemics of the 1940s bears the revealing subtitle: 'A technique for reducing languages to writing.' The ghosts of Bopp, Grimm and company might be forgiven for pointing out that 'reducing languages to writing' is roughly what posterity accused them of doing.

[2] *Language, its Nature, Development and Origin*, p. 46.

Grimm's arithmetic may have been, Bloomfield surpasses him by explaining carefully how to count phonemes, and then getting his own sum wrong (in spite, Grimm's ghost might add, of giving himself the unfair mathematical advantage of choosing in *pin* a manifestly shorter word than *schrift*). According to Bloomfield,[1] in order to ascertain how many phonemes there are in any word of one's native language, it suffices to conduct a few 'experiments' in saying words out loud, and comparing how we pronounce them and how we differentiate them from similar words. Thus in the case of *pin*, our pronunciation experiments will reveal that *pin* begins with the same sound as words such as *pat*, *push* and *peg*. Comparison between *pin* and *in* reveals that *pin* contains the sound of *in*, but adds a further sound at the beginning. Comparison with *man*, *sun* and *hen* reveals that *pin* ends with the same sound as these. Comparison with *dig*, *fish* and *mill* reveals that they all share a middle part with *pin*, but begin and end differently. Bloomfield recommends that these 'experiments' be continued until it is clear that our comparisons have isolated all the 'replaceable parts' in the pronunciation of the word *pin*; that is to say, we are left with units that 'cannot be further analysed by partial resemblances'. Each such unit is 'a minimum unit of distinctive sound-feature, a phoneme'. What is disconcerting about all this is Bloomfield's conclusion: that in *pin* there are just three such units, namely the consonant *p*, the vowel *i* and the consonant *n*. For if we follow exactly the diagnostic procedure Bloomfield recommends, it is difficult to see that this can be the correct result. We cannot avoid finding, for example, that there is a 'partial resemblance' between the sounds at the beginning of *pin* and *bin* which does not obtain between, say, *pin* and *sin*. Bloomfield apparently ignores this 'partial resemblance', but he does not say why. If we ignore it, however, it is difficult to feel confident that we have isolated the 'minimum units of distinctive sound-feature', for the difference between the initial consonants of *pin* and *bin* sounds like a smaller difference than that between the initial consonants of *pin* and *sin*. (This is supported by our observing that saying *pin* and *bin* involves initial lip closure in both cases, but not in *sin*.) So it seems a mistake to suppose that *pin*, *bin* and *sin* can all have the same number of phonemes, given that there is a 'partial resemblance' between *pin* and *bin* which there is not between *pin* and *sin*. Again,

---

[1] L. Bloomfield, *Language*, London 1935, pp. 78-9.

it is puzzling to know why Bloomfield does not draw our attention to the fact that in the pronunciation of *pin* the initial consonant is not immediately followed by the vowel, but separated from it by an aspirate sound which resembles that occurring at the beginning of *hit*. In fact, *pit* sounds like *hit* with a *p* on the front, rather than *it* with a *p* on the front. One wonders why this aspirate sound has apparently been left out of Bloomfield's count. So whichever way we look at it, it seems very unsatisfactory, on the basis of strict comparison, to end up with just three phonemes in *pin*, if 'phoneme' means what Bloomfield says it means. On the other hand, it is easy to see that counting just three phonemes in *pin* produces a very neat correspondence between the phonemic structure of the word and its spelling. Grimm's ghost might well ask whether, if traditional English orthography had recognised an aspirate following the initial consonant and consequently used the spelling *phin* instead of *pin*, Bloomfield would not solemnly have proceeded to discover four phonemes there instead of three, by exactly the same process of comparative experimentation. (He could have invoked the Biblical *hin* to provide a minimal contrast isolating initial *p*.) Considerations of this kind raise the question of how far modern phonology, rather than provide a rigorous, independent analysis of spoken language, was content to settle for a description that would not depart too far from the received wisdom enshrined in traditional orthography. Any quite radical approach to phonology, such as was suggested by J. R. Firth, had to face an impossible uphill struggle against the solid conservatism of the alphabetic tradition. Among the ranks of phonologists who remained faithful to that tradition, the more die-hard objected to any innovation likely to disturb the reassuring parallelism between phonological analysis and alphabetic representation. Their slogan was 'once a phoneme, always a phoneme', which really meant 'once a letter, always a letter'.

The alphabetism of modern phonology thus combined with and reinforced the all-too-easy assumption that the written sentence (e.g. *Mary had a little lamb*) identifies a single unit of spoken syntax. The interlocking of writing and speech was further strengthened in modern linguistic theory by importing into the analysis of the grammatical structure of speech criteria derived, by a not too circuitous route, from the printed page. Perhaps the most blatant example concerns the problem of identifying 'words' as grammatical units in the flow of speech. This problem was still regarded as soluble as late as the 1950s by defining words by reference to 'potential pauses' in a speaker's utterance. That is to say, a spoken word was identified as 'any segment of a sentence bounded by successive points at which pausing is possible'.[1] Theorists who did not like this definition sometimes objected that speakers do not normally pause between words:[2] but an objection on that score is misdirected, since the criterion is explicitly one of potential pause, not of actual pause. A more relevant objection would be to inquire what is meant by 'potential pause'. It can hardly be taken to mean literally 'potential momentary interruption of phonation', since that may occur elsewhere than at word boundaries (e.g. in sing-song recitation: *Ma-ry-had-a-li-ttle-lamb*; or as the result of the speaker's hesitation). If such cases are not to invalidate the definition of a word, a more precise account of 'potential pause' is required. But when an attempt is made to say exactly what counts as a 'pause' for purposes of the definition, it soon becomes evident that the only pauses which will do are those in which it is in principle possible to insert another word (e.g. *Mary (often) had (kept) a (very) little (pet) lamb*). Hence, when the term 'potential pause' is fully explicated, the definition in effect becomes circular: for the notion 'word' is itself required to explain the principle of separability invoked. A word is a segment of a sentence bounded by points at which another word might be inserted. What is interesting about the criterion of 'potential pause' is not what it fails to do (i.e. define words as units in the flow of speech) but what it attempts to do. For it is manifestly an attempt to copy for speech the familiar criterion that obtains in alphabetic writing, i.e. the separation of orthographic words one from another by leaving a blank space in between (a writing convention not well established in Europe until the later medieval period). The search for a phonetic counterpart to the orthographic 'blank space' as a word boundary was by no means new. As far back as the seventeenth century, the Port Royal grammar had tried to combine phonetic and orthographic criteria by defining a word as 'what is pronounced separately and written separately'.[3] Although it is not entirely clear what the Port Royal grammarians meant by 'pro-

---

[1] C. F. Hockett, *A Course in Modern Linguistics*, New York 1958, p. 167.
[2] J. Lyons, *Introduction to Theoretical Linguistics*, Cambridge 1968, p. 199.
[3] *Grammaire générale et raisonnée*, 1660, ch. 4.

nouncing words separately', it is clear enough that their intention was to maintain that there was a parallel between the phonetic status of the word as a unit and its orthographic status. The survival of this tenet into the structural linguistics of the mid-twentieth century simply shows how insistence in principle on the 'primacy of speech' is no prophylactic against the temptation to analyse speaking as if it were writing.

The doctrine of the primacy of speech, apparently so central to modern linguistic theory, is itself a curious amalgam. At least four respects in which speech might be held to 'take precedence' over writing have been distinguished. First, as far as is known, all human communities had a spoken language before they had, if they ever had, a corresponding written language. Secondly, every normal child learns his native language in its spoken form before he learns the corresponding written form. Thirdly, speech serves a wider range of communicational purposes than writing. Fourthly, writing originated as a representation of speech. These four respects have been termed (i) 'phylogenetic priority', (ii) 'ontogenetic priority', (iii) 'functional priority', and (iv) 'structural priority'.[1] But while it is clear that those who claim that language is essentially 'rooted in speech', and quite specifically that nothing is 'a language in the fullest and clearest sense' unless it includes the production, reception and interpretation of sounds originating in the vocal tract,[2] are claiming that writing is in some sense or other parasitic upon speech, it is often less clear which of the various types of priority they consider decisive, or what difference it would make, in their view, if only some or none of these priorities held. For it does not follow from any of the priorities that the use of articulated sound as a medium of expression must be treated as criterial, to the exclusion of writing, in defining what a language is. The kinds of priorities which phylogenetic, ontogenetic, functional and structural priority are merely indicate that for the human species writing is a more advanced and specialised form of adaptive behaviour than speech. But the priorities as such say nothing about the crucial question for any analytic science; namely, the interrelation between the two forms of co-existent behaviour.

[1] J. Lyons, 'Human language', in *Non-Verbal Communication,* ed. R. A. Hinde, Cambridge 1972, pp. 49–85.
[2] M. Black, *The Labyrinth of Language*, Harmondsworth 1972, p. 79.

What is important here is sometimes obscured by an essentially irrelevant argument offered by those who wish to claim that, despite the 'primacy of speech', the use of articulated sound should not be taken to be a criterial feature for defining a language. The argument runs as follows. *Suppose we discovered a community which made no use of vocalisation, but communicated only by means of writing. Suppose that upon analysis this system of writing turned out to have a structure similar to that of our own written languages. Suppose, furthermore, that it served a comparable variety of communicational functions. Should we then refuse to say that this was a community of language-users?*[1] In whatever form this argument is put up, it hinges upon envisaging an imaginary situation in which the crucial properties and functions of a language are embodied in a communication system which *ex hypothesi* is not dependent on or derived from the use of articulated sound. As its critics are not slow to point out, the argument is self-defeating. For the properties and functions which make this hypothetical communication system a plausible candidate for classifying as 'a language' are borrowed directly from familiar systems which are themselves either spoken languages, or known to be parasitic on spoken languages. Hence implicitly the argument concedes the point that speech is an essential feature of the kind of system that provides the paradigm case. Furthermore, this argument and its variants all resort ultimately to question begging. For presumably our readiness or reluctance to agree that the hypothetical community presented for our consideration is a language-using community will depend precisely on the criterial importance we attach to speech. To appeal simply to our readiness or reluctance to abandon that criterion leaves the debate exactly where it was before the argument was offered. Paradoxically, an attempt to persuade us along these lines appears tacitly to concede that no serious argument is available to resolve the issue.

The debate over the criterial status of speech somehow misses the vital point that although *homo loquens* is undoubtedly the precursor of *homo scribens*, the emergence of *homo scribens* makes a radical and henceforward irreversible difference to what a language is, irrespective of the medium employed. Just as the invention of firearms automatically altered the status of bows and arrows by introducing a new concept of what a weapon was, so the invention

[1] J. Lyons, 'Human language', op. cit., p. 64.

of writing, by expanding man's communicational universe, auto-matically introduced a new concept of a language.

Furthermore, the fact that writing developed as it did—from the symbolisation of words, via the symbolisation of syllables, to the symbolisation of still smaller segmental units—provided at each stage a ready-made conceptual matrix for the analysis of speech. As far as is known, the transition from syllabic to alphabetic writing has been made only once in the cultural history of man, and all alphabets are ultimately derived from the same source. Without the transition from syllabic to alphabetic writing, the development of phonemic analysis in modern linguistics would be inconceivable. It is some-times said that whoever invented the alphabet invented the pho-neme. Although that is a picturesque way of putting the matter, it is not quite true. The invention of the alphabet does not presuppose phonemic analysis, although it is certainly the case that anyone who had worked out a prior theory of phonemic analysis would have no difficulty in devising an economical alphabet based upon it. But the boot is on the other foot. The history of the alphabet shows fairly clearly that the critical step was taken when the Greeks bor-rowed from the Phoenicians a notation that turned out to be in various ways not entirely satisfactory for the transcription of Greek, because of structural differences between the two languages. By introducing symbols to represent vowels, which the Phoenicians had not bothered to represent at all, the Greeks by chance came close to having a system of phonemic notation.

Strictly speaking, however, the issue of phonemic analysis only arises when someone asks a question such as: 'What is the minimum number of contrasts it is necessary to recognise in order to dis-tinguish every phonetically non-identical pair of words in the lan-guage?' There is no evidence that this was ever a material question for the inventors of the alphabet. For devising a successful alphabet does not require its solution.[1] It merely requires a sufficient number of symbols having fixed segmental values to ensure the elimination of most practical ambiguities of word identification.[2] Once the

[1] H. A. Gleason, 'Writing systems', *An Introduction to Descriptive Linguistics*, rev. ed., New York 1961, pp. 409–24.

[2] This is evident also from the history of subsequent adaptations of an alphabet to record new languages as e.g. in the transition from Latin to Romance. Cf. R. Harris, 'The Strasburg oaths: a problem of orthographic interpretation', *Revue de linguistique romane*, vol. XXXIV, 1970, pp. 403–6.

practice of representing speech by strings of symbols having fixed
segmental values becomes established, the conceptualisation of the
spoken word as a 'chain' of fixed articulatory positions is inevitable.
But questions concerning the systematisation of segmental contrasts
in speech may still remain unasked, because there is no practical
point in asking them. Hence the long gap in the history of Western
phonetics between Graeco-Roman antiquity and the nineteenth
century. It was not until the twentieth that questions such as that
of the minimum number of segmental contrasts, having at last been
raised, were recognised as not necessarily having straightforward
answers.[1]

A no less fundamental point is that the systematic analysis of
spoken languages depends essentially on their conceptualisation as
systems amenable to representation in a medium other than sound.
Saussure, for all his insistence on the primacy of speech, comes
curiously close to acknowledging this important truth. It is through
writing, he concedes, that the signs of a spoken language take on a
tangible form, and thus become representable; for it would be impossible to photograph them, or capture them in any other way.[2]
But he does not follow up this thought and ask what are its implications for the science of linguistics. None the less, it is an idea to
which he returns uneasily at several points. Although writing is
itself outside the language's internal system, he says, it is impossible
to ignore this process by which the language is constantly represented. And yet he does ignore it, or tries his best to, by denying
to writing any other than a derivative function. The spoken and
the written systems, he says, are two distinct systems of signs: the
second exists for the sole purpose of representing the first. What he
calls the 'linguistic object' is not defined by the combination of the
written word and the spoken word: the latter alone constitutes that
object. But the written word, he concedes, is so intimately bound
up with the spoken word of which it is the image, that in the end it
usurps the principal role: one comes to accord as much importance
or more to the representation of the vocal sign than to this sign
itself. It is as if one believed, says Saussure, that in order to know

---

[1] Yuen-Ren Chao, 'The non-uniqueness of phonemic solutions of phonetic systems',
Bulletin of the Institute of History and Philology, Academia Sinica, 1934, vol. IV, part 4,
pp. 363–97.
[2] Saussure, op. cit., p. 32.

what a person looks like, it is better to study his photograph than his face.[1] The simile as it stands is striking, but inexact. It would be more appropriate if we were to suppose, for purposes of the analogy, that because of the peculiar properties of human vision, we found it much easier to see a two-dimensional photograph than to see a three-dimensional face. In which case, there would be a sense in which it would be right to say that it was only the invention of photography that enabled us to discover what people's faces looked like. But then, clearly, the availability of the study of the human face as a visual object would be a function of the availability of photography.

Again, Saussure admits that whoever consciously deprives himself of the perceptible image supplied by the written word risks being left with a shapeless mass which he does not know what to make of.[2] Detached from their graphic symbols, sounds are only vague, imprecise entities. This, according to Saussure, was why earlier linguists had failed to distinguish between letters and sounds. For them, letting go of the letter meant losing their grasp of language.[3] What Saussure failed to see is, first, that distinguishing carefully between letters and sounds, desirable as that may be, does not in itself amount to 'letting go of the letter'; secondly, that once one had got hold of the letter, however hard one might try, it was in the end impossible to let go of it; and, thirdly, that if, *per impossibile*, one had succeeded in letting go, one would simultaneously have let go of any serious possibility of a systematic analysis of languages.

Thus, regarding written languages as the major source of potential error and confusion for the linguist, Saussure defined the linguistic sign in terms of the pairing of a concept with what he repeatedly described, using a metaphor perhaps unwisely drawn from visual perception, as its 'acoustic image'. By thus consigning the structural elements of the language to an area of the mind or brain hermetically sealed, as it were, against the possible intrusion of all non-vocal forms of expression, but by being willing at the same time to describe what went on in that hermetically sealed area in traditional alphabetically-based terms, Saussure launched modern linguistics on its crypto-scriptist path. Had he been born half a century later, and lived to see the development of sound spectrography, he might well have proceeded otherwise.

[1] ibid., p. 45.   [2] ibid., p. 55.   [3] ibid., p. 55.

With the more recent elaboration of a distinction between 'competence' and 'performance' in linguistic theory, crypto-scriptism has acquired a new dimension. Languages are to be defined by reference to 'ideal speaker-hearers'.[1] What are seen as the typical imperfections of ordinary spoken discourse—phenomena involving hesitations, slips of the tongue, interruptions, syntactic breakdowns, impromptu adaptations to context—are now relegated to 'performance', or, in other words, excluded from 'the language' as such. What is idealised as 'competence', and thus to be accounted for by the linguist's grammar of the language, turns out to be the postulated ability to produce an infinite set of flawless sentences, each complete, well formed, amenable to systematic analysis, having a fixed meaning, and provided with a standard pronunciation uniform for the whole speech community. (The idealisation is one beside which the stigmatised 'classical fallacy' of the grammarians of Alexandria begins to look in retrospect like no idealisation at all, and even to lean in the direction of practical empiricism.) It is no accident that in the modern generative model of sentence-competence, the pronunciation of the sentence is something added at a late stage in its derivation, by a so-called 'interpretive' component of the grammar, which has played no role in the generation of the structure to which it eventually assigns a phonological form. So, despite the 'primacy of speech', pronunciation—according to the generative model—is merely a superficial garb to a basically non-phonic structure. But suppose we strip away this superficial phonetic garb of the sentence, what lies underneath it? Something which must have all its words in place, their order determined, their grammatical relationships established, and their meanings assigned—but which simply lacks phonetic embodiment: a string of words with the sound turned off. In short, a linguistic abstraction for which there is only one conceivable archetype so far in human history; the sentence of writing. What the contemporary generative model of sentence derivation provides, albeit unintentionally, is a revealing anatomy of the difficulties inherent in an essentially literate society's attempt to conceptualise something it has already forgotten, and which cannot be recalled from its cultural past: what an essentially non-written form of language is like.

*   *   *

[1] N. Chomsky, *Aspects of the Theory of Syntax*, Cambridge, Mass. 1965, pp. 3-4.

Less widespread and less obvious forms of cultural conditioning also play a role in the language-user's concept of what a language is. They show up in detailed differences which cross-cultural comparisons bring to light. But it may not be apparent, either at first sight or upon closer investigation, what the source of such differences is.

Most Europeans would be puzzled to know how to reply if asked the question 'What is the word in your language for what people say on Thursdays?', or 'What do you call words spoken at night?', or 'What do you call talk that took place a year ago?' But these questions would make perfectly good sense to a Mayan Indian of Tenejapa, whose language, Tzeltal, provides commonly used designations for all of these.[1] It is not that the European lacks the linguistic resources to make up a translation such as 'Thursday talk', or 'night words'; but rather that he would be at a loss to understand the point of drawing such distinctions. It is not part of his concept of a language that a language should provide you with Thursday talk or night words, and if it does not do that then it need provide no corresponding metalinguistic expressions either.

The European, on the other hand, finds nothing odd about such questions as 'What is the word in your language for the clothes people wear on Sundays?', or 'What do you call a garment worn at night?', or 'What do you call a coat you wear in the winter?' For his concept of clothing, unlike his concept of a language, incorporates the notion of appropriateness to different times of the day, of the week, or of the year. Time is one of the important conceptual parameters in the European's categorisation of clothes, food, and many other things; but a relatively unimportant one in his categorisation of words. Terms like *archaism* and *neologism* belong to the technical lexicon of the scholar, not to the everyday vocabulary of the ordinary language-user.

His everyday vocabulary of speech acts, however, provides ample indication of what the European does expect a language to offer him: appropriate forms of words for apologies, thanks, refusals, congratulations, curses, warnings, promises, and many other purposes. But unlike the metalinguistic vocabulary of Tzeltal it does

[1] B. Stross, 'Speaking of speaking: Tenejapa Tzeltal metalinguistics', in R. Bauman & J. Sherzer (eds), *Explorations in the Ethnography of Speaking*, Cambridge 1974, pp. 213–39.

not make special provision for distinguishing what is said according to the bodily posture of the speaker; for example, sitting down, standing up, lying on one's side, lying on one's back, and kneeling on all fours. Nor for distinguishing according to the location of the speech event or the speaker; for example, between talk in a grassy area, talk on a rock, talk in a canyon, and talk from a speaker who is up a tree. Again, it is not that the European cannot understand the literal sense of expressions like 'grass talk', 'rock talk', 'canyon talk' or 'tree talk'; but rather that he will tend to suppose that the point of having such terms must somehow relate to different social purposes or topics, in ways analogous to such differences as he himself draws between 'talking shop', 'talking business' and 'talking politics'.

Although European culture distinguishes greetings from farewells, congratulations from commiserations, etc., it is interesting that no European language, nor even the technical vocabulary of European-based linguistics, provides any general terms for corresponding distinctions between the words used. While we can describe the difference between the word *children* and the word *kids* as a difference of register, or of formality, or perhaps even of style, we have no parallel way of saying what the difference between *hello* and *goodbye* is a difference of, except—rather lamely—a difference of meaning. This is doubtless not unrelated to the fact that in European speech communities it tends to be rather exceptional forms of speech which are relegated to these specialised functions. The fact that *hello, goodbye, how do you do?, bravo, chin chin*, etc., are expressions which rarely occur except in quite stereotyped social situations, may perhaps favour a tendency to regard them as a kind of appendage to the language, rather than an integral part of it. (The awkwardness which European grammarians feel about accounting for words and phrases of this type is reflected in their frequent consignment to the ragbag categories of 'interjection' and 'idiom'.)

On the other hand, the conscious classification of words into 'parts of speech', according to their form and grammatical function, which is reflected in the metalinguistic vocabulary of all European languages is, by contrast, a feature almost entirely lacking in many non-European languages. Usually such classifications, as the history of grammatical doctrines in Europe well illustrates,[1] are the work

[1] R. H. Robins, *A Short History of Linguistics*, London 1967.

originally of a small class of 'language experts'. But the experts' concept of a language may well, by processes of cultural transmission, become integrated into the linguistic consciousness of a whole community. With language, as with medicine, or religion, what began as a set of specialist's distinctions can become part of the intellectual equipment of Everyman.

The metalinguistic terminology a language provides or does not provide, its resources or lack of resources for talk about language, reflect differences—sometimes subtle and sometimes quite obvious —between the ways in which different cultures treat language-using as a form of behaviour. Someone who agrees that this is so may none the less feel that it is going too far to say that different cultures have different concepts of what a language is. He may not realise that this view may itself be seen as reflecting a particular cultural background. For the European is the inheritor of an intellectual tradition which is strongly biased in favour of regarding languages as superficially different but fundamentally equivalent systems of expression. This assumption reveals itself in a variety of ways, including a willingness to draw a sharp distinction between 'the language' and 'the culture' which the language happens to serve. So when it is pointed out to him that the speaker of Tzeltal, unlike the speaker of German, will, when talking about speech, draw upon a whole system of terminological distinctions concerning when and where the speech took place, which a European would regard as irrelevant or even slightly comic, he is inclined to treat this not as evidence about a difference between concepts of a language, but as evidence about a difference between the cultural patterns which the languages serve. The notion that languages and concepts of languages are themselves constitutive parts of cultural patterns is a notion to which he is not so much antagonistic as oblivious.

To see this is to come at least part of the way towards seeing that 'What is a language?' is not quite the impartial, culture-neutral question that it might be taken for at first sight. Nor do design-feature accounts give it an impartial, culture-neutral answer. For the design-feature strategy implicitly assumes that the question is a taxonomic question, and therefore sets out to supply the kind of answer that Western science favours for taxonomic questions in general; that is to say, by treating languages as constituting a species of the genus 'communication system'. But to proceed thus is not to ensure that the question of the concept of a language is approached without bias. On the contrary, it is already to presuppose the validity of a certain concept of what a language is.

* * *

The belief that, cultural differences notwithstanding, all mankind must somehow share a common concept of what a language is, is sometimes fostered by a failure to distinguish between the two questions 'What is a language?' and 'What is language?'; or the assumption that providing an answer to the second will more or less automatically provide a valid, culture-neutral answer to the first. On this view, individual languages are to be regarded as particular—but in some respects relatively superficial—manifestations of something more basic: the human faculty or activity of language. Language, according to this way of looking at the matter, is what is common to all mankind, even though no one language or type of language is.

If we ask in this context what is meant by 'language', we are likely to be given a very general and seemingly incontrovertible answer, which appears to be supported in equal measure by experience, attentive observation and common sense; e.g., 'Language involves (i) the use of symbols and combinations of symbols, (ii) the assignment of meanings or interpretations to these symbols and their combinations, and (iii) the provision of a means of communication utilisable for a wide variety of purposes in social interaction.' This is a simple version of what is sometimes known as a 'design-feature' account of language; but it reveals the basic structure of all such accounts. A number of parameters are selected (in this case 'formal structuring', 'value assignment' and 'social function') along which the relevant 'design-features' of language are identified. More complex accounts of this type may be constructed by selecting a larger number of parameters and identifying the features in greater detail. Many attempts to give brief textbook definitions of language are, in effect, concise design-feature accounts of this kind.

Various accounts of this type have been proposed, but no purpose would be served in examining them in detail here. However, some commonly discussed design-features of language deserve mention.

One is a feature already discussed in connexion with the doctrine of the primacy of speech, 'vocality', which identifies the vocal tract and the auditory system as the primary physiological bases for language in human beings. Another is 'reciprocity', which emphasises that language is not just one-way communication, but provides for the reciprocal exchange of messages between senders and recipients. A third is 'duality', or 'double articulation', which is identified as a feature of formal structuring such that underlying any combination of meaningful units (words or morphemes) there is a further system of distinctive but non-meaningful units, constituted in the case of spoken languages by the phonemes. A fourth is 'productivity', which emphasises that language is not a limited or closed form of communication, but provides a potentially infinite range of messages for language-users to exchange. Languages thus stand at the opposite end of the communicational scale from systems which are designed simply for the communication of one particular message (as e.g. in the Tristran legend, where hoisting a white sail on the boat is the agreed signal indicating the return of Ysolde, and a black sail her absence). A fifth is 'institutionality', which puts language on a par with other social institutions, such as the family, or the law, which will take different forms in different societies, but are in all cases rooted in the practices and traditions of a community. A sixth feature is 'displacement', by which language typically affords the language-user the possibility of exchanging messages about times, places and circumstances other than those of the immediate situation in which he finds himself. A seventh is 'arbitrariness', which insists on the absence of any inherent or logical connexion between the physical shape of a linguistic sign and its meaning. An eighth is 'transmissibility', which fixes upon the fact that language involves learning; i.e., apprenticeship as a member of a linguistic community is necessary, and normally sufficient, in order to become a competent language-user.

Characteristics of this kind figure prominently in design-feature accounts of language, and it is from the familiarity of such features in human linguistic behaviour that such accounts derive much of their plausibility. However, this is not quite enough if we are hoping that the answer to the question 'What is language?' will at the same time supply a valid transcultural answer to the question 'What is a language?' For design-feature accounts have their own problems.

In the first place, the design-feature approach does not yield an agreed answer to the question 'What is language?' Different accounts select different parameters, and it is clear that reconciling these differences would require prior agreement on the criteria for constructing such accounts. But it appears that the exclusion or inclusion of a given design-feature may itself depend on the theoretical position adopted with regard to the defining characteristics of languages. Thus there is no way of reconciling a design-feature account which includes 'vocality' with one which excludes 'vocality', for the inclusion or exclusion of this feature is essentially bound up with theoretical issues such as the 'primacy of speech'. The matter cannot be settled by 'looking at the facts of linguistic behaviour', for what is controversial here is precisely whether non-vocal communication counts as linguistic behaviour in the full or primary sense.

A problem of a different kind arises from the disparate range of phenomena covered in design-feature accounts. Not all general features of linguistic behaviour appear to be equally relevant to the question 'What is a language?' For example, it is difficult to see that 'reciprocity' is a feature which has any important bearing on the structure of a communication system. From a structural point of view, English would still be English even if a situation developed in which all its speakers happened to be deaf and all its hearers dumb, which would effectively preclude reciprocity. There might then be a problem about how the speakers learned to speak the language, but that is a problem irrelevant to the point at issue. It would still seem very odd to deny that the system of communication in use was English, simply because of the absence of reciprocity. It would be equally odd to deny the lack of reciprocity in such a case, on the ground that although the speakers happened to be deaf and the hearers dumb, none the less their communication system was 'in principle reciprocal'. One might just as well say that in principle courting sticklebacks have a reciprocal communication system, although unfortunately it happens that male sticklebacks never get their abdomens distended by the accumulation of roe, and therefore cannot send certain messages which a female stickleback can send. Reciprocity, in short, is a feature which relates primarily to communication situations and participants, rather than to the system of communication used. Similar considerations apply, *mutatis mutandis*, to design-features such as 'institutionality' and 'transmissibility'.

Different problems again may be illustrated by reference to 'duality', one of the principal points on which design-feature accounts tend to concur. This involves drawing a distinction between meaningful units, or 'pleremes', of which the smallest recognized in grammatical analysis is usually termed the 'morpheme', and distinctive but non-meaningful units, or 'cenemes', of which the 'phoneme' is representative where spoken languages are concerned.[1] Some accounts stress the compositional interrelatedness of the two levels of structure, phonemic and morphemic. Thus the composition of a form like *singing* would be treated as involving a two-stage arrangement. At one stage, there would be an arrangement of meaningful units: 'plerematically', the form would consist of the root *sing-* and the suffix *-ing*. At the other stage, each of these two parts would also be analysable into distinctive but non-meaningful units: 'cenematically', *sing-* would consist of the phonemes /s/, /i/, /ŋ/, and *-ing* of the phonemes /i/, /ŋ/.

However, the duality of structure thus illustrated is to some extent foisted upon the linguistic form by the adoption of a prior theory of structure. The morpheme is a theoretical construct, se up in order to accommodate certain relations between parts of words. But some languages do not have a level of morphemic structuring in the way illustrated by the word *singing*.[2] A way round this difficulty might appear to be feasible by revising the definition of the morpheme so as to introduce a more abstract relationship between phoneme and morpheme. This more abstract relationship would allow us to analyse, e.g., *went* as consisting of two morphemes even though, unlike *going*, *singing*, etc. it is not divisible into two concatenated segments. But if we resort to this more abstract account of the morpheme, what becomes of the claim that duality of structure is common to all languages? If *went* consists of two morphemes, these two morphemes are not composed of phonemes in the way that the morphemes of *sing-* and *-ing* were originally envisaged as composed of phonemes. To treat *went* as bimorphemic preserves parity of analysis with *singing* in one sense; but it does so by introducing a different notion of 'duality of structure'.

[1] 'Plereme' and 'ceneme' are the terms Hockett uses (Hockett, op. cit., p. 575). Bloomfield's corresponding terms were 'glosseme' and 'phememe' respectively (Bloomfield, op. cit., p. 264).

[2] 'The trouble with the morpheme is that, if defined to be a segment of an utteran ce, it is not a unit that is found in all languages' (J. Lyons, 'Human language', op. cit., p. 65).

2

Furthermore, whatever view of the morpheme is adopted, the phoneme is equally a theoretical construct, as is evident from the long history of debate in linguistics over how it should be defined and its 'validity' as a unit. Depending on which definition is adopted, there will be different possible analyses of the phonemic composition of individual forms. One analysis may 'discover' the presence of four phonemes in a word, where another analysis 'discovers' five. It will doubtless be possible to produce reasons for adopting either analysis; but they will be reasons of descriptive convenience. It is as if there were disappearing atoms in the molecular structure of words, which showed up in some lights but not in others. Thus the identification of the cenematic units of language is no less problematic than that of the plerematic units.

In spite of this, it might perhaps be argued that although criticisms can always be levelled at any particular dual-structure analysis, there is some significance in the fact that the choice appears to lie between competing dual-structure analyses. To this it may be replied that various types of phonological analysis are available, some of which dispense with the phoneme altogether, whilst others introduce other non-meaningful units. Equally, it is possible to recognise units of grammatical structure which are composed of phonemes, but which as such have no meanings. It follows that if the insistence that 'duality is found in all languages'[1] is intended to cover all such cases, it becomes a much weakened claim. For it reduces to the contention that 'in some sense or other' (the sense in question being left to the individual analyst or school of analysts) all languages have minimum non-meaningful units from which meaningful combinations may be formed.

It is doubtful, however, whether this is a very interesting claim. If the analyst is given a free enough hand with analytic criteria, it is difficult to see what type of communication system could ultimately resist the imposition of a dual-structure analysis in this very weak sense. For example, it has been maintained that the dance of the honeybee, which conveys information as to the distance and direction of a source of nectar, exhibits no duality of structure. But it does not take much ingenuity to read such a duality into it. Whether we agree that 'the smallest independently meaningful aspects of a given dance are not composed of arrangements of meaningless but dif-

[1] ibid., p. 67.

ferentiative features'[1] will depend on how we distinguish between what is meaningful and what is meaningless. The relevant facts about the so-called 'tail-wagging' dance may be summarised as follows: 'The bee starts the wagging dance by running a short distance in a straight line and wagging her abdomen from side to side. Then she returns in a semicircle to the starting point. Then she repeats the straight run and comes back in a semicircle on the opposite side. The cycle is repeated many times.'[2] Thus the 'sign' the bee makes may be described as a flattened figure 8, in which the two loops are linked by a straight 'wavy' line which they share in common. Such a sign may easily be analysed, if we wish, as a meaningful combination of meaningless elements. The two loops of the figure 8 may be regarded as individually meaningless. But when combined they produce a pattern which is meaningful as an indication of the orientation of the nectar source. (The direction is found from the direction marked by the 'tail wagging' section common to both loops.) To object that the way the two loops combine to form a meaningful symbol does not give an exact parallel to the way in which phonemes combine to produce a morpheme is doubtless correct, but beside the point.[3] The objection merely highlights the extent to which the relation between phoneme and morpheme is being implicitly taken as the paradigm case.

To take a different example, we might choose to say that the courtship ceremony of the black-headed gull consists of a single display sequence which has a fixed meaning; or, alternatively, we might choose to divide it into a tripartite combination of Oblique display, Forward display and Upright display, occurring in a fixed order. Each of the three meaningless elements thus distinguished could be identified as recurring in signalling behaviour other than courtship. None the less, which description of the courtship ceremony makes better sense is quite unclear. Now it might be argued that the case of language is different from this, precisely in that the

---

[1] Hockett, op. cit., p. 577.

[2] K. von Frisch, 'Dialects in the language of the bees', p. 303, in *Animal Behavior*, ed. T. Eisner & E. O. Wilson, San Francisco 1975, pp. 303–7.

[3] A more exact analogy would be graphemic, the 'figure 8' constituting one letter in the apian alphabet. Different letters are provided by the 'round' dance, and by the 'sickle' dance of the Italian honeybee. As C. E. Bazell has pointed out, alphabetic symbols are the equivalent not of phonemes but of morphemes, the cenematic units being the individual strokes, loops, dots, etc. of the letters ('The grapheme', *Litera*, 1956, no. 3, pp. 43–6).

stock of words in a language is not limited by Nature as is, presumably, the display-inventory of the black-headed gull. So we find it easy to imagine an as yet non-existent combination of phonemes acquiring a meaning for the English community: but difficult to imagine an as yet non-existent combination of displays acquiring a meaning for the black-headed gull community. While that may be true, however, it introduces into the argument considerations of a quite different order from duality of structure as such. Indeed, it underscores the point that duality of structure is not some objectively given feature which certain communication systems have, whilst others do not. Duality, like many other things, is in the eye of the beholder.

One could even argue that a communication system as simple as a traffic signal which shows red for 'stop' and green for 'go' exhibits duality of structure. For red means 'stop' only when combined with the absence of green, and green means 'go' only when combined with the absence of red. Thus whichever light shows, the system requires a combination of two cenemes for a meaningful plereme. (This analysis would derive support from the fact that if, through malfunctioning, both red and green lights show together, the resultant combination of cenemes is meaningless.)

It seems, then, that any analysable recurrent pattern in signalling will always be statable, if we wish, in terms of a distinction between meaningless units and their meaningful combinations. So to insist on this as characteristic of language will merely have the effect of tending to equate language with systematic communication in general.

Thus the case of 'duality' illustrates two types of difficulty. One concerns the extent to which design-features relating to the internal structure of communication systems are themselves the artifacts of analytic procedures, and hence of linguistic theories. The other has to do with avoiding the conflation of language with communication in general. Any design-feature account which does not propose to equate language with communication in general is obliged to focus upon communicational features which are not common both to languages and to non-languages as well. In effect, therefore, it must treat language as the special case of 'communication using a language'.

But if language is to be treated as 'communication using a language', it is evidently illusory to suppose that someone seeking an answer to the question 'What is a language?' should start by constructing a design-feature answer to the question 'What is language?' That would be to put the cart before the horse. The question 'What is a language?' must take precedence over the question 'What is language?' Making sense of the concept 'language' depends on first making sense of the concept of 'a language'. Any attempt to reverse this order will risk either failure to distinguish language from communication in general, or else involve the inquiry in circularity.

* * *

Unequivocal insistence on the priority of the concept of 'a language' over that of 'language' is first found in the work of Saussure, although the point has perhaps been obscured for his English readers by the vagaries of translators. The Saussurean term *langage* is sometimes rendered by 'speech', while 'language' is brought in as the English equivalent of *langue*. Sometimes, however, 'speech' is produced as the English translation for *parole*. It has even been claimed that Saussure's *langage* has no exact equivalent in English. In one sense this may be true. But none the less there is a perfectly acceptable translation for *langage* in the way Saussure uses it: it is the word 'language'. The mistake is to start by using 'language' to translate *langue*, and then fail to realise that the distinction Saussure draws by opposing *langage* to *langue* is normally made in English simply by the omission or inclusion respectively of an article. Thus in English one normally speaks of 'language' (without a definite or indefinite article) when one wishes to refer either to a general faculty or to a type of activity; but of 'the language' or 'a language' when wishing to refer to any particular system used by the members of a particular community. Only by failing to respect this distinction can one force Saussure to say what English translators have sometimes made him say, i.e. that 'language is a self-contained whole and a principle of classification'.[1] Nothing could more flagrantly contradict the logic of Saussure's thought. The very last conclusion likely to be reached by someone who is at pains to point out that language is itself too diverse to offer an inherent basis for the ordering of

[1] 'La langue . . . est un tout en soi et un principe de classification' (Saussure, op. cit., p. 25).

linguistic facts is the conclusion that language actually constitutes a principle of classification. What does, in Saussure's view, qualify both as a self-contained whole and as a principle of classification is something that in English is normally called 'a language', e.g. English, French, German, Greek, Swahili, Tzeltal. Language cannot do this. For language, says Saussure, 'is many-sided and heterogeneous: straddling various domains, at the same time physical, physiological and psychological, it belongs both to the individual and to society: it cannot be classified under any category of human facts, because one does not know how to discern its unity.'[1] Only if we set out from the concept of 'a language', in Saussure's view, are we able to introduce order into a complexity which defeats any other attempt at systematisation.

Whether or not one agrees with Saussure on this question of priorities, it is of some significance that not until Saussure does the question 'What is a language?' come into prominence as the central question of linguistic theory. Linguistic theorising throughout the nineteenth century had been addressed to other questions, but not to that one; while in earlier periods it had been the details of how languages worked, their differences and their similarities, which engaged the attention of scholars.

Although it began with Saussure and the question 'What is a language?', modern linguistics did not appear suddenly from nowhere in the middle of a cultural *tabula rasa*. It did not lack an antecedent tradition to predetermine the limits of interpretation for a question like 'What is a language?', novel though the question might be. Saussure in any case was the last person to attempt to look outside the mainstream of European learning for an answer. Following his lead, what was done in the name of linguistic science was to impose a technically sophisticated but essentially Western concept of a language upon the descriptive analysis of all languages. This was not cultural neutrality, but cultural imperialism.

Although European linguists overtly rejected those cruder forms of prejudice, which dismissed Chinese as having 'no grammar', or else 'laboured to find in every language the distinctions recognised

---

[1] 'Pris dans son tout, le langage est multiforme et hétéroclite; à cheval sur plusieurs domaines, à la fois physique, physiologique et psychique, il appartient encore au domaine individuel et au domaine social; il ne se laisse classer dans aucune catégorie des faits humains, parce qu'on ne sait comment dégager son unité' (ibid., p. 25).

in Latin',[1] none the less descriptive fallacies of the same stamp persisted and persist in subtler forms at higher levels of abstraction. They have acquired a kind of academic immunity, by becoming part of the technical apparatus of linguistic science.

But it would be illusory to suppose that in any culture there is ever a break of continuity between 'popular' and 'technical' concepts of what a language is. The concept of a language may find expression in various ways and at various levels. It may take the form of myth, legend, or folklore. It may also in certain circumstances become the focal point of an explicit body of knowledge, doctrines, practices and methods of inquiry, tending towards the establishment of what is nowadays usually called a 'study', or 'discipline', or 'science', overtly concerned with linguistic matters. In the course of recorded history, this kind of development has taken place independently at different times in various civilisations. Linguistics, as recognised in contemporary Western culture, is the outcome of one such development.

Certainly, the concept of a language itself undergoes elaboration in the process of transition towards what we now call 'science'. But science, as Benjamin Farrington reminds us, does not and cannot exist in a social vacuum.

'Science, whatever be its ultimate developments, has its origin in techniques, in arts and crafts, in the various activities by which man keeps body and soul together. Its source is experience, its aims practical, its only test that it works. Science arises in contact with things, it is dependent on the evidence of the senses, and however far it seems to move from them, must always come back to them. It requires logic and the elaboration of theory, but its strictest logic and choicest theory must be proved in practice. Science in the practical sense is the necessary basis for abstract and speculative science.

As thus conceived, science develops in close correspondence with the stages of man's social progress and becomes progressively more self-conscious as man's whole way of life becomes more purposive. A food-gatherer has one kind of knowledge of his environment, a

---

[1] O. Jespersen, *The Philosophy of Grammar*, London 1924, p. 47. Easily held up to ridicule were grammars which detected the case system of Latin in the English noun, and hence listed paradigms like: *table* (Nominative), *o table!* (Vocative), *table* (Accusative), *of a table* (Genitive), *to a table* (Dative), and *from a table* (Ablative). Aunt Sallies like these offered a comforting reassurance that at last all cultural blinkers had been removed from the study of languages.

food-producer another. The latter is more active and purposive in his relation to mother earth. Increased mastery of the environment brings increased productivity, which, in its turn, brings social change. The science of gentile or tribal society cannot be the same as the science of political society . . . Fully to understand the science of any society, we must be acquainted with the degree of its material advancement and with its political structure. There is no such thing as science *in vacuo*. There is only the science of a particular society at a particular place and time. The history of science can only be understood as a function of the total life of society.[1]

To the extent that this is true of science in general, it is true of linguistic science in particular. Our verbal behaviour, no less than other forms of behaviour, may, under certain social conditions, give rise to the practice of particular techniques and form the subject matter for intellectual inquiry and the elaboration of theory. But this will not and cannot happen *in vacuo*. How it happens, and exactly what happens, will inevitably reflect in various ways the cultural context in which it happens.

[1] *Greek Science*, vol. 1, Harmondsworth 1944, pp. 14–15.

2

One may be tempted to call Language a kind of Picture of the Universe, where the Words are as the Figures or Images of all particulars.

The concept of a language which survived as part of the intellectual inheritance of modern linguistics first took shape in Graeco-Roman antiquity. There the foundations were laid for a view of man as a language-user which was to provide the basis for all subsequent linguistic studies in Europe for the next two thousand years. But while the continuity of that tradition justifies speaking here of the development of one concept of a language, it is necessary to distinguish various conceptual strands which form part of it.

The first of these strands which claims attention is the idea that words are essentially surrogates or substitutes for other things. Languages are thus surrogational systems, which provide the language-user with a set of verbal tokens which stand for, or take the place of, non-verbal items of various kinds. Accordingly, it is the relation between words and what they stand for which is central to understanding how languages work.

The concept of languages as surrogational systems has as its principal component a doctrine of names which goes back to the very beginnings of the Western tradition. In the Judaeo-Christian branch of that tradition it is embodied in one of the most influential etymological myths ever told: the account given in ch. 2 of the Book of Genesis of how Adam gave the animals names. In the Graeco-Roman branch, it makes its first appearance in the extended discussion of words presented in Plato's dialogue *Cratylus*.

Genesis and *Cratylus* make an interesting comparison, both in

2*

what they say, and in what they do not say, but take for granted, about names.

The writer of Genesis, with characteristic and tantalising brevity, says simply:

> And out of the ground the Lord God formed every beast of the field, and every fowl of the air; and brought them unto Adam to see what he would call them: and whatsoever Adam called every living creature, that was the name thereof.
> And Adam gave names to all cattle, and to the fowl of the air, and to every beast of the field.[1]

Plato's dialogue refers to the mythical activities of a figure who is called simply 'the name-maker'. Who he is, or might have been, remains a mystery. The dialogue is concerned not with his identity, but with how he fulfilled his task; that is to say, with the general principles on which the name-maker, whoever he was, allocated names. In particular, it is concerned with the question of the 'correctness of names'. From the very way this question is introduced, it is evident that the subject is regarded as controversial. One of the participants in the dialogue, Cratylus, expounds a view which we may call 'natural nomenclaturism'. He holds that 'everything has a right name of its own, which comes by nature, and that a name is not whatever people call a thing by agreement, just a piece of their own voice applied to the thing, but that there is a kind of inherent correctness in names, which is the same for all men, both Greeks and barbarians'.[2]

Cratylus makes his point initially with the startling and paradoxical claim that his opponent in the debate, Hermogenes, is not correctly named 'Hermogenes': 'Your name is not Hermogenes, even if all mankind call you so.'[3] The point of this gibe, it appears, rests on the fact that 'Hermogenes' means, literally, 'son of Hermes', Hermes being the patron deity of traders and bankers, whereas the Hermogenes with whom Cratylus is in dispute was in real life a failure at making money. Hence Cratylus' claim that Hermogenes was given the wrong name. It is on a par with making fun of a bankrupt whose name happens to be Richman.

[1] Genesis 2: 19–20.
[2] *Cratylus* 383A (tr. H. N. Fowler, Loeb Classical Library edition).
[3] *Cratylus* 383B.

No such problem is raised in the Biblical account. There is no question as to whether Adam named the animals 'correctly'. On the contrary, what the Bible says seems at first sight to imply precisely the opposite of Cratylus' contention: that is, that far from every thing having, by nature, a right name of its own, it had no name at all until Adam, at God's instigation, gave it one. According to the writer of Genesis, God never refused to accept what Adam called any of the animals, or rebuked him for misnaming them, or considered some of Adam's efforts better than others. This was not a test which God devised to see whether Adam could get the names right. Far from it: 'whatsoever Adam called every living creature, that was the name thereof.' Thus it might appear that the Bible implicitly supports the position maintained by Hermogenes, Cratylus' opponent, who holds the view that 'whatever name you give to a thing is its right name'.[1]

This, however, would be to read back into the Biblical story a controversy which is not there. The point of Cratylus' argument is that there are connexions between words and things which transcend particular languages. Whereas in the context of the Biblical account, there are no particular languages to be transcended. We are present, as it were, at the birth of language itself, when hitherto nameless things are first given names. The possibility of their having different names in different languages does not yet arise.

To treat the story of Adam as favourable to the view held by Hermogenes would in any case be doubly mistaken, since there is no question of Adam's seeking a social agreement about the names of the animals. At that stage in the Creation, Adam had no peers with whom such an agreement might be negotiated. Whether Adam called the animals whatever first came into his head, or whether in any sense he attempted systematically to make the name fit the animal we simply are not told.

The conflict between a theory of natural names and a theory of arbitrary names is one which has implications for the concept of a language which it will be necessary to consider in greater detail. But for the moment it is enough to note that there is a measure of agreement between Genesis and *Cratylus*, at least in the following respects. Names are treated as vocables standing in a certain relationship to things, and the things in question are antecedently

[1] *Cratylus* 384D.

given; that is, exist independently either of their being named at all, or of what they are named. God brought the animals to Adam before they had names. Hermogenes is the person he is, irrespective of whether or not he is correctly called 'Hermogenes'. Thus, in a fundamental sense, what is named is prior, and the name is secondary. This is the assumption on the basis of which it makes sense to discuss whether or not things are correctly named. There is, then, what we may call an implied 'priority of the nominatum'.

This much is common ground to the natural nomenclaturist and his opponent, whom we may call, for purposes of discussion, the non-natural nomenclaturist. The debate between them might be thought a curious starting point for inquiry into the nature of human linguistic activities, and the issue one which in any case had long since ceased to be of relevance to linguistic theorising. But it should not be lightly dismissed.

Natural nomenclaturism can still be detected in various guises in work representative of certain trends in contemporary linguistics. For example, considerable attention has been paid during recent years to the structure of numerical expressions in different languages.[1] A computer programme has been devised to simulate the learning of numerical expressions for languages as diverse as English, Japanese and Mixtec.[2] The obvious attraction of numerical expressions as a field of investigation is that they appear to constitute sets which can be compared across languages without raising any of the awkward questions of comparability which hinder attempts to make interlingually valid statements about other lexical subsystems. So if the analyst takes the cardinal series *one, two, three, four*, etc. and compares it with the corresponding French series *un, deux, trois, quatre*, etc., he can write systems of rules which generate sets of English numerical expressions and sets of French numerical expressions, and point out how similar or dissimilar these rule systems are, without running any grave risk that some sceptic will reject the comparison as invalid.[3] It turns out that the whole of the

[1] E.g. J. R. Hurford, *The Linguistic Theory of Numerals*, Cambridge 1975; D. Stampe, 'Cardinal number systems', *Proceedings of the 12th Annual Conference of the Chicago Linguistics Society*, 1976.

[2] R. J. D. Power & H. C. Longuet-Higgins, 'Learning to count: a computational model of language acquisition', *Proceedings of the Royal Society*, 1978, pp. 391–417.

[3] The risk cannot be eliminated entirely, since different languages deploy their numerical expressions in different ways. In some languages there are distinct numerical

English cardinal series up to 999,999 and the whole of the corresponding French series may be generated by relatively simple systems of rules—systems which can easily be written down on a postcard.[1] The interesting point about these studies, in the context of the present discussion, is that most of them seem to be based implicitly on the assumption that numerical expressions like *one, two, three, four*, etc., are in fact names.[2] Furthermore, they are proper names in the sense that each is the name of some unique thing. The thing in question is an abstract entity called a 'number'. With this qualification, the interpretation offered is basically nomenclaturist. The numerical expression is said to 'stand for' the number.[3]

The thing a numerical expression stands for is not envisaged as belonging to any particular language, any more than the bearer of an ordinary proper name such as *New York* or *Shakespeare*, even though the names *New York* and *Shakespeare* are English names. It is therefore in principle possible that the bearers of these names have other names in other languages. Thus we are told that 'the English name for 503 is the numeral *five hundred and three*';[4] or that 'it is beyond dispute that *soixante-dix* in French and *seventy* in English both denote the number which is symbolized by the Arabic numeral 70.'[5] Learning numerical expressions is envisaged as something separable from learning the systems of calculation from which these expressions derive their use.[6] Sometimes it is claimed that

---

series for various types of countable objects. Even English and French differ marginally (cf. *Louis Quatorze*, but *Henry the Eighth: le trois mai*, but *the third of May*). Hence (see below) the assumption that numerical expressions are comparable 'as names' is not vacuous.

[1] Power & Longuet-Higgins, op. cit.

[2] This occasionally emerges quite clearly. For example, the collection of papers edited by H. B. Corstius in 1968 (Foundations of Language Suppl. Series, no. 7) is entitled not *Grammars for Numerals*, or *Grammars for Numerical Expressions*, but *Grammars for Number Names*. 'Number-names' is also the term used by Hurford (loc. cit.) for expressions of the type which belong to what is referred to in English as the 'cardinal' series: *one, two, three, four*, etc. A speaker's competence in using them is represented by what Hurford calls 'number-name grammars', which are subparts of the grammar of some natural language which the speaker has mastered.

[3] Power & Longuet-Higgins, op. cit., p. 392.

[4] Power & Longuet-Higgins, op. cit., p. 392 fn.

[5] Power & Longuet-Higgins, op. cit., p. 392.

[6] 'A foreigner learning English is not at the same time learning arithmetic. He already has a clear idea of the relationships between the concepts underlying the English words *eight, nine, ten*; he is merely learning new names for them.' (Hurford, op. cit., p. 2.)

numerical expressions stand for concepts which are universal.[1] Rarely, however, is any attempt made to explicate what kind of concept it is that could function as the bearer of a 'number name'. Presumably, this is assumed to be already clear to everybody, or else irrelevant. All that matters is that we accept that each member of a given series like *one, two, three, four*, etc. stands for a certain abstract item, and this abstract item is something which the word in question and any equivalent words in other languages all stand for. In short, numerical expressions are conceived of as forming complete surrogational linguistic subsystems, and numbers as things that Adam might have got round to naming after he had dealt with all the beasts of the field, if God had seen fit to bring them along for Adam's inspection.

Furthermore, the grammatical and semantic analyses which are proposed for numerical expressions involve a tenet which bears a striking resemblance to the doctrine expounded by Cratylus: that is to say, the assumption that every number has a right name or names of its own, which come by nature. The proposition is not put in quite such Platonic terms, and it does not take the crude form of supposing that if the English word *three* is the right name for a certain number, then the French word *trois* must somehow be wrong, or at least not the right name for the very same number. But what is assumed is that, within each separate language, every number has at least one 'naturally correct' name, i.e. a name that is ideally predictable for it. The notion of 'ideal predictability' here must be understood as encompassing the kind of irregularity presented by French *quatre-vingts*. That is, there is a sense in which one might expect the French word corresponding to English *eighty* to be *huitante*; and that form is in fact used in some dialects, although not in standard French. But *quatre-vingts*, although irregular in that respect, is not actually incorrect. Whereas if the French expression corresponding to English *eighty* were *soixante-dix*, while the equivalent to English *seventy* was *quatre-vingts*, that state of affairs in French would be not merely irregular but incorrect. In short, the

---

[1] E.g. 'The concepts of particular numbers seem to be universal' (Hurford, op. cit., p. 2). It is not always clear what such universality claims amount to. If they are intended to entail that everyone has e.g. the concept of the number 999,999, or that there are at least some numbers such that everyone has the concept of them, they are claims which would require making out a much more detailed case than is usually provided to support them.

assumption is that numbers have naturally correct names in the sense that each name not merely stands for but somehow reflects the identity of its number, in ways which accord with the assumed universal laws of arithmetic. This is natural nomenclaturism just as deeply rooted, perhaps more deeply, than the variety propounded by Cratylus. Its fundamental conviction is that any number-name must be wrong if it fails to correspond to the nature of its number. That is exactly on a par with the idea that the whale is incorrectly called *Walfisch* in German, since the whale is not in fact a fish. Therefore, the name misrepresents the reality.

Since the nomenclaturist interpretation of numerical expressions assumes that the name has to fit the number in some natural way, it is obliged to invent semantic rules which explain how the names are appropriate. Thus, for example, the expression *twenty-two* may be explained as comprising a 'major term' (*twenty*) and a 'minor term' (*two*) conjoined in a construction of which the meaning is defined as 'sum'.[1] In other words, the semantic component of a speaker's grammar contains a rule which enables him to identify the meaning of that expression by performing the appropriate arithmetical computation on the two components. What postulating such a rule accounts for about the speaker's mastery of his language it is very difficult to see. He could certainly use the word-string *twenty-two* correctly for all counting purposes without making any such analysis, just as he can use the expression *five* correctly without analysing it into two parts meaning 'four' and 'one'. On the other hand, the rule does solve the typically nomenclaturist problem of explaining in what the 'correctness' of the name consists. The name is held to be correct because the expression *twenty-two* means 'twenty-plus-two', and twenty plus two adds up to twenty-two, the number we first thought of. It is an etymology which would have delighted Varro, who held that a bee was called *apis* in Latin because *apis* really meant *a* 'without', *pis* 'foot': and bees, as is well known, have no feet.

Explanation is also needed, on the nomenclaturist interpretation, for such facts as that *fifty-nine*, and not **forty-nineteen*, is the English numerical expression which occupies the slot between *fifty-eight* and *sixty*. The explanation may be supplied by postulating

---

[1] Power & Longuet-Higgins, op. cit., p. 395.

rules of the grammar which have the effect of eliminating *forty-nineteen* in favour of *fifty-eight*, and so on. But the need for postulating such rules would never have arisen in the first place, but for the typically nomenclaturist assumption that *forty-nineteen* is in principle a name which is naturally correct for the number in question, since it reflects the nature of that number just as accurately as the expression *fifty-nine*. Hence, the non-occurrence of *forty-nineteen* as a number-name calls for explanation. It is rather like asking why in English frogs are not called *pondhoppers*. For anyone who is not a natural nomenclaturist, the question does not arise. The fact is simply that in English frogs are called *frogs*. There is no need to postulate that English speakers have mastered some rule which has the effect of eliminating the expression *pondhopper* from their vocabulary.

The use of a nomenclaturist terminology in discussing numerical expressions cannot be justified as a harmless *façon de parler*. For at the very least it favours a misleading assimilation of the role played by numerical expressions to the role played by other words. To think of learning the numerical expressions of a language as a process of discovering 'how to name the numbers' is implicitly to adopt a surrogational concept of that part of the language. It is as if learning the numerical expressions were a kind of elementary botany, which involved identifying various specimens provided by Nature, and finding out what each is called. Whereas for most language-users the basic learning of numerical expressions is a quite different kind of enterprise. They are used primarily for counting people, things and events. There are also secondary uses, which do not involve counting people, or things, or events. But even a parachutist who recites aloud 'one, two, three, four, five, six, seven, eight, nine, ten' before pulling the ripcord is not engaged in some abstract naming exercise, as someone would be if, for example, he decided to see if he could list all the other householders living in his street. What the parachutist is doing is nothing like that: he is just counting. To ask 'But what is he counting?' is already a misguided question. To reply that he is counting the numbers would be to give an even more misguided answer.

*   *   *

'1 ne survival of nomenclaturism, whether of the natural or non-natural variety, also claims our attention on the score that the two most influential figures in twentieth-century thought about language, Wittgenstein and Saussure, both set out to attack it.

At the beginning of the *Philosophical Investigations*,[1] Wittgenstein criticises the account given by St. Augustine in Book I of the *Confessions* of how, as a child, Augustine learnt the meanings of words by observing the verbal behaviour of his elders. This account, according to Wittgenstein, is based upon and exemplifies an erroneous concept of what a language is.

The relevant passage in the *Confessions* runs as follows:

> When they (my elders) named some object, and accordingly moved towards something, I saw this and I grasped that the thing was called by the sound they uttered when they meant to point it out. Their intention was shown by their bodily movements, as it were the natural language of all peoples: the expression of the face, the play of the eyes, the movement of other parts of the body, and the tone of voice which expresses our state of mind in seeking, having, rejecting or avoiding something. Thus, as I heard words repeatedly used in their proper places in various sentences, I gradually learned to understand what objects they signified; and after I had trained my mouth to form these signs, I used them to express my own desires.[2]

Such an account of language-learning, says Wittgenstein, embodies a certain idea of what a language is, but 'it is the idea of a language more primitive than ours'.[3] Specifically, it is the idea of a language in which the individual words name objects, and sentences are combinations of such names.[4] Wittgenstein goes on to consider

---

[1] *Philosophische Untersuchungen*. References are to the revised edition and translation by G. E. M. Anscombe (Oxford 1958).

[2] *Confessions* I. 8. 'Cum ipsi (majores homines) appellabant rem aliquam, et cum secundum eam vocem corpus ad aliquid movebant, videbam, et tenebam hoc ab eis vocari rem illam, quod sonabant, cum eam vellent ostendere. Hoc autem eos velle ex motu corporis aperiebatur: tamquam verbis naturalibus omnium gentium, quae fiunt vultu et nutu oculorum, ceterorumque membrorum actu, et sonitu vocis indicante affectionem animi in petendis, habendis, rejiciendis, fugiendisve rebus. Ita verba in variis sententiis locis suis posita, et crebro audita, quarum rerum signa essent, paulatim colligebam, measque jam voluntates, edomito in eis signis ore, per haec enuntiabam.'

[3] 'die Vorstellung einer primitiveren Sprache, als der unsern', *Philosophische Untersuchungen*, §2.

[4] 'Die Wörter der Sprache benennen Gegenstände—Sätze sind Verbindungen von solchen Benennungen', ibid., §1.

what a language would be like if in fact it worked in the way he takes to be implied by Augustine's remarks. He invites the reader to imagine a language which fits Augustine's description: it is a language meant to serve for communication between a builder and his assistant. The builder uses four types of building materials: blocks, pillars, slabs and beams. His assistant has to fetch them in the order the builder requires. They use a language consisting of the four words: *block*, *pillar*, *slab*, and *beam*. The builder calls out a word, whereupon his assistant brings him an item of the corresponding type. 'Conceive this,' says Wittgenstein, 'as a complete primitive language.'[1]

There is perhaps a temptation to object straight away to Wittgenstein's example and say that it is absurd to ask us to conceive this system as a complete language, primitive or otherwise.[2] Our concept of a language will accommodate four-letter words, but it will not accommodate four-word languages. If explorers discovered a lost tribe in New Guinea using just this verbal equipment, or its equivalent, should we not be inclined to say not that there was one more language to add to the list of four thousand or so already known, but rather that this was the first recorded instance of a civilisation which had no language at all?

However, objections along these lines would be misguided for at least two reasons. First, it is not essential to insist that the system Wittgenstein's builders have be called 'a language'; the term can easily be withheld without harm to the example. None the less, what we call a language will presumably occupy some position in a hierarchy of possible communication systems, of which the one used by Wittgenstein's builders exemplifies a certain basic type. Exactly which range of possible systems in the hierarchy we agree to call 'languages' is, it might be argued, a terminological point which is ultimately of no great importance.

Secondly, the objection itself concedes one of the main points which Wittgenstein seems concerned to make. Although we can imagine a primitive communication system of the type he describes,

---

[1] 'Fasse dies als vollständige primitive Sprache auf', ibid., §2.

[2] A. Kenny, *Wittgenstein*, London 1973, p. 168 et seq. The 'builder's language' is not only of extreme structural simplicity, but also fails to meet several of the criteria favoured by 'design-feature' theorists, including 'reciprocity', 'institutionality' and 'displacement'. On the other hand, it meets the requirements of 'vocality', 'arbitrariness' and 'duality'.

and although we can think of communication situations in which
such a system would be perfectly viable, none the less we need only
have the details spelt out crudely for us in this way to recognise
at once that such a model fails to capture very many features which
seem essential to languages as we know them. English, or French,
or Swahili, we realise, cannot in the final analysis be elaborate systems of names for objects, even though in certain circumstances it
may seem from the way they work that that is just what they are.

A very similar point about languages was made by Saussure. In
fact, it is made no less than three times in the *Cours de linguistique
générale*. A language, says Saussure, is sometimes treated as if it
were simply a nomenclature. This is initially presented as one of
the factors inhibiting the development of an autonomous science of
linguistics.[1] It is a misconception which stands in the way of our
seeing clearly what a language is, for it stifles, says Saussure, all
research into the true nature of languages.

This condemnation may strike the reader at first as surprisingly
sweeping, or even exaggerated, the more so since initially it is left
without amplification or qualification of any kind. But why and how
does the concept of a language as a nomenclature provide such a
formidable impediment to our understanding of what languages really
are? The answers to these questions are left in abeyance until we
come to the chapter on the nature of the linguistic sign. Here the
point is developed,[2] and we begin to see for the first time exactly
how the concept of languages as systems of names for objects is not
merely erroneous, from Saussure's point of view, but offers indeed
the exact antithesis to a correct understanding of what languages are.
For one thing, it obscures the nature of the relationship which it
purports to clarify, since it allows an ambiguity as to whether words
are to be considered as entities in the mind, or as concrete vocalisa-
tions. For Saussure, it is important to insist that 'the linguistic sign
unites not a thing and a name, but a concept and an acoustic image'.[3]
Secondly, it fosters the illusion that the connexion between thing and
name is a quite simple relation, which is far from being the case.
But thirdly, and most importantly, it presupposes that there are
units given in advance, namely words and things, between which a

---

[1] *Cours de linguistique générale*, 2nd ed., p. 34.   [2] ibid., pp. 97-8.
[3] 'Le signe linguistique unit non une chose et un nom, mais un concept et une image
acoustique', ibid., p. 98.

language merely establishes certain correlations, thereby instituting a given word as the name (in that language) of the given thing.

This last point is eventually treated at greater length in the chapter on 'La valeur linguistique',[1] where the essential message of Saussurean structuralism is expounded in its definitive form. In this chapter, Saussure explains that nothing is to be regarded as given in advance of the language; for it is the structure of the language itself which creates on the one hand the divisions of sounds which we identify as words, and on the other hand, the divisions of thought by which we classify the world of things. And these are not two separate processes, but facets of one and the same process. In short, a language, as Saussure's dictum puts it, can only be a 'system of pure values'.

*   *   *

The surrogationalism condemned by Saussure and Wittgenstein appears in two different basic forms throughout the Western tradition. What may be called 'reocentric surrogationalism' supposes that the things words stand for are to be located 'out there' in the world external to the individual language-user. On the other hand, what may be called 'psychocentric surrogationalism' supposes that what words stand for is to be located internally, that is to say in the mind of the language-user. (Various possible compromises between these two varieties of surrogationalism can readily be envisaged.)

Reocentric surrogationalism has an importance in Western thought which is by no means confined to debate on strictly linguistic topics. It goes much further. Indeed, it would be difficult to exaggerate the extent to which it permeates Western attitudes. It is central to much of Western philosophy of science. In so far as science is conceived of as providing—or involving the provision of —'correct' reports of reality, the Pandora's box of problems which are the inseparable concomitants of reocentric surrogationalism is already open. What is it for a report of reality to be accurate? How must the words stand in relation to the alleged describienda in order that there shall be no misrepresentation of what they purport to describe?

Fortunately or unfortunately, science in the West developed a

[1] ibid., p. 155 et seq.

methodology which, at least on one level, managed to circumvent such problems, or at least prevent them from assuming proportions which would induce total stagnation. This mode of circumvention was the experimental method itself. In other words, for many scientific purposes a report of reality is simply accepted as correct if what it appears to claim can be replicated experimentally with the same results. However, this solution is not available in areas of science which are, for various reasons, not amenable to the experimental method. It is in these areas that we typically encounter debates as to whether the investigation in question belongs to science or not, and debates as to how the correspondence between report and reality can be made to rest upon a surer foundation.

One illustration of this is offered by modern developments in the social sciences. Traditional ethnography is criticised on the ground that its reports of social reality are unreliable, not in the trivial sense that the reporters are careless, or fail to understand what they observe, but in the sense that ethnographic reports have an endemic unreliability, however competent the individual reporter may be. The essential features of this criticism are embodied in what may be called the 'travellers' tales' argument. Travellers' tales, it is argued, are unreliable in the first place because the traveller, through no fault of his own, tends to be struck by the exotic. He is relatively unimpressed by what is familiar, and may not even notice it, much less examine its significance. Just so the ethnographer in his field work automatically concentrates on the exotic features of whatever he is studying, whether within his own culture or in an alien culture. Within his own culture he will tend to choose as his field of study aspects of social organisation within one of the less-than-everyday situations—court proceedings, or job interviews, or medical and quasi-medical investigations. These are less-than-everyday situations not in the sense that they cannot be found every day of the week, but in that they do not occur every day of the week for the great majority of the population. Secondly, even in respect of reporting the exotic, the traveller will necessarily leave out of his tale a great deal of what he observed, and of what in principle he could have included, but for fear of boring his audience, or failing to conform to the culturally determined norms for travellers' tales. Similarly, it is argued, the ethnographer must necessarily condense and summarise his field notes, in order to present what is regarded as an acceptable report. For whatever the traveller observes provides material for potentially endless description. But the traveller's tale is a finite description, and therefore must omit at least part of what might have been included. Thirdly, whatever the traveller observes and includes in his tale might in principle have been described in some other way than the way he chooses to describe it. Similarly, it is suggested, since the ethnographer has a choice between different ways of reporting his observations, the way he eventually chooses must be determined by factors other than the social reality he is purportedly describing. Traditional ethnography, therefore, falls foul of at least three problems in the reporting of social reality: the problem of 'focus', the problem of 'omission', and the problem of 'slant'.

The thrust of the travellers' tales argument in the social sciences has had significant practical and theoretical consequences; e.g., it is one of the factors behind the emergence of ethnomethodology.[1] In one sense, ethnomethodology can be interpreted as implying a radical critique of the surrogational view of languages: both negatively, by its rejection of conventional reports upon the social world, and also positively, by its insistence on the priority of analysing the methods people use to participate in and make sense of verbal interaction. The result is a redirection of attention away from the correlation between words and what they allegedly stand for in the external world, since this is implicitly dismissed as an inadequate model for understanding what is going on in verbal activity. It is trust in this inadequate model which misleads the social scientist into believing that he can simply inspect any selected segment of the social world and produce a correct, objective, descriptive summary of what it contains. The point which is of relevance to the present discussion, however, is that the travellers' tales debate would be inconceivable in a culture which accorded no credibility at all to surrogationalism. It would be quite meaningless to argue about whether social phenomena had been correctly reported, unless it were taken for granted that a correct report was in principle possible. If words were not assumed to stand for things in such a way as to project the possibility of this ideal report, omitting nothing and distorting nothing, then the objections to the defi-

[1] Cf. the points of view formulated in, e.g., H. Sacks, 'Sociological description', *Berkeley Journal of Sociology*, 1963; H. Garfinkel, *Studies in Ethnomethodology*, 1967.

ciencies of travellers' tales would hardly make sense. The problem
of 'focus', the problem of 'omission', and the problem of 'slant'
become problems only against a background which assumes that
reality is not just what we happen to notice; that words are in
principle available to represent the totality of what is real; and that
any given segment of reality may give rise to alternative verbal
representations. But these are assumptions about how languages
work, and about the relations between words and things.

An analogous example is provided by contemporary movements
in literary stylistics. Here we see attempts to circumvent the alleged
subjectivity of stylistic analysis by introducing an objective determination of the stylistically prominent features of a literary work.
For the travellers' tales argument may be applied equally to reports
about experiences of reading poems and novels. One attempt to
rebut such criticism is by appeal to a kind of collective literary
jury, personified in a so-called *archilecteur*.[1] The point about the
archilecteur is not that he is a fiction of literary theory, but that his
creation would never have been felt necessary except in the context
of a tradition in which the words of the literary critic may be seen
as amenable to assessment primarily in the dimension of correspondence to reality. Whether the *archilecteur* provides an adequate
basis on which to found stylistic analysis is irrelevant: it is the
theoretical strategy *per se* which merits attention. The appeal to a
collective literary competence which readers share is the literary
counterpart of ethnomethodology.[2] It makes sense only as an
attempt to resolve the typically surrogationalist problem of how to
judge whether what the literary critic says corresponds to the reality
of the literary work.

*   *   *

The idea that the 'things' of the external world about us constitute the enduring reality from which words, as mere vocal labels,
must ultimately derive their meanings is so entrenched in the
Western tradition as to seem almost to stand in no serious need of
substantiation. Yet the extent to which such an assumption is part

[1] Michael Riffaterre, *Essais de stylistique structurale*, Paris 1971, pp. 46–7.
[2] With the qualification that in the case of the *archilecteur* how readers interpret what
they read is discounted. It is, as it were, the syntax of their reading which is retained as
evidence, not the semantics.

of a cultural inheritance should not be underestimated. It becomes apparent if we consider, for comparison, the Confucian doctrine known as *cheng ming*, or 'rectification of names', which appears to take for granted exactly the opposite assumption. That is to say, things are conceived of as conforming to the natural order not in themselves, but in virtue of corresponding to their names. When things for any reason fail to correspond to the essence represented by their names, disorder ensues; and this can be rectified only by bringing things back into correspondence with what they are called, and hence what they should be. For Confucius, an example of non-conformity between name and thing was the use of the word *ku*, traditionally designating a type of drinking goblet with corners, but which came to be made without corners. Rather than treating this as a case where the word was no longer appropriate to the thing, or an example of a word changing its meaning, Confucius appears to have regarded it as a case of the thing no longer being appropriate to the word. It is as if, to take an English parallel, one described the situation in which the word *manuscript* is no longer applied exclusively to documents written by hand, but also to what is type-written, by saying not that the word *manuscript* had altered or extended its meaning, but instead that manuscripts were often nowadays wrongly made (i.e. by using typewriters). Or as if one said not that in the phrase *tin box* the word *box* had lost its etymological sense of 'boxwood'; but instead that there were no tin boxes. (The lady who objected to having the surname *Cooperman* and had it legally altered to *Cooperperson* presumably believed in the doctrines of Women's Lib. If she had believed in the doctrine of *cheng ming*, she would have had a sex-change operation instead.) When asked about the principles of government, Confucius is reported as replying: 'Let the ruler be ruler, the minister minister, let the father be father and the son son.' That is to say, society will be well governed if the ruler conforms to the name of 'ruler', the minister to the name of 'minister', the father to the name of 'father', and the son to the name of 'son'.[1] In short, names are regarded as representing the permanent or true state of the world, from which things derive their meaning.

Here we glimpse the possibility of a totally logocentric view of

[1] Fung Yu-Lan, *A History of Chinese Philosophy*, tr. D. Bodde, 2nd ed., Princeton 1952–3, vol. 1, pp. 59–60.

reality: that is, a view according to which words hold the key to things, and language provides the patterns to which reality must conform.[1] Its antithetical counterpart is a reocentric view of language: that is, a view according to which things hold the key to words, and reality provides the patterns to which language must conform.

The Western intellectual tradition has been mainly dominated by reocentric thinking, from Plato's theory of Forms onwards. To treat beauty, virtue, honesty, etc., as real things, even if not things of the ordinary, everyday kind, is characteristically reocentric. To say this is not to imply that Plato was naïve enough to suppose that because words like *Athens, Socrates, earth, water*, etc., were names of real things, words like *beauty, virtue, honesty*, etc., must also somehow be names of real things. But it is to suggest, first, that the attractiveness of postulating some abstract reality which is the Form of Beauty, or Virtue, or Honesty is difficult to comprehend except in an intellectual context where the paradigm for explaining names is to relate them to things; and, secondly, that the Platonic theory of Forms can be viewed as an attempt to solve problems which arise essentially out of a reocentric view of names. The problems are set by the evident disparity between the various particular things to which one and the same general name can be applied, and the evident disparity between the various general names which may be applied to one and the same particular thing. If one considers the obvious differences between, say a Yorkshire terrier and a Borzoi, can it be right to apply the same general name *dog* to both creatures? For to use the same name implies, from a reocentric point of view, that we are talking about the same thing. And yet the Yorkshire terrier and the Borzoi are manifestly not the same thing. Equally, to either we may apply not only the general name *dog*, but other general names, such as *quadruped*, or *animal*, which can be used of many other creatures than dogs. Again, how can this be correct, granted that the dog is one creature, and not many? One difficulty is that of finding a source of recurrent sameness in the face of superficial diversity, and another that of finding a source of co-existent diversity in the face of apparent unity.

The elegance of a Platonic theory of Forms lies in resolving both

---

[1] The term *logocentric* is here used in a different sense from that which will be familiar to readers of Derrida.

difficulties at a single stroke. The answer offered in the *Parmenides* is that there is nothing to marvel at in the fact that two things may be alike in certain respects, but unlike in others. Socrates argues that inasmuch as things partake in likeness they will be alike, and inasmuch as they partake in unlikeness they will be unlike. But if anyone could show that likeness and unlikeness themselves partook of each other, that would indeed be a wonder. Similarly, a thing may in some respects be one, but in other respects many. Socrates says, if someone wishes to show that I am both one and many he will proceed as follows. 'He will say, when he wishes to show that I am many, that there are my right parts and my left parts, my front parts and my back parts, likewise upper and lower, all different: for I do, I suppose, partake of multitude; and when he wishes to show that I am one, he will say that we here are seven persons, of whom I am one, a man, partaking also of unity; and so he shows that both assertions are true.'[1] But this, argues Socrates, is not surprising either. What would be surprising is a demonstration that unity itself is in reality many, or multitude itself in reality unity. Thus the mystery is created by failing to distinguish between particular things and the abstract Forms of which particular things partake. Once this distinction is drawn, the mystery evaporates.

The distinction between the abstract Form and the particular which partakes of it is applied also by Socrates to conceptions such as Justice, Beauty and Goodness. But when Parmenides asks him whether there is a Form of Man, apart from all individual men, or of Fire, or of Water, Socrates seems to be less sure; and he agrees that it would be absurd to think of hair, or mud, or dirt as having abstract Forms. 'And yet,' he adds, 'I am sometimes disturbed by the thought that perhaps what is true of one thing is true of all'[2]— a remark of which the self-critical irony can hardly be ignored; for once one embarks upon the explanatory postulation of Forms, there is no obvious place to stop short of extending similar explanations to cover the whole gamut of general names.

A limited extension can be seen in, for example, the *Meno*, where Socrates rejects Meno's attempt to define what virtue is by giving examples of virtue. To show why this is a mistake, Socrates considers the question 'What is a bee?' and points out that though

---

[1] *Parmenides* 129C,D (tr. H. N. Fowler, Loeb Classical Library edition).
[2] *Parmenides* 130D.

there are different kinds of bees, listing all the varieties will not tell us what a bee is, because bees do not differ as bees. In order to answer the question we have to make some attempt to say what it is that all bees have in common which makes them bees. And the same holds for virtue. However diverse the virtues may be, they all share a characteristic form, an εἶδος, which makes them virtues, and it is to this, says Socrates, not to the particular virtues, that one must look if one wishes to say what virtue is.[1] From this argument, it appears that the distinction between particulars and abstract Forms applies to moral qualities and to natural species alike.

More explicitly still, a well-known passage in Epistle VII (if the attribution to Plato is correct) appears to sanction applying the same distinction to virtually everything in the world of ordinary experience, including specifically geometrical shapes, colours, moral concepts, all bodies whether natural or manufactured, all living creatures and all moral actions or passions of the soul.[2] In this passage, the thing itself, in its ultimate essence or Form, is distinguished from, firstly, its name; secondly, its definition; thirdly, its manifestation in particular examples; and fourthly, our knowledge of any of these.

In the *Parmenides* Socrates does not express his thesis in overtly semantic terms; but when asked by Parmenides whether he thinks that the things which partake of the Forms are named therefrom, 'as, for instance, those that partake of likeness become like, those that partake of greatness great, those that partake of beauty and justice just and beautiful',[3] he agrees that this is so. So he agrees, it appears, that the existence of the Forms supplies the ultimate justification for the correct application of the general name.

This seems to fit with the assumption invoked in the *Republic*[4] that there is one Form corresponding to every set of things which are called by the same name. We need not go into the controversy which hinges on Aristotle's claim that Plato recognised only Forms of what exists in Nature,[5] nor the question of the extent to which Plato revised his theory of Forms. It suffices in the present context to make two general points. One is: that to say that the Form underlies and explains the application of the general name is not to saddle Plato with the doctrine that the name represents just the Form. In

[1] *Meno*, 72C.   [2] *Epistles* VII. 342.   [3] *Parmenides* 130E–131.   [4] *Republic* 596A.
[5] Cf. W. D. Ross, *Plato's Theory of Ideas*, Oxford 1951, p. 79 and references.

other words, it would not follow that if the same Form were to underlie two distinct names, those names would be automatically synonymous. For, as we are told in Epistle VII, there is a 'weakness inherent in language', by which names do not express simply the essence of things, but also qualities of things.[1] And this weakness is adduced as a reason why the true philosopher would never be so rash as to commit his serious views to writing.

The second point, which is more important for the general theme of this discussion, is that whatever the truth may be about the evolution and crystallisation of Plato's views, the *Parmenides* gives us as clear a piece of evidence as we could wish for the existence of a phase in which intangibles such as beauty and virtue have Forms postulated to supply the reality they apparently lack, whereas no comparable postulation is felt necessary in regard to more immediately accessible things, such as chairs, tables or human beings. Now such a compromise would be totally incomprehensible in the context of a logocentric framework of thought; for beauty, virtue, etc., occupy no special status from a logocentric point of view. Something would be beautiful in so far as it conformed to the name of *beauty*, just as something would be a chair in so far as it conformed to the name of *chair*. But in a type of theorising which is fundamentally reocentric, such a compromise is readily understandable, granted that words like *beauty* and *virtue* lack things of which they are the names, more obviously and more mysteriously than words for material objects lack things of which they are the names.

Whatever reservations may be entertained about points of detail, what emerges very clearly from the Platonic mode of reasoning is that the general reocentric strategy of looking for a thing which the name stands for is assumed to be right. In cases where it is difficult to find an obvious nominatum, the conclusion reached is that there must be some more basic stratum of reality, or realm of things, other than the one immediately accessible to observation, since the immediately accessible realm is populated only with unsatisfactorily imperfect examples.

But this is, as it were, doubly reocentric—reocentricism coming to the rescue of its own deficiencies. Instead of concluding that perhaps certain names do not stand for things after all, recourse is had

---

[1] *Epistles* VII. 342E–343A.

to invoking abstract realities when observable realities fail to meet the requirements demanded of them.

Whatever we may think of the solution offered by a Platonic theory of Forms, the question raised involves a stronger hypothesis about languages than merely that languages are systems of names. For we can imagine a system of names which does not give rise to any such problem. Wittgenstein's builder's language might be one example. Or imagine an even more primitive language-game played with the same verbal equipment. Suppose A has a stockpile of blocks, pillars, slabs and beams. One block is to all intents and purposes indistinguishable from another block, one pillar from another pillar, and so on. A selects an object at random from his stockpile and holds it up for B to see. B then calls out the appropriate word, *block, pillar, slab* or *beam*, as the case may be. When he has done that, A selects another object. And so the game continues.

Someone may object: 'But at least Wittgenstein's language-game had some end in view. It enabled the builders to co-operate in the building operation. Whereas this new language game would be quite silly.' Silly or not, it does curiously resemble the language-games mothers play with their children,[1] or the language-games we are sometimes invited to play when learning foreign languages.[2] But the point here is that the rules of the game are set up in such a way that one name does only one job in relation to the world of things. If the languages we use in everyday life were all like that, it is safe to say that the Platonic theory of forms would never have been formulated. The theory only makes sense in a context in which it is taken for granted that languages are not merely systems of names, but, more importantly, systems which allow the same name to be applied to things which are not qualitatively identical, and different names to be applied to one and the same thing.

Suppose, for instance, we augment the four-word vocabulary *block, pillar, slab* and *beam* in the following way. We introduce a word *blom*, which can be applied to any block or any beam, and also a word *plab*, which can be applied to any pillar or any slab. When A holds up an object chosen at random, B's role in the game is now

[1] A. Ninio & J. Bruner, 'The achievement and antecedents of labelling', *Journal of Child Language*, vol. 5, 1978, pp. 1-15.
[2] For example, what are called 'identifying games' in W. R. Lee, *Language-Teaching Games and Contests*, Oxford 1965.

significantly different. For each object he has a choice between two correct words to utter.

This new situation may be regarded as providing the minimum language model in relation to which a Platonic theory of Forms makes sense. It is as if someone asked: 'But how can the same word *blom* be the right name for B to utter when A holds up either a block or a beam; and how can the same word *plab* be the right name for either a pillar or a slab? For are not blocks, beams, pillars and slabs all different? And how can one object which A holds up be correctly called by B either *block* or *blom*? For surely it is only one object, not two.'

Now whatever we may think of such questions, they are clearly questions which concern the rules of the language-game. The answers which a Platonic theory of Forms would supply would be answers which suggested that although blocks, pillars, slabs and beams were all that was visible, the reality of the game-world included also bloms and plabs, although examples of these were never actually encountered in a pure state, but only in particular blocks, pillars, slabs and beams; and that once we accept that, then we can see how it is legitimate for B to call the object which A holds up either *block* or *blom*, and likewise legitimate for him to call by the same name *blom* both blocks and beams indifferently.

Whatever we think of such answers, they are clearly responses quite different in kind from saying 'What a stupid question to ask!', or 'Those are just the rules of the game'. They are answers which presuppose a different concept of what a language is. To have a concept of a language necessarily involves going beyond mere understanding of what the acceptable verbal moves are, even in the case where what is claimed is that to know a language is just to know the acceptable verbal moves. A concept of a language involves, and is most often clearly manifest in, acceptance or rejection of what requires explanation about the ways in which languages work. This means that a concept of a language cannot stand isolated in an intellectual no-man's-land. It is inevitably part of some more intricate complex of views about how certain verbal activities stand in relation to other human activities, and hence, ultimately, about man's place in society and in nature. The moment we try to ask ourselves what a language is without situating the question in such a perspective, we ask a question which may sound as if it leaves open a whole range of possible answers, but to which it turns out to be impossible to give any answer at all.

* * *

The view of the natural nomenclaturist, that things have naturally correct names, even though men may not always use them, is one for which it is not easy to make out a convincing case. It requires some attempt to explain exactly how a name is to be regarded as fitting its nominatum; in other words, an attempt to elaborate a doctrine of natural affinity between words and things.

The most plausible cases of natural affinity which a language offers are usually those of imitative or echoic words, where, as for example in the case of the English word *cuckoo*, a creature is named after its characteristic call, or a sound is called by a combination of vowels and consonants which evoke a similar auditory impression, as in the case of words such as *tinkle* or *bang*. This relatively small class of cases can be considerably enlarged by invoking a theory of mimetic transposition, which allows the similarity to hold not merely between sound and meaning, but also between articulation and meaning. Accordingly, the individual articulations of a language are held to have characteristic mimetic functions. In this way, words can be interpreted as imitations of things in virtue of their pronunciation, irrespective of whether the resultant sound bears any striking resemblance to a sound associated with the object named.

Such a theory is discussed in Plato's *Cratylus*. It is suggested, for example, that because the sound /l/, the Greek lambda, is produced with a gliding movement of the tongue, this is why the Greek words meaning 'glide', 'level', and 'sleek' all contain a lambda. Likewise the Greek fricative consonants phi, psi, sigma and zeta are all 'pronounced with much breath' as if in imitation of the action of blowing, and this is why Greek words meaning, for example, 'cold, shivering', 'seething', 'shake' and 'shock' contain these consonants. Similarly the vowel /o/, Greek omicron, is associated with roundness, and /r/, Greek rho, being allegedly the consonant involving greatest agitation of the tongue, is associated with the ideas of motion and rapidity. Thus the theory of mimetic transposition holds that each name is a combination of sounds, and each sound, because it is formed by the organs of speech in a particular way, is suited to express a certain notion. From some such basic set of sound-and-sense associations the appropriate names of all things are formed.

One might expect the theory of mimetic transposition to have died a natural death in Classical antiquity; but it turns up again much later in the Western tradition in full vigour, for example in eighteenth-century France. Charles de Brosses explains the principles of word formation in the following terms:[1]

> In this small number of germs or articulations [he is referring to the speech sounds of which the human vocal apparatus is capable] the choice of those to be utilised in the construction of a word, that is to say the name of a real object, is physically determined by the nature and quality of the object itself; in such a way as to depict, as far as possible, the object as it is; for otherwise the word would give no idea of it; so that any man who is in the position of imposing the first name on something that is rough will employ a rough sound and not a soft one; just as, from among the seven primary colours, a painter who wishes to depict grass is obliged to choose green, and not violet. Without looking further, one can see this from the words *rude* and *doux*: is not the one rough and the other soft? Let us suppose that a native of the Caribbean wishes to designate, for the benefit of an Algonquin Indian, a cannon shot, something which neither has encountered before, and suppose that neither speaks the other's language. He will not call it *nizalie* but *poutoue*.
>
> Thus the system of the original making of human language and the imposition of names on things is not arbitrary and conventional, as is customarily imagined; but a genuine system of necessity determined by two causes. One is the construction of the vocal organs which can render only certain sounds analogous to their shape. The other is the necessity and property of the real things one wishes to name. This requires one to employ as their names sounds which depict them, establishing between the thing and the word a connexion by which the word may conjure up an idea of the thing.
>
> Thus the original making of human language must have consisted, as both experience and observation bear witness, in a more or less complete depiction of the things named; in so far as it was possible for the vocal organs to accomplish it by a sound imitative of the real objects . . .
>
> Thus . . . there exists a primitive, organic, physical and necessary language, which is known and practised by no people in the world in

[1] *Traité de la formation méchanique des langues et des principes physiques de l'étymologie,* 1765, p. xi et seq.

its pristine simplicity: but which all men none the less speak, and
which constitutes the basis of language in all countries . . .

The example illustrates how what is regarded as requiring explanation about languages, and how it is explained, may be determined
by the way in which languages are seen as fitting in to some broader
theoretical schema. What underlies this resurrection of natural
nomenclaturism in eighteenth-century France is the commitment
of certain *philosophes* to showing that all things human could be
explained without the postulation of divine intervention. In the
case of languages, this appeared necessary in order to refute the
'orthodox' view (as expressed, for example, by Jean Frain du
Tremblay[1]) that man had received from God the gift of speech.
Both Condillac and de Brosses saw in the theory that words were
originally vocal imitations of things a way of providing a 'natural'
explanation of the origin and development of languages, owing
nothing to divine assistance. The treatise on languages that de
Brosses wrote reveals this preoccupation even in its title (*Treatise
on the Mechanical Formation of Languages*). Moreover, writers like
Rousseau and Beauzée,[2] who seem to have found it difficult to
accept a purely human origin for languages, were none the less
concerned to accommodate and explain the existence of languages
within a more general systematic account of the nature of man and
human knowledge.

However well it may fit in to certain philosophical frameworks,
or explain a limited number of correspondences, a theory of natural
affinities between words and the things they stand for is eventually
doomed to founder, first of all, on the difficulty of explaining the
mimetic appropriateness not merely of some but of every articulatory constituent of a given word; and secondly, on the manifest
disparity of nomenclature between different languages. If some
natural system of affinities were operative, one would expect a much
greater degree of similarity between the names for the same object
in different languages. At this point the natural nomenclaturist may
be tempted to fall back on the position that his theory is intended

---

[1] *Traité des langues*, 1709, ch. 4.
[2] In the *Encyclopédie* article 'Langue'. The article is signed with the initials 'B.E.R.M.'.
Juliard (*Philosophies of Language in Eighteenth-Century France*, The Hague 1970, p. 23)
regards the authorship as uncertain. But 'E.R.M.' stands for Ecole Royale Militaire,
where Beauzée taught grammar. Cf. the article 'Syntaxe', which is signed 'E.R.M.B.'.

to explain only the original names given to things, and claim that corruption of the original pronunciation over the course of time accounts for the apparent counterexamples in current usage. However, any compromise of this kind must in the end be self-defeating for the natural nomenclaturist. Once it is admitted that a name can function as a name in spite of a corrupt (i.e. non-natural) pronunciation, and even that the majority of names are in some degree corrupt, any theory of natural affinity is to a large extent robbed of its *raison d'être*, since it has been conceded, in effect, that a name need not imitate its nominatum. Whether or not it originally did becomes a matter of merely historical interest.[1]

The flaws in the natural nomenclaturist's thesis are so evident as to make one realise that any semblance of plausibility must be borrowed from elsewhere. Its very weaknesses offer a striking confirmation of the extent to which a surrogational concept of languages, nurtured in an intellectual context which is reocentrically oriented, may generate a powerful drive to 'explain', at the risk of courting absurdity, how words derive their authenticity from Nature. An equivalent drive, in a logocentrically oriented culture, would give rise to pseudo-science: the attempt to explain how, in spite of appearances, things were really as described by the language. It would favour a biology which explained how, in spite of appearing to be insects, silverfish really are fish; and a botany which explained how the buttercup is actually a receptacle for butter.

When such a drive is operative, the inadequacy of the explanation in detail will tend to be swallowed up by the profound conviction that in general the approach is on the right lines, since that is how languages must work. Part of that conviction may derive from the desire to avoid at all costs what may be seen as the intolerable alternative: that languages afford no access to the nature of reality at all. In short, the use of words is just play. It is no accident that Wittgenstein chose precisely the metaphor of games to epitomise his own eventual convictions about language. For on one view the most radical alternative to a surrogational concept of languages is to deny altogether the validity of looking outside the language-using in search of any explanation of its significance.

In an attenuated form, natural nomenclaturism continues and

---

[1] This is not to deny that the historical question may itself be regarded as having important philosophical implications, as it did for the *philosophes*.

thrives in the etymological speculations of the grammarians of antiquity. *Lucus a non lucendo*[1] survives as a stale joke enjoyed by modern scholarship at the expense of its academic ancestry. But, as Wittgenstein perceived, the same concept of a language which produced *lucus a non lucendo* produced also a far more influential theory of meaning and truth. The message of the *Philosophical Investigations* is imbued with the irony that a tradition which strained at the gnat of Classical etymology could nevertheless swallow the camel of Classical logic. For it is the surrogational concept of a language which sanctions the belief that a true proposition is a faithful representation of reality, and thus establishes the basis of all logical strategies for proceeding from truth to truth via words. The validity of argument is grounded in the assumption that something outside language guarantees the stability of verbal meanings. There must be things other than words for words to stand for. The sounds we utter are thus envisaged as rather like I.O.Us or figures in a ledger, which are only trustworthy in so far as something more solid is available to back them up. That foundation in a reality outside language is just the difference between spending a million pounds and playing Monopoly.

Reocentric surrogationalism discerns the principal utility of languages as residing in the facility they offer for representing the external world in a manner appropriate for human discourse. This was the view held by the professors of the grand academy of Lagado, who based upon it their project for devising an alternative system of communication which would render languages superfluous. The thinking behind this project was that

> since words are only names for things, it would be more convenient for all men to carry about them, such things as were necessary to express the particular business they are to discourse on. And this invention [reports Gulliver] would certainly have taken place, to the great ease as well as health of the subject, if the women in conjunction with the vulgar and illiterate had not threatened to raise a rebellion, unless they might be allowed the liberty to speak with their tongues, after the manner of their forefathers: such constant irreconcilable enemies to science are the common people. However, many of the most learned and wise adhere to the new scheme of expressing themselves by things; which hath only this inconvenience attending

[1] 'A grove is so called from the absence of light' (Lat. *lucus* 'grove', *lucere* 'to shine').

it; that if a man's business be very great, and of various kinds, he must be obliged in proportion to carry a greater bundle of things upon his back, unless he can afford one or two strong servants to attend him. I have often beheld two of these sages almost sinking under their packs, like pedlars among us; who, when they met in the streets would lay down their loads, open their sacks, and hold conversation for an hour together; then put up their implements, help each other to resume their burthens, and take their leave.

But, for short conversations, a man may carry implements in his pockets and under his arms, enough to supply him, and in his house he cannot be at a loss; therefore the room where company meet who practise this art, is full of all things ready at hand, requisite to furnish matter for this kind of artificial converse.[1]

An important facet of surrogationalism closely related to that which Swift chose to ridicule concerns the role of language in the service of rational thought.

The surrogational concept of a language fosters the belief that reasoning is essentially analogous to working out a complex business transaction on paper, instead of going to the trouble of actually exchanging goods or money at every step. The check on whether the sums have been done correctly could always be provided, if necessary, by moving the goods and money involved, instead of juggling with figures. Ultimately, indeed, no other kind of checking is envisaged as possible. If A has to give B nine pounds, and then B has to give A twelve pounds, a calculation will tell them that the outcome is that B owes A three pounds. But if they distrust the calculation, they can reach the right result without it, by A actually handing over nine pound notes and then B handing back twelve pound notes. In the same way as figures for pound notes, words are supposed to stand proxy for things in the calculations of logic.

Now languages are only reliable for this purpose if words and their combinations do give the right results when checked against reality, just as a system of arithmetic is no good, at least for business purposes, if its sums produce the wrong answers when measured against the business transactions they are supposed to mirror. But since it cannot be supposed that the verbal manipulations happen to work out right each time by chance, any more than that arithmetical calculations regularly happen to work out right by chance, it might

---

[1] Jonathan Swift, *Gulliver's Travels*, part III, ch. 5.

seem that there must be some natural connexion between words and things which explains this, and which guarantees that we can reliably use words as proxies for things. Much of Greek thought in antiquity is devoted to the search for this connexion, and the ideas put forward in Plato's *Cratylus* are part of that search. Within the confines of reocentric theorising, it would seem natural to suppose that the guarantee must somehow reside in the capacity of words and their combinations, when correctly used, to represent or conform accurately to the things they stand for. Even if a mimetic theory of the relation between languages and reality is rejected in the crude form presented by the natural nomenclaturist, it can still seem plausible in the less crude form adopted by the logician. Indeed, the overt rejection of the claim that words are mimetic representations of things at the phonetic level may even serve to allay objections to the fact that words are still being treated as mimetic representations of things at the propositional level. But the underlying strategy of understanding remains the same: the surrogational concept of a language merely assumes a more abstract guise.

*   *   *

In the Western tradition, the early recognition of natural nomenclaturism as the unacceptable face of a philosophy of language based on surrogational assumptions seems to have done little more than sanction and facilitate the progressive entrenchment of its counterpart, non-natural nomenclaturism. Instead of Augustine, Wittgenstein might have chosen as his initial target in the *Philosophical Investigations* any one of a number of thinkers who subscribe to the thesis that words have meanings by standing as names for things, and subscribe to it more overtly and unequivocally than Augustine does.

One was Hobbes, who in chapter 4 of *Leviathan* explicitly equates the invention of speech with the invention of names and combinations of names. Hobbes says:

> The most noble and profitable invention of all other, was that of SPEECH, consisting of *Names* or *Appellations*, and their Connexion.

He goes on to distinguish two kinds of names.

Of Names, some are *Proper*, and singular to one onely thing: as *Peter*, *John*, *This man*, *this Tree*: and some are *Common* to many things; as *Man, Horse, Tree*; every of which though but one Name, is never-theless the name of diverse particular things; in respect of all which together, it is called an *Universall*; there being nothing in the world Universall but Names; for the things named, are every one of them Individuall and Singular.

Since, furthermore, it is clear that Hobbes regards a declarative sentence like *A man is a living creature* as the joining together of two names (the name *man* and the name *living creature*), it would seem that his view conforms to what Wittgenstein identifies as the idea underlying Augustine's account of language-learning, the idea of a language in which 'the words name objects, and sentences are com-binations of such names'.

Or to take a nineteenth-century example, John Stuart Mill held that languages could be regarded as providing men with the means of expressing their beliefs about the world, whether the beliefs them-selves were well founded or erroneous. Any belief, Mill held, when put into words, must take the form of what he calls a Proposition, such as *Gold is yellow* or *Franklin was not born in England*, and 'every proposition consists of two names'.[1] A proposition, Mill claims, affirms or denies one of the names of the other. What it is that is affirmed or denied must depend on what the names are names of. There must be at least two names involved, since single names in isolation do not admit of belief or disbelief: 'in every act of belief *two* objects are in some manner taken cognizance of.'[2] For instance, if I say *the sun*, that word has a meaning, which the listener can grasp, but to ask the listener whether he believes what was said makes no sense, for, says Mill, 'there is as yet nothing to believe, or to disbelieve'. For that, some other name must be combined with *the sun*. And what is affirmed or denied will then depend on what the second name is the name of. Moreover, according to Mill, it would be illusory to hope to undertake any enumeration and classification of things, except by starting from their names. 'We must begin,' he says, 'by recognising the distinctions made in ordinary language.'

As to what it is, in general, that names are names of, Mill is equally forthright. Names are names of things, not, as some people

---

[1] *System of Logic*, I. §3.   [2] ibid., I. §2.

suppose, names of ideas in the mind. He supports this contention by the following argument. When a name is used for the purpose of expressing a belief, the belief in question is a belief concerning the thing itself, not concerning an idea of the thing. Thus to say *The sun is the cause of day* is not to affirm that the speaker's idea of the sun is the cause of the speaker's idea of day; but rather that a certain physical fact, the sun, causes another physical fact, day.

We must distinguish, according to Mill, between words which are themselves names, and words which are merely parts of names, like *of*, *to*, *truly* and *often*. For these are words which do not express anything of which something can be affirmed or denied, unless they are taken as names of words themselves, as when we say, for instance, *'Truly' is an English word*. In the case of adjectives, it must be admitted that we cannot say, for example, *Heavy fell* or *Round is easily moved*. None the less, an adjective can stand by itself as predicate of a proposition, and we can say *White is an agreeable colour*, just as well as *A white colour is agreeable* or *The colour white is agreeable*. So the difference between *Round is easily moved* and *A round object is easily moved* may be regarded as merely 'grammatical', and not a difference of meaning. The rules of ellipsis in English might have been such as to allow the former as well as the latter. So as between *round* and *a round object*, says Mill, 'it is only custom which prescribes that on any given occasion one shall be used and not the other'.[1] Hence, adjectives may be treated as names, whether —as Mill puts it—'in their own right', or as representatives of 'more circuitous forms of expression'.

Mill makes passing reference here to the principal tenet of 'psychocentric surrogationalism'. It differs from that which Mill defends by identifying what words immediately stand for as the ideas expressed by means of words. This does not necessarily imply an outright rejection of a connexion between words and things. It may simply involve the contention that words stand for things not directly but indirectly, by way of standing for ideas which conform to the things in question. This view is perhaps best represented in the Western tradition by Locke,[2] but was formulated by the modistic

---

[1] ibid., II. §4.

[2] It may be argued, however, that Locke's version of the thesis that words stand for ideas is not one which is open to the kind of objection raised by Mill. Cf. N. Kretzmann, 'The main thesis of Locke's semantic theory', *History of Linguistic Thought and Contemporary Linguistics*, ed. H. Parret, 1976, pp. 331–47.

grammarians of the Middle Ages, and goes back ultimately to antiquity.

Aristotle had described spoken words as 'symbols or signs of affections of the soul'.[1] Furthermore, he held that these affections were 'representations, likenesses, images, or copies' of things. Just as the external world of things was the same for all mankind, so also was the inner world of affections; even though speech itself differed among the different races of men.

However, if the affections were complete and faithful representations of things, and words in turn were complete and faithful representations of affections, there ought to be simpler correlations between a language and the external world than in practice we appear to find. For not only does a language offer, in any particular instance, a variety of possible descriptions of what exists, but it also offers the possibility of describing what does not exist at all. Furthermore if, as the diversity of languages appears to show, words are merely arbitrary sounds, not in themselves connected with what they stand for, how can one be sure that the structure of reality is faithfully represented in language at all? And if it is, just how? These questions leave surrogationalism with some awkward explanatory gaps to fill.

It was not until the later Middle Ages that a general theory of language was elaborated that made a systematic attempt to fill these gaps. This distinctive contribution of the *modistae*, while remaining Aristotelian in approach and no less surrogationalist in its assumptions, was part of a more comprehensive synthesis of knowledge based upon the epistemology of medieval Catholicism. The ultimate aim was to explain how everything—including language—fitted in to the perfect schema of the universe devised by its Creator. In particular, where language was concerned, the purpose was to demonstrate that, appearances notwithstanding, there was no underlying discrepancy between words and non-verbal reality. The former provided a consistent and accurate system of representation of the latter; the whole being designed for the expression of rational thought in man. It followed that the modistic grammarians were utterly uninterested in differences between languages, or in usages which did not appear to reflect logical processes, or in the diversity of human communicational purposes. Attention to any or all of

[1] *De Interpretatione* 16A.

these, from their point of view, would only obscure an appreciation of the systematic harmony between the organisation of external reality and the organisation of language. The key to this appreciation lay in understanding the various modes of signifying (*modi significandi*) by which sound was enabled to function as an adequate medium of representation.

Starting from Aristotle's position that a name is not inherent in its sound, but that a sound only becomes a name by becoming a symbol,[1] the *modistae* disclaim any interest in sounds as such. 'Grammar,' says Thomas of Erfurt, 'deals with signs of things.'[2] Since being a sign is accidental to sound, sound is taken into account accidentally. However, 'sound, as sound, is not considered by the grammarian.'[3] This view may be contrasted with that taken by the grammarian of antiquity, for whom, as Quintilian tells us,[4] the classification of sounds into vowels and consonants, correct pronunciation, and the adequacy of the representation of sounds by the letters of the alphabet, were all topics which required examination and discussion. The change of emphasis reflects the extent to which by the fourteenth century grammar was no longer simply a propaedeutic to rhetorical and literary studies.

According to the *modistae*, the business of the grammarian is to explain how the intellect has created a grammatical system through which sound acquires the potentiality of signifying. In order to do this, the system must mirror reality as grasped by the understanding. In the context of this system, a given unit of sound becomes a sign (*signum*). Specifically, it becomes a word (*dictio*), when considered simply in its capacity for designating something; a part of speech (*pars orationis*), when, in addition, considered as having an active mode of signifying; and finally a term (*terminus*), when considered as subject or predicate of a proposition.[5] In this way, grammar links up with logic, and is envisaged as its foundation. For an expression could not be a term unless it were also a grammatical element, and *ipso facto* part of a system by which the mind expresses its understanding of reality. Herein lies the guarantee that the syllogism is not just an empty word-game, but has a validity which is

---

[1] *De Interpretatione* 16A.

[2] 'grammatica est de signis rerum', *Grammatica Speculativa*, ed. G. L. Bursill-Hall, London 1972, VI. 12.

[3] 'vox, inquantum vox, non consideratur a grammatico', ibid., VI. 12.

[4] *Institutio Oratoria* I. iv. 6-8.   [5] Thomas of Erfurt, op. cit., VI. 11.

ultimately underwritten by the very structure of the universe. If God had allowed mankind to get its grammar wrong, rationality would be a mockery.

Since the many individual things that go to make up the physical world are not isolated one from another, but interrelated in various ways, the sounds that stand for them must reflect this fact, and this they do by not merely signifying, but also 'consignifying' (*consignificare*); that is to say, by relating to other sounds in ways which afford a basis for combination in sentences. Thus the intellect 'attributes to sound a double function'. Inasmuch as it signifies, it is formally a word (*dictio*): inasmuch as it consignifies, it is formally a part of speech (*pars orationis*).[1] Much of modistic grammar is taken up with the detailed analysis and explanation of the Latin parts of speech. For according to the *modistae*, this is not just a convenient classification imposed by the grammarian (as it had often been considered in antiquity),[2] but reflects the articulation of reality, as the mind understands it. Thus they are forced by the logic of their own position to assume that all languages have essentially the same grammatical system as Latin. Otherwise there would be an inexplicable non-conformity between reality—which is the same for all men—and the way in which the mind expresses its understanding of reality through the modes of signifying.

Modes of signifying pertain both to expressions and to the things they stand for. An 'active' mode of signifying (*modus activus*) is a mode or property of the expression by which it signifies a property of the thing. A 'passive' mode of signifying (*modus passivus*) is a mode or property of the thing, insofar as it is signified by the expression.[3] Although active and passive modes of signifying are thus complementary, they are not equipollent, and it is here that the reocentric bias of surrogationalism emerges. The active modes of signifying themselves originate from some property of the thing:[4] they are not merely intellectual figments (*figmenta*). For understanding is a passive capacity (*virtus passiva*). When the intellect assigns an expression to an active mode of signifying, this is not

---

[1] ibid., I. 3.

[2] Varro, *De Lingua Latina* viii. 44; Priscian, *Institutiones Grammaticae* I (ed. H. Keil, *Grammatici Latini*, Leipzig 1855, vol. 2, pp. 54–5).

[3] ibid., I. 2.

[4] 'oportet omnem modum significandi activum ab aliqua rei proprietate radicaliter oriri', ibid., II. 4.

arbitrary, but is based on a property of the thing.[1] Thus 'the active modes of signifying are derived immediately from the passive modes of understanding; for the active modes of signifying are not derived from the modes of being, unless these modes of being have been grasped by the mind'.[2] In this way, the relation between word and thing is an indirect, not a direct one. This is essentially the position taken much later by Locke, except that for Locke the relation is even more indirect, since the mind in turn is dependent on the information supplied by the senses.

As developed by Locke, surrogationalism is an integral part of a theory of knowledge and of perception. The mind is held to receive impressions or simple ideas conveyed by sense perceptions, and to be able to form judgments about them. Since thinking is an internal, mental process, it was necessary that in order to communicate with his fellows man should devise 'external sensible signs, whereof these invisible ideas, which his thoughts are made up of, might be made known to others'. For this purpose, words 'came to be made use of by men as the signs of their ideas'.

Locke rejects the view of the natural nomenclaturist, and maintains that there is no natural connexion 'between particular articulate sounds and certain ideas'. For if that were the case, he argues, 'then there would be but one language amongst all men'. What is involved is 'a voluntary imposition, whereby such a word is made arbitrarily the mark of such an idea'. Thus, says Locke, the use of words 'is to be sensible marks of ideas; and the ideas they stand for are their proper and immediate signification'. Again, 'words, in their primary or immediate signification, stand for nothing but *the ideas in the mind of him that uses them,* how imperfectly soever or

[1] Thomas of Erfurt's explanation of the fact that there are meaningful words (e.g. *chimaera*) which apparently stand for non-existent things is that they can signify in virtue of the fact that the figments they represent are conceived of as having parts (e.g. the head of a lion, the tail of a dragon) which in fact do exist (op. cit., II. 5). But it is difficult to see how this is ultimately compatible with modistic surrogationalism, since although the parts may exist in reality, there is no structure of reality in which they are combined, and from which the whole could be apprehended by the passive faculty of the understanding. Hence the problem of where this whole comes from remains unresolved. This appears to require retreat to an 'atomistic' position, in which there is only a guarantee that a language correctly represents the basic units of reality, but no guarantee that it represents their 'molecular' combinations correctly.

[2] modi significandi activi sumuntur immediate a modis intelligendi passivis; quia modi significandi activi non sumuntur a modis essendi, nisi ut hi modi essendi ab intellectu apprehenduntur: ibid., III. 7.

carelessly those ideas are collected from the things which they are supposed to represent'.[1]

On such a view as that advocated by Locke, it would evidently be a mistake to suppose that words directly reflect or correspond to the nature of things: any correspondence must depend ultimately on how far the mind had first gathered complete and correct ideas about things via the senses.

An important feature of this account of how words have meanings is Locke's doctrine of generalisation. For it is evident that although our sense impressions are impressions derived from particular things, somehow men have managed to make words fit for general purposes. Precisely what languages do not do is provide unique expressions for all the separate thoughts that may call for communication. Languages economise by making the same words usable over and over again for indefinitely many instances.

This economy, according to Locke, is the product of two processes. One process relates to words for simple sensory qualities, such as *white, red, hot* or *cold*. In the world of external reality, things present themselves as complex and indissoluble combinations of such features. Yet the corresponding ideas registered in the mind are distinct and unconfused. Locke claims that they 'enter by the senses simple and unmixed'.[2] Thus we are able to make 'the particular ideas received from particular objects to become general', that is by considering them 'separate from all other existences, and the circumstances of real existence, as time, place, or any other concomitant ideas.'[3] This is what abstraction is. The idea thus abstracted, i.e. of 'white', or 'red', or 'hot', or 'cold', will serve as a standard by which to judge later ideas received from particular objects, and in so far as the later ideas conform, the particular objects in question will in principle be judged to be white, or red, or hot, or cold.

The second process relates to words like *man*, or *horse*, or *chair*. These are evidently not like words for simple sensory qualities, since the corresponding ideas are highly complex. Yet, again, languages manage to effect a remarkable economy of expression. In this type of case, according to Locke, we frame a general idea by simply leaving out of each particular complex idea what is peculiar

---

[1] *An Essay concerning Human Understanding*, bk. III, ch. ii, sections 1–2.
[2] ibid., bk. II, ch. ii, sect. 1.   [3] ibid., bk. II, ch. xi, sect. 9.

to each, while retaining what is common to all. Thus words like *man*, or *horse*, or *chair* stand for general ideas which include what is common to indefinitely many ideas of particular men, particular horses and particular chairs. This second process, in Locke's view, is not an easy one. To form the general idea of a triangle, he argues, we have to arrive at something which is 'neither oblique nor rectangle, neither equilateral, equicrural, nor scalenon; but all and none of these at once'.[1]

What Locke says about this second process leaves him open to the objection that what is required for generalisation is not merely difficult but impossible. For it appears that in order to provide the meaning which links the general term *triangle* to any and every triangle, an idea is required that either combines all possible features of triangles, or else excludes every feature which might distinguish one triangle from another. Berkeley criticised Locke on the ground that it makes no sense to speak of any idea answering to a triangle which is not equilateral, nor isosceles, nor scalene, nor any other specific triangular shape; and it makes no sense either to speak of framing the idea of a triangle which is all of these together: this is precisely what Locke's theory seems to demand, and the demand is self-contradictory.[2]

The difficulties which Locke's theory encounters are typically surrogationalist, and specifically nomenclaturist difficulties. They are generated by the assumption that a general term must have its meaning by being the name of whatever it stands for, and then finding that it is extremely difficult to give any coherent account at all of any one entity which it could be the name of. Locke clearly realised that in the real world there are no general things which general words could be names of. There is no general object called *white*, or *man*, or *horse*; but only particular white things, particular men and particular horses. Locke's psychocentric surrogationalism is an attempt to solve this problem by proposing that the meaning of a general word is not a general thing, since general things do not exist, but a general idea. However, if Berkeley is right, it seems highly doubtful whether a general idea of the kind Locke's theory requires could exist either. Psychocentric surrogationalism

---

[1] ibid., bk. IV, ch. vii, sect. 9.
[2] *Principles of Human Knowledge*, Introduction §13. Cf. G. J. Warnock, *Berkeley*, Harmondsworth 1953, ch. 4.

encounters difficulties no less acute than its reocentric counterpart.

Locke's strategy is reversed in the more radical form of psycho-centric surrogationalism which has emerged in contemporary linguistics, with the claim that it would be impossible ever to learn what words mean without the prior availability of mental schemata for representing meanings. The postulated schemata are held to require no learning themselves, since they are genetically provided. Thus Wittgenstein is regarded as mistaken in criticising Augustine in *Philosophical Investigations* §32 for describing the first steps in language acquisition as if the child 'already had a language, only not this one'. On just this point, it is claimed, 'Augustine was precisely and demonstrably right',[1] and Wittgenstein wrong. In other words, the contention is that learning a language is impossible unless one already has a language.[2] The language the child already possesses, as Augustine saw but Wittgenstein failed to see, is the 'language of thought'; and that language is innate.[3]

According to this modern version of surrogationalism, the fact that Augustine must be right is held to be shown by the following argument. Learning a language involves learning (i) what the predicates of the language mean. Learning (i) involves learning (ii), a determination of the extension of the predicates. Learning (ii) involves learning (iii), the 'truth rules' for the predicates. But (iii) cannot be learned unless a language is available in which the predicates and the truth rules can be represented. But the language that is about to be learned is not yet available for that purpose. Therefore a prior language is necessary in order to learn the predicates of any given language.[4]

Whereas Locke introduced psychocentric surrogationalism to solve the problems raised by reocentric surrogationalism, here it is the other way round. Reocentric surrogationalism, in the form of the assumption that to know the meaning of a predicate is to know its truth conditions, is used to provide an argument intended to justify identifying a language as a system of mental structures. In brief, we cannot learn what a word stands for unless there is already something in the mind to stand for what it stands for. Thus a surrogational concept of languages is, as it were, projected inward to provide a model for the mental equipment which will in turn explain

---

[1] J. A. Fodor, *The Language of Thought*, Hassocks 1976, p. 64.
[2] ibid., p. 64.   [3] ibid., p. 65.   [4] ibid., pp. 63-4.

how the relations between words and the outside world can be grasped. Surrogationalism in one form is again vindicated by invoking surrogationalism in another form.

Whether or not we are inclined to accept any defence of Augustine along these lines, it can hardly be denied that the version of surrogationalism attributed to him in the *Philosophical Investigations* is a starkly unsubtle one. According to Augustine, it would seem, it is a simple fact of life that words are names of things; and, moreover, a fact of life which the child, in his earliest attempts to communicate with those about him, soon discovers for himself.

Even for Hobbes, whose surrogationalism is of a crude enough variety, there is more to it than that. The reader of Hobbes cannot fail to be struck by the fact that the nomenclature thesis is part of a general explanation of the nature of truth and of reasoning. According to Hobbes: 'When a man *Reasoneth*, hee does nothing else but conceive a summe totall, from *Addition* of parcels; or conceive a Remainder, from *Subtraction* of one summe from another: which (if it be done by Words), is conceiving of the consequence of the names of all the parts, to the name of the whole; or from the names of the whole and one part, to the name of the other part.'[1] On this view, an Aristotelian syllogism—*Men are mortal: Socrates is a man: Therefore Socrates is mortal*—is simply a piece of arithmetic. But it is an arithmetic done with names instead of figures.

Hobbes claims that '*truth* consisteth in the right ordering of names in our affirmations'. Here he evidently has in mind the fact that whereas such sentences as *Whales are mammals* and *Mammals are whales* are both formed by the joining together of the same names, none the less they are not truth-conditionally equivalent. Accordingly, says Hobbes, 'a man that seeketh precise *truth*, had need to remember what every name he uses stands for; and to place it accordingly; or else he will find himselfe entangled in words, as a bird in lime-twiggs; the more he struggles, the more belimed.'[2] Thus the doctrine of names in Hobbes is not to be separated from the doctrine of truth.

This is equally apparent in the case of Mill. 'All truth and all error lie in propositions,' says Mill.[3] 'What, by a convenient application of an arbitrary term, we call a Truth, means simply a True Proposition; and errors are false propositions.' Logic, in Mill's

[1] *Leviathan*, part I, ch. 5.   [2] *Leviathan*, part I, ch. 4.   [3] *System of Logic*, I. §2.

view, has as its object to examine how we arrive at knowledge which is not intuitive; that is to say, how we distinguish between what is proven and not proven. It is concerned, therefore, with questions which require consideration of evidence; and since the answer to every question it is possible to ask must be expressible in the form of a proposition, the logician is obliged to inquire into the meanings of words; since otherwise he cannot analyse propositions. For to understand a proposition requires in Mill's view an understanding of what things the names contained in the proposition are names of.

Now Wittgenstein is concerned no less than Hobbes or Mill about the connexion between an account of language and an account of truth. The *Philosophical Investigations* takes a position on this issue which contrasts sharply with that adopted in the immediately ante-cedent philosophical tradition, notably by Frege, by Russell, and by Wittgenstein himself in the *Tractatus*.

Whereas Frege's philosophical semantics may be seen as an attempt to improve the credibility of a surrogational analysis of how languages work, by providing an extended ontology of things for words to stand for, such an attempt, from the standpoint of the *Philosophical Investigations*, is both futile and fundamentally mis-guided. Frege's replacement of the traditional subject-predicate analysis by a function-argument analysis borrowed from mathe-matics, and his application of the notion of a function to whole propositions, enabled him to consider 'Wellington defeated Napo-leon at Waterloo' as standing for the True, and 'Napoleon defeated Wellington at Waterloo' as standing for the False. But precisely this treatment of sentences as complex names of truth-values may be seen as demonstrating just how narrowly nomenclaturist Frege's view of language was, and how closely his conception of what it was for an expression to mean something was tied to the basic model of the proper name.

In Frege we see modern surrogationalism retreating to a position where the foundations of language rest in part upon a mysterious correspondence not between words and material objects, nor be-tween words and ideas, but between words and 'thoughts'. Thoughts, Frege argues in *Der Gedanke*,[1] constitute a third realm,

---

[1] First published in 1918 in *Beiträge zur Philosophie des deutschen Idealismus*. Quota-tions and page references are to the English translation by P. T. Geach in *Logical Inves-tigations* (Oxford 1977).

which is neither that of the physical universe nor that of the individual consciousness. Thoughts have in common with ideas that they cannot be perceived by the senses, whereas material objects can. But they have in common with material objects that they exist independently of the thinker.[1] It is thoughts which are true or not true, and if true timelessly true, irrespective of their expression by a particular form of words on a particular occasion. Frege gives no detailed account of the other functions of a language, although he assumes it to be possible to identify the expression of a thought among various concomitant verbal functions. The thought he describes as what is—or is contained in—the content common to an assertoric sentence and its corresponding 'yes/no' question. Frege does not explain why languages should afford such indirect and in some respects obscure mechanisms for achieving this essential task of expressing thoughts. Indeed, he appears to regard the actual workings of languages as a hindrance rather than a help. If A and B know different sets of facts about London, then although they may both use the sentence *London is the capital of England* they are not strictly, according to Frege, speaking the same language.[2] Here we see at its most naked the insistence that what 'a language' is be interpreted in terms of anchoring words unambiguously to non-linguistic correlates of a stable, permanent kind. If the non-linguistic correlates are different, the languages must be different, even though the form of words used may be, deceptively, identical. 'One fights against language,' Frege says revealingly at one point,[3] but never appears to realise that perhaps the struggle in question is generated by the many ways in which language resists attempts to force it into the Procrustean bed of surrogational analysis.

From the standpoint of the *Philosophical Investigations*, Russell would be, by self-confessed philosophical allegiance, representative of a somewhat less mystical brand of surrogationalism. When, in a well-known passage,[4] Russell divides philosophers into three groups—those who infer properties of the world from properties of language, those who maintain that knowledge is only of words, and those who maintain that there is knowledge which cannot be expressed in words, but who none the less use words to tell us what this knowledge is—he places himself in the first group, expressing

[1] ibid., p. 17.   [2] ibid., p. 12.   [3] ibid., p. 13 fn. 4.
[4] *An Inquiry into Meaning and Truth*, 1940, p. 322.

his belief that 'with sufficient caution, the properties of language may help us to understand the structure of the world'. This implies acceptance of a basically surrogational view of what languages are; but the caution is necessary because certain crude forms of surrogational analysis may hinder rather than help. It is part of Russell's thesis that languages have certain words, such as *Socrates, horse* and *yellow*, which have meanings which can be learnt directly by confrontation with appropriate objects, the objects in question being what the words mean, or instances of what the words mean. These are the words which give us, as it were, the most direct access to the connexions between words and the non-linguistic realities for which words stand: and it is therefore here, according to Russell, that any explanation of 'meaning' must begin.[1] But when Russell claims that there is a 'discoverable' relation between the structure of sentences and the structure of the occurrences to which the sentences refer,[2] his use of the word *discoverable* serves to emphasise that the relation is not immediately apparent. The form of words available to direct observation is only an imperfect representation of what is meant. Penetrating beneath the superficial appearances of verbal grammar is a task to which the philosopher must address himself. In *Principia Mathematica*, Russell had argued that whenever, as in a case like 'The round square does not exist', the grammatical subject of a proposition can be supposed not to exist without thereby rendering the proposition meaningless, this shows that the grammatical subject is not a proper name, 'i.e. not a name directly representing some object'.[3] He also pointed out the error of supposing that an expression like *the author of Waverley* stands for something in exactly the same way as an expression like *Scott*. But his theory of definite descriptions was not an attack on surrogationalism, but a rescue operation. By demonstrating how sentences containing expressions like *the author of Waverley* can be analysed into combinations of predicates and quantifiers, the theory of definite descriptions showed how the impression that *the author of Waverley* is a complex name is merely a *trompe-l'œil* effect created by surface grammar. Thus much of Russell's philosophy of language may be regarded as devoted to showing that a surrogational concept of languages, although it may initially appear inadequate, none the less provides at a deeper level the only correct analysis of how languages work.

[1] ibid., p. 23. [2] ibid., p. 322. [3] *Principia Mathematica*, Introduction, ch. III (I).

Finally, Wittgenstein's *Tractatus* advocates yet another version of surrogationalism. Here a language is treated as a totality of sentences.[1] Only sentences have a sense (*Sinn*).[2] Their constituent names have a reference (*Bedeutung*),[3] this reference being the object with which the name is correlated.[4] The sense of a sentence is its conformity or nonconformity to possible states of affairs.[5] Such a position is anti-mentalist, not in the sense that thought is denied to be involved in language, nor that there is nothing left for psychology to discover about language-using,[6] but rather in that it apparently makes little difference what psychology may discover. Words and things, combinations of words and combinations of things, are all that need to be taken into account. It is also a reocentric position, in that words are held to be dependent on things, and things alone, for their linguistic role. The nature of the dependence of words on things is summed up in the claim that sentences are 'pictures of reality'.[7] There must be something identical in a picture and what is depicted thereby in order for the picture to be a picture of it.[8] A given picture either agrees with reality, in which case it is a true picture, or fails to agree, in which case it is a false picture.[9] In order to tell whether a picture represents reality, there is no other way than to compare it with reality.[10] These are the essential theses of the *Tractatus*. In short, languages are essentially systems which provide us with names for objects and, in sentences, with quasi-pictorial surrogates for possible states of affairs.

With these less remote candidates available, it is at first surprising that in the *Philosophical Investigations* it should be Augustine who is elected representative of the surrogational tradition. The choice perhaps reflects on the one hand Wittgenstein's preference for an initial formulation which is not merely vague but also purely anecdotal and biographical. What Augustine says serves no ulterior purpose. It is, in other words, a more innocent, a less philosophically contaminated version of surrogationalism than Hobbes, or Mill, or Frege, or Russell could have provided. At the same time, the choice

---

[1] *Tractatus Logico-Philosophicus*, §4.001.
[2] ibid., §3.3.   [3] ibid., §3.3.   [4] ibid., §3.203.   [5] ibid., §4.2.
[6] As indicated by Wittgenstein's reply to Russell's question concerning the constituents of a thought. (*Notebooks 1914–1916*, p. 129.)
[7] *Tractatus Logico-Philosophicus*, §4.01.
[8] ibid., §2.161.   [9] ibid., §2.21.   [10] ibid., §2.223.

perhaps indicates Wittgenstein's concern to represent surrogational-ism not as a narrowly philosophical misconception, but as an error deeply rooted in quite ordinary, everyday views about what a language is. Doubtless eradication of that error would not have assumed the importance it has for Wittgenstein unless modern philosophers had founded such ambitious theories upon it. None the less, Wittgenstein's choice of exemplification seems calculated to point out that it is an error of quite humble origins, since it can occur quite unbidden in philosophically unsophisticated recollections of childhood. Augustine's mistake, Wittgenstein seems to imply, is a mistake any of us could have made. We are thus brought to consider whether surrogationalism is based simply on an everyday misconception about words. If so, how does the misconception arise?

Wittgenstein throws out various hints as to possible sources. Sometimes he appears to regard it as the product of a kind of lexical myopia: an inability to see further than words of a certain kind. Anyone who describes language-learning in the way Augustine does, he suggests, must be thinking primarily of nouns like *table*, *chair* and *bread*, and of personal names, and only secondarily of the name of certain actions and properties, and not at all of other kinds of words.[1] From this we might infer that the mistake, in Wittgenstein's view, is to extrapolate from the learning of one type of word to language-learning in general. But the original question then arises at one remove. For it remains unexplained why there should be any temptation to effect that extrapolation.

Or we might infer that the source of the error lies in the conflation of how we learn what a word means with what it is for a word to have a meaning. Since it is perhaps easiest to think we understand how the meanings of words like *table*, *chair* and *bread* are learned, our notion of how these words are learned is then pressed into service when an account of what it is for any word to have a meaning is required. But again the original question arises at one remove. For it is not at all clear why in the first place there should be any inclination to mistake questions about meaning for questions about language-learning.

Might it not be, then, that it is putting the cart before the horse to regard surrogationalism as a symptom of 'lexical myopia'? Perhaps the 'lexical myopia' is itself a symptom of surrogationalism,

[1] *Philosophical Investigations*, §1.

words like *table*, *chair* and *bread* being fastened upon because they appear to provide ideal cases to illustrate the aptness of a surrogational analysis of languages.

It is certainly the noun which, in the structure of European languages, provides the least controversial example of a part of speech of which the function can plausibly be stated in overtly surrogational terms. In the fourth century A.D., when Donatus, in his *Ars Minor*, summed up the received wisdom of scholarly antiquity by defining the *nomen* as 'that part of speech with case flexion which signifies an object or thing (*corpus aut rem*) whether individually or in general (*proprie communiterve*)'[1] he established a foothold for surrogationalism in Western grammar from which it has never been dislodged. Twentieth-century English schoolboys who learn their Latin from Kennedy's *Shorter Latin Primer* are still taught that nouns are 'names of persons, places, things or qualities',[2] these four categories being exemplified by the words *Caesar* 'Caesar', *Roma* 'Rome', *sol* 'sun' and *fortitudo* 'bravery'. This is not presumably because educational theorists hold the *avant-garde* view that if one is learning a dead language one ought to learn it in a suitably antiquated way. Nor because they are neo-Whorfians, who hold that you cannot learn an alien tongue unless you learn to analyse it in the same way as the aliens themselves. But simply because the definition of what a noun is has not basically changed in the Western tradition for two thousand years.

An interesting thing about this definition is that it has long since ceased to correspond, if it ever did, to anything which ordinary language-users actually believe in, as evidenced by their observable behaviour. The typical procedure in current European culture for finding out the meaning of a noun does not involve going to a museum and searching for a display case containing a specimen of the thing so labelled. The typical procedure is to look in a dictionary. Furthermore, it would be a grotesque misreading of European history to suggest either that dictionaries developed as pocket substitutes for museums; or that museums developed as scientifically more respectable substitutes for dictionaries. The specimen in a

[1] 'Pars orationis cum casu corpus aut rem proprie communiterve significans' (*Grammatici Latini*, ed. H. Keil, vol. iv, 1864, p. 355).

[2] B. H. Kennedy, *The Shorter Latin Primer* (revised by Sir James Mountford), London, 3rd impression 1966, p. 3.

museum case we do not regard as the meaning of the word on the label. The word on the label is regarded as telling what the specimen in the case is—which is quite a different matter.

The dictionary, which has become one of the most influential and significant institutions of European culture, does not assign any privileged position to words like *chair*, *table* and *bread* which, according to Wittgenstein, provide the paradigm for the mistaken view of meaning characteristic of surrogationalism. Nor does the dictionary attempt to deal with meanings as if all words were names. On the contrary, words which are names in the most obvious sense, like *Socrates*, *Peter*, or *Manchester*, normally find no place there. The dictionary, in short, embodies a semantics which is in some respects the complete antithesis of surrogational semantics. The meanings the dictionary gives for words like *chair*, *table* and *bread* are neither physical objects nor ideas; but simply other words. In a civilisation with a thoroughgoing surrogationalist attitude to language, the dictionary as we know it would be inconceivable. Whereas the fact is that in Europe the dictionary came to be seen as the repository of verbal meanings *par excellence*, regarded with a veneration and respect for authority amounting in certain cases almost to superstition. Such a development would be impossible if a surrogational view of languages prevailed twenty-four hours a day and seven days a week.

If we are interested in understanding surrogationalism, we are obliged to situate it in a broader context than Wittgenstein shows any inclination to do. The question to ask is not 'What kind of mistake is it based on?', but 'What is its source and role in Western culture?' And to put that question in its proper perspective, it is important first to see how surrogationalism intertwines with other strands in the traditional Western concept of a language.

3

It so happens, in the constitution of human affairs, that it is not sufficient merely to declare ourselves to others. We find it often expedient, from a consciousness of our inability, to address them after a manner more interesting to ourselves.

If we look carefully at the passage from Augustine's *Confessions* which Wittgenstein quotes at the beginning of the *Philosophical Investigations* we can find in it, perhaps in addition to—or perhaps in contradiction with—that picture of 'the essence of human language' which Wittgenstein finds there, a significantly different concept of what a language is. For while it is true that Augustine describes the key to his understanding of what was going on in the communication situation as his realisation that 'the thing was called by the sound uttered', it is also true that this realisation is explicitly situated within a context of intentional behaviour. Augustine speaks of people uttering the sounds in seeking, having, rejecting or avoiding the things in question. His realisation was not intuitive, but a rational process of putting two and two together, or rather putting together one, one and one; for each of three components is carefully distinguished in Augustine's account.

First, there is the sound. And this, it should be noted, is not 'given' to immediate apprehension as a unit. Augustine's picture is not, *pace* Wittgenstein, one of a simplistic world in which the inhabitants go around Tarzan-like, communicating in sparse monosyllables, like 'Fire', 'Rain', 'Tree', 'Slab', 'Beam' and so on. Augustine speaks of hearing words 'used in their proper places in different sentences', and frequently so used. This implies that essential to his realisation was the recognition of recurrent items as being the same items embedded in different sequences of sounds. But nothing he says implies that this recognition was prior to his association of the word with its corresponding object.

Secondly, there is the object. This is identified as the focus of attention correlated with the recurrence of a particular sound within the variety of sound sequences which accompany human action.

Thirdly, there are the aims underlying the accompanying actions. These, according to Augustine, he was able to identify in a quasi-intuitive fashion. They were obvious from movements, expressions of the face, tone of voice, gestures and so on. In a striking phrase he refers to a 'universal language' of the human body ('tamquam verbis naturalibus omnium gentium').

Now it is the identification of these aims which holds the key to establishing the correlation between word and object in Augustine's account: for what he observed as a child was the spectacle of those around him manifestly achieving certain communicational objectives by using sound systematically in connexion with objects. Without the recognition of purpose in this vocal activity, there would have been no basis for grasping the connexions. Mere regularity of spatio-temporal concomitance, as e.g., between thunder and lightning, is not what is presented in Augustine's account as yielding the realisation that there was a particular recurrent sound which was what a certain repeatedly-talked-about thing was called.

It verges on misrepresentation to appear to suggest that Augustine views the correlation between word and thing as existing in its own right, independently of human desires. On the contrary, he seems at pains to make it clear that the reference of words to things occurs only as an intrinsic part of verbal and non-verbal behaviour in which the speaker has some specific communicational objective in view. In short, in Augustine's remarks about language-learning, what is said about the connexions between words and things is only part of—and cannot, without distortion, be decontextualised from— a view of language as purposeful activity which is perhaps best characterised not as 'surrogationalist' but as 'instrumentalist'. That is to say, words are envisaged as instruments for accomplishing human communicational objectives, rather than standing for things or ideas. Language-using is seen as analogous to tool-using, rather than as analogous to labelling.

This interpretation is borne out by what Augustine says in the passage immediately preceding that which Wittgenstein quotes.[1] Here Augustine recounts how, at an earlier stage of communicational experimenting, he had endeavoured as a child, with groans and other forms of vocalisation (gemitibus et vocibus variis) and by gesture (variis membrorum motibus) to express what he wanted, in order that his wishes might be obeyed (ut voluntati paretur). Thus it is clear that it was not merely natural instinct for—or spontaneous delight in—vocal expression, but the achievement of practical ends, which motivated the child's attempts to communicate. The frustration of these first attempts brought him to look about him to see how others achieved success; and thus he was led by empirical observation and inference to hit upon the solution to the problem of communication.

Whether or not we think Augustine's account of this first breakthrough to language is plausible is beside the point. What is very clear is that it is an account in which names are seen not primarily as depictions or representations of things, but as instruments for achieving human intentions in relation to things. That which correlates the name with the thing is not some intrinsic likeness or affinity, as the natural nomenclaturist holds, but its use to further some human purpose. It is the furtherance of such purposes which provides the essential link. The difference between this view of names and the natural nomenclaturist's would be analogous to the difference between supposing that a knife is shaped as it is primarily in order to allow the user to cut with it, and supposing that the shape of the knife is somehow intended to depict or represent the cutting or what is cut.

Doubtless one reason why Wittgenstein plays down the instrumentalism in Augustine's view of 'the essence of human language' is that instrumentalism is itself an important element in the view of language presented in the *Philosophical Investigations*. The metaphor of words as tools is closely bound up with Wittgenstein's theory of meaning as use. In the *Philosophical Investigations*, the diversity of

---

[1] 'And this I well remember, and I afterwards observed how I first learned to speak. For my elders did not teach me this ability, by giving me words in any certain order of teaching (as they did letters afterwards), but by that mind which thou, my God, gavest me, I myself with gruntings, varieties of voices, and various motions of my body, strove to express the conceits of my own heart, that my desire might be obeyed; but could not bring it out, either all I would have, or with all the signs I would', *Confessions* I. vii, tr. W. Watts (Loeb Classical Library edition).

the functions of words is compared to the diversity of the functions
of the contents of a tool-box: hammer, pliers, saw, screw-driver,
ruler, glue-pot, glue, nails and screws.[1] No one, however obtuse or
unpractical, would suppose that such diverse objects all served
more or less the same purpose. Why, then, should this be supposed
in the case of words? To this question Wittgenstein gives what at
first sounds like one of the least convincing answers to be found
anywhere in his writings. What misleads us, he suggests, is 'the
uniform appearance of words when we hear them spoken or meet
them in script and print'. It sounds rather like suggesting that we
might get confused about the difference between a five-pound note,
a wedding invitation, and a postcard of the Tower of London
because they all came in the form of oblong pieces of paper.
Conceivably, such an explanation might have some plausibility if
European languages failed to distinguish morphologically between
functionally different word classes. Even then it could hardly be
supposed that language-users would be totally deceived by morphological uniformity into believing that there were no functional
differences between words. One can make more sense of Wittgenstein's suggestion by supposing that what he had in mind was the
misleading assumption that all words, simply because they are
words, must somehow have the same kind of function, or at least a
common basic function *qua* words. For he asks what would be
gained by insisting, for example, that since the hammer modifies the
position of the nail, and the saw the shape of the board, and the
rule our knowledge of a thing's length, all tools therefore serve to
modify something.[2] Again, he compares looking at a language to
looking into the cabin of a locomotive. The handles we see in the
locomotive cabin all look more or less alike, which is hardly surprising, since they are all handles. None the less, this similarity
conceals many differences of function; e.g. between a crank which
can be moved continuously, a switch which has only two positions,
a brake-lever, and so on.[3] These two 'instrumental' comparisons
of the tool-box and the locomotive cabin complement each other.
Instruments may look alike, or they may look unalike. Wittgenstein's point seems to be that both the general similarities which
words appear to share as words (whatever these may be), and also
the formal similarities which words of a certain type or class may

[1] *Philosophical Investigations*, §11.   [2] ibid., §14.   [3] ibid., §12.

appear to share, may be equally misleading, in that they may distract attention from very important differences between how words are used. But while this interpretation may make Wittgenstein's explanation of our failure to see the instrumental diversity of words sound rather less unconvincing, it makes even more conspicuous Wittgenstein's disinclination to situate the question of how we look at language in any specific cultural context. It is as if all language-users were, *qua* language-users, in exactly the same position, trying to grapple with exactly the same problem of understanding the mechanisms of language, and, moreover, each grappling with it on his own.

It may be asked why Wittgenstein's builder's language seems designed to capture only one part of Augustine's alleged misconception, which is to regard words as names of things, while omitting the complementary part of the misconception as Wittgenstein identifies it, which is to regard sentences as combinations of names. For the builder's language, it might be said, has no syntax. Indeed, it may be objected 'that unless a language-game is at least complicated enough to allow a distinction between words and sentences to be drawn, then it does not really deserve to be called a *language*-game at all'.[1] Two preliminary points need to be made in this connexion. The first is that if 'syntax' is to be understood as implying word-concatenation, that should not be equated with what allows a distinction between words and sentences to be drawn. On the other hand, if 'syntax' is to be understood as whatever structural features allow a distinction between words and sentences to be drawn, that should not be taken as necessarily implying word-concatenation. What allows a distinction between word and sentence to be drawn is the difference in linguistic structure between (to use convenient Bloomfieldian terms) phonemic and taxemic contrasts. Thus in 'Stop!' we have an utterance which involves no word-concatenation, but which exemplifies a sentence none the less. If a necessary condition for sentences were word-concatenation, to describe 'Stop!' as a one-word sentence would be a contradiction in terms. From the mere fact that the words of a language may each stand as a single sentence, it would not follow, in one sense of 'syntax', that the language had no syntax. The second point is that this would not follow for the other sense of the term 'syntax' either. Wittgenstein

[1] A. Kenny, *Wittgenstein*, London 1973, p. 168.

makes it clear[1] that the correct execution of the assistant's duties involves bringing the building materials in the order in which the builder requires them. Hence word order must be accounted significant in this communication system, since it is the only device available to encode information relevant to that aspect of the assistant's duties. To say 'Slab! Beam! Block!' is to issue a different instruction or set of instructions from that issued by saying 'Beam! Slab! Block!' It makes no difference to this point that the builder may decline to run the risk of having the slab, the beam and the block brought in the wrong order, by waiting until the assistant has brought one item before he issues an instruction for the next. There remains a significant contrast of word order, whether the builder does this or not. Similarly, in this language 'Block! Block!' presumably means that the builder wants two blocks, not that he is impatient for one block. So to deny that word-concatenation plays any role in the builder's language would be to deny that there are any rules governing word order or word repetition, and this is manifestly not the case. The reason why we may feel some reluctance to accept 'Slab! Beam! Block!' as a 'sentence' has nothing to do with this. It relates to the fact that in the languages with which we are familiar, sentences typically involve the concatenation of words with different grammatical roles, and not the concatenation of words with the same grammatical role. But had Wittgenstein allowed his builder's language sufficient grammatical complexity to achieve this, it would have incurred the objection that it did not consist just of names.

A paradoxical feature of Wittgenstein's example is that in spite of this precaution, or rather because of it, the builder's language in the end does not consist just of names; at least, not of names in the sense required to make the charge of surrogationalism against Augustine stick. For words as used in the builder's language are not just vocal labels attached to things. In Wittgenstein's fable, the builder's language is essentially a practical language, a language for getting things done. It contains no idle or merely ancillary grammatical machinery of any kind. Everything is geared to the fetching of building materials. So much so that if we are asked to say what, for instance, *block* means in this language, there is a strong temptation to reply not that it stands for a piece of wood or other material,

---

[1] *Philosophical Investigations*, §2.

which would be the typical nomenclaturist answer, but instead that it indicates that the builder wants his assistant to fetch him a block, which would be the typical instrumentalist answer. So that, contrary to expectation, Wittgenstein's own exemplification of Augustine's mistaken account of how languages work actually appears to exculpate Augustine from the error with which he was charged. Words are not just object-labels in this language, but instruments for achieving human purposes.

How has this come about, and was it quite what Wittgenstein intended? Here we must consider the implications of the fact that the words of the builder's language are explicitly presented as constituting a closed system. Wittgenstein tells us to imagine this as 'a complete primitive language'. Exactly what this means is perhaps not entirely clear, but at least it seems that any other words the builder and his assistant may know the use of do not belong to this particular language. Furthermore, although this is less certain, we are to understand that the four words are used, or usable, only in connexion with the cycle of activities Wittgenstein describes. But then it would appear that it is the 'closure' of the language which lets Augustine escape from the charge of surrogationalism; although Augustine himself makes no reference to word-thing correlations as constituting closed systems. Inasmuch as the introduction of the notion of a closed language is Wittgenstein's move, he might seem to have bungled the prosecution against Augustine by his own court-room tactics. He has left the way open for opposing counsel to construct a defence of Augustine along the following lines. First, Augustine did not claim that names constitute closed communicational systems. Secondly, even if he had offered an account of languages faithfully exemplified by the language Wittgenstein's builder and his assistant use, that would appear to show him not to be a surrogationalist at all, but on the contrary an instrumentalist.

Wittgenstein himself raises the question of the status of the words in the builder's language. For he asks whether 'Slab!' is a sentence or a word,[1] and suggests that if it is a word, it can hardly mean the same as our ordinary word *slab*, since in the builder's language it functions only as a command; whereas if it is a sentence, it can hardly be the same as the ordinary elliptical sentence 'Slab!', since in the builder's language there is no fuller sentence for it to

[1] ibid., §19.

be an elliptical version of. But why, he asks, can we not say that 'Bring me a slab!' is an expanded version of the sentence 'Slab', rather than saying that 'Slab!' is a shortened version of 'Bring me a slab!'? Perhaps, he suggests, 'Slab!' in the builder's language can be called a word and also a sentence. Or perhaps 'Bring me a slab!' in our ordinary language could be considered one long word instead of four. Evidently, our analysis will depend on what other expressions we are implicitly contrasting our examples with. But that has nothing to do with what we have in mind when we use an expression. If we consider a sentence 'elliptical', says Wittgenstein, it is 'not because it leaves out something that we think when we utter it, but because it is shortened—in comparison with a particular paradigm of our grammar'.[1]

Having said this, Wittgenstein seems to be almost on the verge of making the Saussurean point that it is only structural contrast within a given system which constitutes the identity of a given sign within that system, and hence its identity as a sign *simpliciter*. For a Saussurean, the question whether any utterance in the builder's language is a word or a sentence only makes sense to the extent that the system is complex enough to afford the possibility of contrast. Likewise, the question whether the meanings of the expressions are things or instructions is meaningful only if the system is sufficiently sophisticated to allow that distinction. But Wittgenstein seems more concerned with using the question to expose the fallacy of looking for some concomitant mental activity as the basis for determining whether an expression means one thing or another.

It is difficult to exculpate Wittgenstein from the commission of a tactical error here. By introducing the notion of a closed system, he makes it impossible to construct even a hypothetical example of what a language would be like if it consisted just of names of things. There is no system of names of things, even hypothetically, except as part of some larger system which is not just a system of names. At the same time, it should be noted that this tactical error is forced upon Wittgenstein by a tactical dilemma. For without introducing the notion of a closed system, he cannot clinch the accusation that Augustine is guilty of a misconception about how languages work. If the words the builder uses are not the whole of the language, but just a part of it, there is no way in which the example involves any

[1] ibid., §20.

blatant misrepresentation of the function of words at all. So it is the closure of the language which has to make this into an apposite illustration of the surrogational fallacy. In case anyone objects, 'But surely the builder is just using ordinary words in their everyday meanings, and what is there peculiar about that?', it has to be possible to reply, 'But suppose that was all there was of the language!' Unfortunately, the tactic misfires, in that once the language is considered closed at just this point, that move lets the surrogationalist off the very hook on which it was intended to catch him.

The moral of Wittgenstein's fable is the wrong moral, because his fable attempts an impossibility. The impossibility is to construct a model of what a language would be like if it consisted solely of names of things; that is to say, of words which functioned intrinsically as names of things, as distinct from words which might be described, in a chosen metalanguage, as names of things. For as soon as we allow that the word can be used to further some purposeful activity in connexion with the thing, then it ceases to be merely a name, and is open to an instrumentalist interpretation. On the other hand, if we stipulate that the words of our hypothetical language must not be used to further any kind of thing-oriented purpose, we have constructed the nonsense of a language based on relations totally irrelevant to its employment: or, more simply, an unusable language. For although it might be possible to save appearances by stipulating that the language could be used for some purpose apparently unconnected with its consisting of names for things, e.g. just for frightening away evil spirits, or for constructing the lyrics of nonsense songs, such a stipulation itself gives the game away. The problem would then be to explain in what sense it was true to say that the language did consist of names of the things it was claimed its words were names of.

The failure of Wittgenstein's fable, however, itself points to an important feature of the relationship between surrogationalism and instrumentalism. The latter is not to be regarded as an enrichment or elaboration of the former. On the contrary surrogationalism, of whatever variety, is based on an impoverishment or simplification of the instrumentalist account of how words have meanings. The essence of the simplification lies in the omission of purposeful activity as the connecting link between word and thing; and hence the institution of a search for some more direct correspondence uniting name to reality. But why this search should be instituted in the first place, or why its goals should be considered attractive, are not questions with obvious answers. They ask more than merely how surrogationalism manages not to do justice to the complexity of the ways in which words fulfil their communicational purposes.

*   *   *

An essential difference between surrogationalism and instrumentalism may be regarded as turning on the willingness of the surrogationalist to abstract from the flux of purposeful activity of which speech is part, and concentrate attention solely upon the connexions between, on the one hand, words, and, on the other, the things or ideas or events or states of affairs which words supposedly stand for. These connexions, for the typical surrogationalist, may be envisaged as obtaining independently of the intentions of the language-users. By concentrating upon these connexions, he believes he is able to command a clear view of all the linguistic essentials. The surrogationalist will not deny that language is a form of human activity and as such reflects the pursuit of human objectives; but he tends to regard these objectives, in so far as they are relevant, as being already adequately institutionalised in linguistic form. Thus in defining what, say, the word *chair* means, he will regard it as superfluous to mention the purposes which language-users may achieve by having this word available in their language, such purposes being too obvious to need spelling out. All that needs to be stated, for the surrogationalist, is the connexion between the word *chair* and a certain type of furniture. Provided this is done, language-users' purposes can be left to look after themselves. Similarly, the meaning of the sentence *It is raining* can be given by specifying the meteorological state of affairs connected with it, and the time-relation between its utterance and the actualisation of the said state of affairs. No need is felt to say anything further about the communicational objectives which may be—or customarily are—pursued by uttering the sentence: these can be assumed to be self-evident. Whereas for the typical instrumentalist, we may hypothesise, no such assumption can be made; for him, to leave out of account the purposes of the language-users, or to believe that one can in some way take them for granted, is already to create a distorted image of what a language is.

Because of this divergence of emphasis, surrogationalism and instrumentalism differ considerably in their capacity to provide a basis for philosophical and sociological theorising concerning the role of languages in human affairs, although these theoretical implications remain latent for most of the history of Western thought, and do not appear clearly until the contemporary period. Even when they do, so deeply entrenched is surrogationalism in the Western tradition that the form of instrumentalism which emerges may be founded on a partial compromise with the opposing point of view.

Such a compromise can be seen in the work of Austin, the title of whose Harvard lectures of 1955, *How to do things with words*,[1] epitomises their instrumentalist approach. In them one recognises a familiar twentieth-century philosophical suspicion that in ordinary language all is not what it appears to be, and that the superficial grammar of sentences may be misleading. But in the cases of Frege, Russell and the early Wittgenstein, this suspicion had led to the view that natural languages contained various 'imperfections', which a careful logical analysis would reveal, and which could be eliminated in the construction of an ideal language. Moreover, this ideal language (ideal, that is, from a logical point of view) was regarded as providing the model to which natural languages aspired. Russell had written: 'The whole function of language is to have meaning, and it only fulfils this function in proportion as it approaches to the ideal language which we postulate.'[2] Furthermore, Russell added, 'the essential business of language is to assert or deny facts.' In Austin's view, on the other hand, this philosophical preoccupation with an ideal language geared to asserting and denying facts had led philosophers to overlook many cases where what appeared by grammatical criteria to be fact-stating sentences were in practice used for a quite different purpose. But instead of adding them to the waiting-list of 'imperfections' to be dealt with by logical surgery, Austin used these cases as a basis for criticising the assumptions underlying what he called the 'constative fallacy'. By implication, the ideal language of previous philosophers was rejected as embodying an erroneous concept of what a language is.

In *How to do things with words*, Austin's contention is not that

[1] Ed. J. O. Urmson, Oxford 1962.
[2] In his Introduction to Wittgenstein's *Tractatus Logico-Philosophicus*.

4

'truth' is an impossible notion on which to found an explanation of how the words we use mean what they do, but that it provides at the very least a curiously limited basis for doing so. For in a wide range of cases it makes very little sense to ask whether what someone said was true, if by that is understood asking whether things stand exactly as he claims. This is because in so many instances of an everyday kind it is very odd to start from the presumption that what the speaker is doing is making a claim about some state of affairs at all, or at least that he is primarily making such a claim. Typical instances where this doubt arises are those falling under what Austin termed 'explicit performatives'. When someone says 'I will' at the appropriate juncture in the marriage ceremony, or 'I name this ship the *Queen Elizabeth*' when smashing the bottle against the stem, or puts in his will 'I give and bequeath my watch to my brother', or says to an acquaintance 'I bet you sixpence it will rain tomorrow', he is using a sentence which overtly has a normal declarative form, but, Austin claims, the words as used do not describe or report anything, even though they may in part serve to inform hearers about what is going on. Hence there is no question of what was said being true or false. This, says Austin, is not something which needs to be argued, any more than it needs to be argued whether saying *damn* is saying something true or false.[1]

Furthermore, even when people say things which are intended to be taken primarily as descriptive, Austin points out that it would be naïve to suppose that we can make a sensible appraisal simply by looking to the facts supposedly described, without taking into consideration what the speaker was trying to do in making the statement. Thus if someone says 'France is hexagonal', we may reasonably suppose that he is trying to say something about the shape of a certain country. But we are at a loss to know which facts we ought to set against this statement in order to decide, in the final analysis, whether it is true or false. A more sensible question concerns its utility. It is a description which might be good enough for a top-ranking general, but not for a geographer. We can say, claims Austin, that it is a rough description; but it is not a true or false one.[2] Whether this rough description is any good for our purposes will depend crucially on what our particular purposes are.

---

[1] op. cit., pp. 5–6.   [2] ibid., p. 142.

Austin's instrumentalism, however, was not sufficiently thorough-going to make do without the support of a surrogationalist founda-tion, in the form of what Austin designated 'locutionary' (as distinct from 'illocutionary' and 'perlocutionary') acts. The illocutionary act, for Austin, was the act one performed in saying something, e.g. the act of promising, or requesting, or apologising. The perlocutionary act was the act one performed by saying something, e.g. the act of persuading, or convincing, or preventing. But both of these were based upon the locutionary act, which was the act of uttering certain words as having a certain meaning, i.e. a certain sense and reference in accordance with the rules of the language to which they belong. To take one of Austin's own examples,[1] if someone says 'Shoot her!', we specify the locutionary act by, e.g., defining the relevant sense of the verb *shoot* and identifying the referent on this occasion of the pronoun *her*. We specify the illocutionary act by saying what was done in performing it, e.g. that X urged (or advised, ordered, etc.) Y to shoot her. We specify the perlocutionary act by saying what the immediate effect was, e.g. that X persuaded Y to shoot her. Thus both illocutionary and perlocutionary act depend on the locutionary act being what it is, and thus, *inter alia*, on the estab-lished connexion between the verb *shoot* and a certain form of action with a fire-arm. Austin himself never claimed that the meaning of *shoot* depended on the illocutionary or perlocutionary force of utterances like 'Shoot her!' (although claims of this kind were sub-sequently advanced by Austin's followers). Nor did he clarify the relationship between the locutionary act and the other two, but was content provisionally, as he put it, to take ' "sense and reference" on the strength of current views'.[2] This failure left the way open for his critics to claim that Austin's notion of illocutionary force was vacuous,[3] on the ground that once an adequate account is given of the meaning of an utterance and of the effect it has, there is no room left for attributing to it an illocutionary force as well. Austin can thus be represented as an over-enthusiastic surrogationalist, whose mistake was to be tempted, by noticing the great variety of things that can be done with words, and the great variety of things that can be left unsaid, into inventing a quite fictitious dimension

[1] ibid., p. 101.   [2] ibid., p. 148.
[3] L. J. Cohen, 'Do illocutionary forces exist?', in *Symposium on J. L. Austin*, ed. K. T. Fann, London 1969, pp. 420–44.

of verbal interpretation, which he supposed everyone else had over-looked.

However, although it was never worked out in detail by its originator, and although later attempts by linguists to incorporate some of its features into transformational grammar showed, more than anything else, how easy it was to use Austin's terminology while missing the point of his distinctions, the theory of illocutionary acts suggested the possibility of new foundations for linguistic analysis. Its main contention was that words are instrumental in accomplishing not just one purpose, but a variety of purposes simultaneously. This feature of our use of words is obscured, rather than brought out, by the surrogational assumption that words have fixed meanings, in the form of the things they stand for, or the facts they are designed to assert and deny.

The potential of this critique was never developed by Austin to the full, in the first place because he permitted the locutionary act to remain as the basis for explaining illocutionary and perlocutionary acts; and in the second place because he allowed that what is in-volved in judging truth and falsity may be seen as a different mode of assessment from what is involved in judging the utterance as a performance.[1] In the former case he suggests that what is being aimed at is 'the ideal of what would be right to say in all circum-stances, for any purpose, to any audience'. Whereas in the latter case we attend 'as much as possible to the illocutionary force of the utterance, and abstract from the dimension of correspondence with facts'.

That Austin felt it necessary to make any such compromise is itself no mean indication of the philosophical prestige enjoyed by the concept of a language which his method implicitly threatens. In the end the compromise is as unnecessary as it is valueless. It gets us nowhere to reserve the terms 'true' and 'false' for valid use in a mode of assessment which sets out to ignore what the speaker is attempting to do in the particular instance, and concentrate simply on the direct correspondence between what is said and the facts. For just what is called in question once an instrumental con-cept of languages is adopted is the validity of postulating an inde-pendent relationship of 'correspondence with facts'.

*　　*　　*

[1] ibid., pp. 144-5.

A quite different but no less interesting example of the clash between instrumentalism and surrogationalism is to be found in Bernstein's work on the sociology of education. Like Austin's, Bernstein's approach to language is fundamentally instrumentalist.[1] It is this which enables Bernstein to identify a linguistic factor affecting the varying educational attainments of children. Mastery of verbal skills is seen in terms of the achievements which in practice they enable the language-user to accomplish in the context of social interaction. The only linguistic source of educational failure which a surrogationalist could identify would have to be a difference between children either in their quantitative or in their qualitative understanding of what words stand for. In so far as differences in educational performance could be correlated with differences in social class, the surrogationalist would have to suppose that this was because of inequality either of opportunity or of intellectual capacity for establishing the right connexions between words and things, or words and ideas. By contrast, the essence of a Bernsteinian explanation of educational failure is that mastery of words serves different purposes for children of different types of social background. These differences arise because children's grasp of what words are for is differently shaped by their family upbringing. Hence the experience of education is qualitatively different, depending on previous experience of the function of language.

According to Bernstein,[2] the English acquired by the post-war generation of English children reveals, upon analysis, the existence of two distinct 'codes'. These are distinguished by the terms 'elaborated' and 'restricted'.[3] Characteristic of the 'elaborated' code are said to be such features as accurate grammatical construction, frequent use of prepositions (indicating logical as well as temporal and

---

[1] The term 'instrumental', however, is used by Bernstein in a quite restricted technical sense. The 'instrumental order' is the organisational structure of a school controlling curricula, pedagogy and assessment, as distinct from the 'expressive order' controlling conduct, character and manner.

[2] B. B. Bernstein, 'Linguistic codes, hesitation phenomena and intelligence', *Language and Speech*, vol. 5, 1962; 'Social class, linguistic codes and grammatical elements', *Language and Speech*, vol. 5, 1962; 'A critique of compensatory education', in *Education for Democracy*, ed. D. Rubinstein & C. Stoneman, Harmondsworth 1970; 'A brief account of the theory of codes', in V. Lee, *Social Relationships and Language: Some Aspects of the Work of Basil Bernstein*, Open University Press 1973.

[3] They replace the terms 'formal language' and 'public language' used in earlier papers.

spatial relationships), and frequent use of impersonal constructions. Characteristic of its opposite, the 'restricted' code, are said to be poor grammatical construction, unfinished sentences, infrequent use of impersonal constructions, repetition of conjunctions, limited use of adjectives and adverbs, and reliance on pronouns in preference to nouns for referential purposes. Various objections to the ways in which the distinction between elaborated and restricted codes is drawn may be raised,[1] but for present purposes these details are of no consequence.

The important issue was Bernstein's claim that children from working-class homes and children from middle-class homes did not have equal mastery of these two codes of English. The working-class child's disappointing educational performance was held to be accounted for by his having access to the restricted code only, whereas the educational system presupposed access to the elaborated code.

Use of the restricted code only is seen, in Bernstein's theory, as reflecting a process of socialisation in which words have a relatively limited role to play in life. Broadly speaking, they are not used if alternative means of communication will suffice to achieve the immediate purpose, and their use is heavily context-dependent. Whereas use of the elaborated code is seen as reflecting a process of socialisation in which there is emphasis on constructing, by means of words, an explicit, systematic and rational categorisation of experience, and on understanding the reasons for and the place of particular events within that categorisation.

Although it is clear that there are profound differences between Bernstein's view of language and Austin's, it is also fair to say that they share a common focus of attention upon the extent to which certain things may be understood but not overtly expressed in the words used. In Austin's case, this leads to the distinction between explicit and implicit performatives, and the theory of illocutionary force. In Bernstein's case, on the other hand, the outcome is a theory of codes, in which 'the basic thesis has been that forms of communication may be distinguished in terms of what is rendered implicit and what is rendered explicit'.[2]

[1] Cf. for example the criticisms in ch. 5 of D. Lawton, *Social Class, Language and Education*, London 1968.
[2] Lee, op. cit., p. 70.

Since it is easy enough in the area with which Bernstein's work is concerned to allow moral and political considerations to obscure what is relevant, it may be worth emphasising that it would make no difference, as far as the present discussion is concerned, if the social allocation of elaborated and restricted codes were reversed, or they were distributed on a quite different economic basis. Nor is agreement or disagreement with Bernstein's views of social class, or of education as an agency of social control, involved. Bernstein's elaborated and restricted codes have their origin in Durkheim's two forms of solidarity, mechanical and organic.[1] They are based on the ways in which people relate to each other through similarity of function in a society, as distinct from relationship through dissimilarity of function. Bernstein himself asserts that elaborated codes are not necessarily middle-class communication procedures, nor do they function automatically as reinforcing a particular class structure.[2] What he does contend is that in industrialised societies, how codes function in relation to class structure depends on how their transmission is controlled in the educational system.

Whatever view one may take of the validity of Bernstein's explanation of the social differentiation of educational performance, it is evident that it presupposes that what is involved in language-learning cannot be simply an understanding of the correlations between words and things, or alternatively between words and concepts, nor the consequent pairing of sentences with possible states of affairs. What is involved is no less than the integration of an individual into his social world. How that is achieved is envisaged as depending at least in part on the fact that the predominant functions of language-using are not socially invariant.

A surrogational concept of languages would not be merely inadequate for the type of thesis which Bernstein proposes: it is ultimately incompatible with such a thesis. For the surrogationalist assumption is that speaking the same language is a matter of sharing the same set of correlations between words and their surrogates. Whereas Bernstein's point is precisely that merely speaking what would count as the same language from a surrogationalist point of view does not guarantee equality of access to the content of an educational programme ostensibly formulated in that language And the reason for this is that children from different social

<hr>

[1] ibid., p. 66.   [2] ibid., p. 69.

backgrounds do not treat a language as the same kind of operational instrument, even though it apparently offers them the same range of verbal equipment.

However, the sharpness of this point is blunted by Bernstein's own theoretical compromise with surrogationalism, which takes the form of refraining from saying that, e.g., middle-class English children and working-class English children do not speak the same language. He insists that his distinction between codes relates to linguistic performance only, and not to linguistic competence in English; he is not concerned with differences between social groups as reflecting differences which have their origins in the 'basic tacit understanding of the linguistic rule system'.[1] Thus, like Austin, he draws back from developing an instrumentalist approach to language into a radical critique of the bases of surrogationalism. But this compromise, just as with Austin, is what gives the critic an opportunity to step in and reject the validity of the distinction on which the entire thesis rests. In Bernstein's case, the critic's objection will be that the difference between elaborated and restricted codes is a reflection of nothing more than the 'superficial stylistics of middle-class and working-class forms of conversational behaviour'.[2] Although Bernstein protests that this objection involves a 'travesty' of his thesis, the protest is robbed of its force by his own insistence that all that is involved in distinguishing between codes relates to linguistic performance only, and not to mastery of 'the language' as such. As in Austin's case, the compromise with surrogationalism is as unnecessary as it is valueless. Once it is made, the theory of codes is placed in the paradoxical position of claiming that although all members of the community are playing exactly the same language-game, some sections of the community do not understand how the language-game of other sections of the community is played. Precisely what is called in question as soon as this lack of comprehension is conceded is whether the game *is* the same, even though it may be called by the same name (e.g. 'English').

*　　　*　　　*

The instrumentalist concept of a language as a system designed for the achievement of communicational purposes in human inter-

[1] ibid., p. 70.　　[2] ibid., p. 69.

course finds its clearest expression throughout the history of Western culture at the practical level of education in verbal skills. The
rights and wrongs of how to use words, as taught in the classrooms
of modern Europe, derive from a long-established pedagogical tradition which goes back through the medieval schools and univer-
sities to the educational system of antiquity. The basic philosophy
of this pedagogical tradition is thoroughly instrumentalist. It
presents the study of grammar not as an end in itself, but as a means
to enable one to express one's thoughts well. But since there is no
pedagogically viable way of inspecting thoughts in order to test
whether they have been well expressed, the practical criterion used
is invariably the communicational effect which the words have upon
a hearer. Thus, for example, the 'rule of proximity' which generations of English children learned was usually formulated in terms
of the association of thoughts: e.g. 'things which are to be thought
of together must be mentioned together.'[1] But the examples given of
infringements of this rule, e.g. *A piano is for sale by a lady about
to cross the Channel in an oak case with carved legs,*[2] make it clear
that the point of the rule was to avoid the production of unintended
communicational effects for the hearer. This is entirely in keeping
with an instrumentalist criterion of 'effective speech' which comes
straight from the rhetorical theorists of Greece and Rome. Thus it
is hardly surprising to find a twentieth-century manual still quoting
Quintilian in order to explain to English schoolboys what clarity of
expression is. And what Quintilian says is that we must try to use
words in such a way that our audience not merely be able to understand what we say, but *must* understand it, whether they want to
or not.[3]

From the beginning, instrumentalism was the professional creed
of the rhetorician, and the rhetorician took the whole discourse, not
the sentence, as his unit. This is evident from the traditional division of Classical rhetoric into its five parts.[4] The first part, 'invention' (εὕρεσις, *inventio*), is concerned with the subject matter of the
speech, of which three principal types are recognised: deliberative,
forensic and epideictic. Of these, forensic speeches occupied the

---

[1] J. C. Nesfield, *Manual of English Grammar and Composition*, London, 23rd repr.
1922 (1st ed. 1898), p. 126.
[2] ibid., p. 126.   [3] ibid., p. 178.
[4] G. Kennedy, *The Art of Persuasion in Greece*, Princeton 1963, p. 10 et seq.
4*

most important place and were the most systematically analysed. Under the head of 'invention' falls consideration of what is at issue, and how it may best be demonstrated or refuted. The second part, 'arrangement' (τάξις, *dispositio*), is concerned with the division of the speech into sections (introduction, narration, proof, epilogue) and the functions of each section as a contribution to the whole. The third, 'style' (λέξις, *elocutio*), is concerned with the appropriateness of tropes, figures, diction, construction and rhythm to the various kinds of speech and their aims. The fourth, 'memory' (μνήμη, *memoria*), concerns mnemonic devices for the orator. The fifth, 'delivery' (ὑπόκρισις, *actio*), concerns the manner of speaking, including voice production, stance, and gesture.

The internal logic of this five-part schema shows how the system of rhetoric was founded on a primary evaluation of the communicational purpose to be served by the discourse as a whole. It is from this that the communicational purposes of the various parts, their organisation and appropriate techniques all follow. Thus the rhetorician recognised what the modern communication theorist calls a 'hierarchy of communicational goals'.[1] Each subordinate goal is determined by a superordinate goal, of which the highest depends ultimately on who is addressing whom, and in what social context. These are the key questions; their answers supply the framework within which any consideration of how the communicational purposes can best be achieved must be situated. These answers may often be taken for granted, as in the Ciceronian assumption that rhetoric is a branch of politics; but they cannot be dispensed with. For without them, the rhetorician would have nowhere to start from. Furthermore, inasmuch as the answer to the question of who is addressing whom must be a generalisable answer, if the art is to be teachable at all, Western rhetoric may be regarded as in effect based upon an implicit theory of communicational roles. No communicational purpose can properly be analysed without specifying for whom the message is intended. Speaking is envisaged as an essentially audience-directed activity, and its success or failure are to be measured by what in Austinian terms are classified as perlocutionary effects.

This instrumentalist approach enabled Western rhetoric to retain an open-ended flexibility and sensitivity to social change, since the

[1] D. Parisi and C. Castelfranchi, *The Discourse as a Hierarchy of Goals*, Urbino 1976.

typology of communicational roles is infinitely adaptable. Any new development in communication requirements could in principle be accommodated, and usually was, provided that the consumer demand for instruction warranted pedagogical systematisation. Thus the Middle Ages was able to elaborate rhetorical techniques unknown to Aristotle or Cicero. One of the most interesting of the medieval developments, the *ars dictaminis*, involves a radical departure from the assumption of the Classical rhetoricians that communication is oral, and reflects the increasing importance of writing in Western culture. But the integration of the *ars dictaminis* into the domain of rhetoric presents no problem once an appropriate system of communicational roles is worked out. This had already been done before the year 1200 at Monte Cassino.[1] It remained the organising principle of the art of correspondence for many centuries. Victorian manuals such as *Beeton's Complete Letter Writer* were descended from a long line of medieval and post-medieval treatises, going back to Alberic's *Dictaminum Radii*. Although the social context had changed a great deal, the underlying theory had not. The question of who is addressing whom was still basic. The medieval treatises were usually concerned with whether one was writing to a superior, an inferior, or an equal; whereas *Beeton* classifies all letters into two types, depending on whether the writers are 'ladies' or 'gentlemen'. In this it remains entirely faithful to the theory of the *ars dictaminis*, since the distinction between lady writers and gentleman writers provides the most fundamental division of communicational purposes that *Beeton* recognises. For instance, whereas both the list of possible 'Ladies' letters' and the list of possible 'Gentlemen's letters' include a 'School' section (since, clearly, ladies as well as gentlemen may have children away at school), in 'Ladies' letters' there is no 'Borrowing and Lending Money' section (since, clearly, borrowing or lending money are not among the communicational purposes for which ladies write letters).[2]

Similarly, the European pedagogical tradition has always treated it as an intrinsic part of instruction in foreign languages that the learner must be taught to distinguish what may appropriately be said to whom and on what occasion. This gives rise to a classification of phrases and sentences which survives in the modern 'traveller's

---

[1] J. J. Murphy, *Rhetoric in the Middle Ages*, Berkeley 1974, p. 203 et seq.
[2] *Beeton's Complete Letter Writer*, new and revised ed., London n.d. (1894).

phrase-book'. But the principle was already known to the author of the earliest extant medieval French conversation manual,[1] who arranges his material according to whether the intended addressee is, e.g., a lady, an innkeeper, a merchant, or a passer-by, and includes an interesting but possibly injudicious selection of strong language for use to rogues and scoundrels.

In principle, if the communicational purpose is sufficiently closely defined, systematisation of the kind the European tradition developed makes possible an entirely automatic generation of the discourses that may be required. In practice, rhetoricians usually did not go this far since, quite apart from the laborious analysis involved, they preferred to emphasise the creative aspects of their art rather than its mechanical character. None the less, it is worth pointing out that precisely this step, which is basic to modern theories of generative grammar, was already taken within the scope of the *ars dictaminis* at the beginning of the fourteenth century by Lawrence of Aquilegia. Lawrence reduced letter-writing to a system which could easily be formulated as a set of rewrite rules of the type employed in the phrase-structure part of a transformational grammar. His system of communicational roles postulates seven types of addressee, which cover a wide range from popes down to heretics. For each type of addressee he provides a tabulation of alternative phrases and clauses, arranged consecutively in groups, in such a way that one item from each group must be selected at each successive stage in the derivation of a letter. It is the 'Dear Sir/Madam' principle carried to its logical conclusion. This has the advantage, from the scribe's point of view, that it is no longer necessary to invent any materials, or consider the order of parts, or choice of words. Provided one can find one's way through the epistolary chart provided, writing a letter, as one commentator has pointed out,[2] does not even require the writer to know the language.

This medieval anticipation of the notion of the language-user as a programmed automaton is intriguingly paradoxical. The pursuit of methods of instruction which will enable the learner to improve his ability to use words effectively leads to a system which dispenses with this ability altogether. But it should be noted that the possi-

[1] E. Stengel, 'Die ältesten Anleitungsschriften zur Erlernung der französischen Sprache', *Zeitschrift für neufranzösische Sprache und Literatur*, vol. 1, 1879, pp. 10–15.
[2] Murphy, op. cit., p. 259.

bility of mechanisation of word-use emerges here under the aegis of an instrumentalist view of language. What is presupposed is that one can define the communicational objective in view in a specific social setting. There is no suggestion that a completely general mechanisation of language-producing procedures makes any sense at all. The point of departure is the whole discourse in its communicational environment, not the decontextualised sentence.

As one proceeds down the scale from discourse to word, from larger to smaller units, the analysis of audience-directed aims begins to merge with that of the mechanics of sentence construction. In traditional grammar, an instrumentalist differentiation of functions in terms of communicational purpose is most clearly reflected in the terminology of sentence-types and clause-types. The differences between declarative, interrogative and imperative sentences are explained by appeal to a simple typology of communicative acts. The function of a declarative sentence is identified as that of asserting, or describing, or informing. The function of an interrogative sentence is identified as that of asking a question. The function of an imperative sentence is identified as that of issuing a command. Similarly, the function of certain subordinate clauses may be explained as asking 'indirect questions', or issuing 'indirect commands'. Other subordinate clauses may be designated as 'causal', 'concessive', 'conditional', and so on. Evidently such terms are intended to have an explanatory value, and this tells us something about how the syntactic structure of languages is seen as relatable to the reasons for which people exchange verbal messages. It is noticeable that below the level of the clause, this grammatical terminology based on communicational purposes peters out, as if the instrumentalist at this point had abandoned the attempt to correlate linguistic units directly with the achievement of independently specifiable aims. Thus the traditional terminology of the parts of speech is not basically instrumentalist, even though partially instrumentalist definitions may sometimes be associated with the terms in question. The parts of speech system in the form it had developed by Priscian's time, although incorporating in a piecemeal fashion individual features of diverse origin, belongs as a whole neither to the surrogationalist nor to the instrumentalist, but reflects a different view again of what languages are.

4

*Many Words, possessing their Significations (as it were)
under the same Compact, unite in constituting a particular
Language.*

There is a third main strand in the traditional Western concept of
a language, which needs to be distinguished both from surrogationalism and from instrumentalism. It is no less important than
either of these; for it too goes back to the beginnings of Western
linguistic thought, and already provides one of the main lines of
argument to be found in Plato's *Cratylus*.

'I cannot come to the conclusion,' says Hermogenes, 'that there is
any correctness of names other than convention and agreement.'[1]
In so saying, Hermogenes declares which side he is on in the great
debate of Greek antiquity between the rival claims of φύσις and θέσις;
between those who held that the Greek language was the product
of Nature, and those who held it to be the invention of Man. For
when Hermogenes speaks of 'convention' and 'agreement', he
clearly has in mind the kind of convention and the kind of agreement upon which the fabric of human society is based, its practices,
its customs, its standards of social behaviour, and its laws. In short,
he champions what we may call a 'contractualist' view of languages.
Their main function is to enable a society to co-ordinate interper-
sonal exchanges between its members. A language is thus envisaged
as the manifestation of a tacit collective understanding between
members of a community as to how a certain range of social affairs
shall be conducted. It is essentially a form of social contract. The
key word here is 'essentially' (as opposed to 'incidentally'): for

[1] *Cratylus* 384C,D.

according to Hermogenes it is not merely coincidence that Greeks agree as to how a thing shall be called. On the contrary, it *is* their agreement which alone determines how a thing shall be called. There is no other standard of 'correctness'.

Modern scholarship has been on the whole unfavourably inclined to the terms of this debate. According to one authority, 'the nature-convention discussion does not seem properly framed or very fruitful as far as language is concerned'.[1] The significance of the controversy is held to be of merely historical interest. Emphasis is placed on its role in the early development of linguistic theorising, and on the stimulus it provided to a more detailed analysis of the Greek language.[2] This lack of modern sympathy is itself interesting evidence of the extent to which the cultural context of inquiry into how languages work has altered. The twentieth-century assumption tends to be, simply, that Hermogenes was obviously right, and there is little profit to be gained even from entertaining the possibility that he might have been wrong. The issue is envisaged as being roughly on a par with that which divides Pythagoreans from flat-earthists, or democrats from believers in the divine right of kings.

What Hermogenes says appears *prima facie* to be supported by a wide range of linguistic observations which make the existence of any universal principles of sound-and-sense association capable of providing the basis for an alternative theory seem highly unlikely.

First, different languages often have quite different names for the same or similar things. It is difficult for a non-conventionalist theory to explain why the same animal should be called *dog* in English, *chien* in French, and *Hund* in German, or why the same piece of cloth should be called *zakdoek* in Dutch, *fazzoletto* in Italian and *handkerchief* in English.

Secondly, different languages often have the same or similarly pronounced names for quite disparate things. German *Bau* means 'building' while English *bough* designates the main branch of a tree. English *peel* means 'fruit rind', while French *pile* means 'battery'.

Thirdly, languages have randomly associated homonyms. The English word *bank*, meaning 'financial institution', has a homonym *bank* meaning 'river edge'. There is apparently no obstacle to the co-existence of both words, even though there is evidently no connexion between the two meanings. The French word *banque* meaning

[1] R. H. Robins, *A Short History of Linguistics*, London 1967, p. 18.   [2] ibid., p. 19.

'financial institution' has no homonymic partner meaning 'river edge'. These facts are difficult for a non-conventionalist theory to explain, since the same sounds apparently fulfil quite different nomenclature functions with equal efficiency within the same language, while between different languages there is no parallelism of homonymic pairings.

Fourthly, languages also have randomly associated synonyms. It is difficult to see what non-conventionalist explanation is available to account for the fact that the word *furze* designates the same plant as the word *gorse*.

Fifthly, over the course of time things may change their names. The vegetable which used to be called the *neep*, and still is in some parts of England, is now more generally known as the *turnip*. *Gossima* was the original name of the game now called *ping-pong* or *table-tennis*.

Sixth, over the course of time names may change their nominata. The English word *meat* once designated food in general. The Latin name for the butterfly (*papilio*) came to be used to designate a type of tent (Fr. *pavillon*). Facts of this kind argue that the association between name and thing is not intrinsically permanent, but subject to continuous ratification by the linguistic community.

Seventh, when conditions of cultural contact are appropriate, one linguistic community may borrow a name from another. The number of such borrowings as *le jazz* and *le week-end* in the vocabulary of contemporary French is such as to arouse much criticism and condemnation from French academic purists.[1] That the borrowing continues in spite of such criticisms suggests that disagreement from individuals is not strong enough to override the collective arbitration of the community.

Finally, the establishment of a new name for a new thing is often preceded by a period in which various rival possibilities compete for acceptance, and the community takes time to come to a final decision. The term *velocipede*, which English eventually rejected for *bicycle*, found favour in French. Lexical competition may often continue unresolved for a considerable length of time. In current British English, *launderette* seems to be winning over *laundromat* as the preferred name for a shop where the customer can do his own

---

[1] Reflected, for example, in the pejorative title of R. Etiemble's book *Parlez-vous franglais?* (Paris 1964).

washing in a coin-operated machine; but the preference is only slowly becoming established.

All the lexical phenomena mentioned above serve to highlight difficulties for any non-conventionalist theory, and to suggest that the adoption of a name is eventually a matter of acceptance or collective agreement by the linguistic community.

Like natural nomenclaturism, the theory of names by convention is only one manifestation of a more general and far-reaching view about what languages are. For the contractualist, languages are sets of social conventions, on exactly the same footing as other conventions. Unlike the surrogationalist, he is not tempted to look to what words stand for in order to provide an explanation of why various features of linguistic structure are as they are. Unlike the instrumentalist, he is not tempted to seek such an explanation by analysing human communicational intentions either. Typically, the contractualist emphasises what is arbitrary about the way languages work. The very fact that different languages appear to express very similar ideas in quite dissimilar ways is to him an evident demonstration that the surrogationalist is wrong. Linguistic knowledge, for the contractualist, does not reach out to the structure of reality; it is simply knowledge of what the contract is.

This is the characteristic position of the grammarian in the Graeco-Roman world. It reflects the pragmatic attitude of the language teacher, whose primary aim is exposition rather than explanation. However, it is a position which, although avoiding some of the difficulties which the surrogationalist and the instrumentalist encounter, generates problems of its own. If it is agreement among the linguistic community which constitutes the linguistic contract, what is to be said of cases where there is disagreement? When there are manifest divergences of linguistic usage within the community on certain specific points, does this mean that there is no contract, or that the contract has broken down? Or does it mean that certain practices are in breach of contract? Or does it mean that there are a number of different but equally valid contracts operative?

In antiquity, the contractualist solution to such problems took the form of what has been called the 'classical fallacy',[1] although it long outlived the period which that designation may suggest. This solution consists in opting for one standard of linguistic practice

[1] J. Lyons, *Introduction to Theoretical Linguistics*, Cambridge 1968, p. 9.

as 'correct' or 'good', and regarding deviations from this as 'incorrect' or 'bad'. It is essentially an authoritarian solution, but one which has certain obvious pedagogical advantages. It requires some person or persons to be in a position to compare and evaluate different linguistic usages: in practice, it presupposes a class of professional 'language experts'. Moreover, since language experts are unlikely to condemn their own linguistic practices as incorrect, selecting a standard merges inevitably with setting one. Hence contractualism leads almost automatically to a 'prescriptive' or 'normative' view of language-using. In turn, this will have sociological implications, inasmuch as it gives rise to the view 'that the "purity" of a language is maintained by the usage of the educated, and "corrupted" by the illiterate'.[1] Inevitably too, to the extent that education is identified with literacy, a scriptist bias will operate to condemn spoken usages which have no support in writing; and where a body of prestigious texts has already been handed down from earlier generations, these texts will tend to be regarded as authoritative in respect of linguistic matters.

This bias is nowhere more evident than in the programme which Quintilian lays down for the *grammaticus* of imperial Rome.[2] It is a programme clearly based upon the linguistic standard set by the Classical authors. The reading aloud of passages from their works, together with comment, questions and explanation, is its foundation. To this, various tasks which Quintilian enumerates are directly related. The grammarian will explain how vowels differ from consonants; how semivowels differ from mutes; how the pronunciation of words has altered in the course of time; what the various parts of speech are; and how nouns are declined and verbs conjugated. He will distinguish between native words and foreign borrowings, simple words and compounds, and between literal and metaphorical terms. He will proscribe barbarisms and solecisms. He will correct errors of prosody and other faults of pronunciation. He will point out common errors of gender, tense, person, mood and number. He will show how the etymology of a word may be of use in determining its correct interpretation. He will acquaint his pupils with the archaic spellings of the works of writers of past ages. He will teach them how to read poetry differently from prose; where to pause for breath, how to make breaks in accordance with the sense of the text,

[1] ibid., p. 9.   [2] *Institutio Oratoria* I.

when to raise or lower the voice, and when to increase or diminish
the speed of delivery. He will supply them with a good range of
reading, beginning with Homer and Vergil, and including tragic
verse and lyrics. He will teach them about figures of speech and all
devices of style. He will school his pupils in paraphrase, beginning
with Aesop's fables, and proceeding from a simple line-by-line
paraphrase to free paraphrase, in which the original text is abridged
or even embellished. He will also teach them the art of aphorisms,
and how to write simple types of prose composition.

Such a programme shows the 'classical fallacy' translated into a
systematic course of instruction. What this instruction sounded like
in the classroom we can judge from Priscian's revealing *Partitiones*,
which begins by quoting the first line of Vergil's *Aeneid*:

> *Arma virumque cano Troiae qui primus ab oris*

and then gives a full enumeration of all the questions that a pupil
could be asked about this line, together with the correct answers.
How many caesuras? . . . Which are they? . . . How many feet? . . .
How many parts of speech? . . . How many nouns? . . . Which are
they? . . . How many verbs? . . . Which are they? . . . And then,
proceeding word by word: What part of speech is *arma*? A noun.
What kind of noun? Appellative. What kind of appellative? General.
What gender? Neuter. How do you know? Because all nouns which
end in the plural in *-a* are neuter in gender without exception . . .[1]

This rigid catechism is less attractive than the urbane arguments of
Hermogenes, but it demonstrates the consequences of accepting
them: it shows us contractualism in practice. For although in Plato's
Cratylus Hermogenes does not seek to generalise his case beyond the
conventionality of names, it is very easily open to generalisation. If
names are no more than an arbitrary convenience, and what matters
is simply that men should reach agreement as to the names they will
use, the same can apply to any and every item in the whole linguistic
contract. It will make no difference how men form the past tense,
or construct subordinate clauses, provided they agree among themselves how it should be done. Thus may contractualist theory in the
end justify a practical policy of leaving it all to the grammarian.

[1] *Partitiones Duodecim Versuum Aeneidos Principalium*, in H. Keil, *Grammatici Latini*,
Leipzig, vol. III, 1858, p. 459 et seq.

Indeed, having grammarians for just that purpose may be seen as a great improvement in society's conduct of affairs, just as having judges, priests, or consuls may be seen as an improvement over other forms of social anarchy.

The advance of contractualism in the field of grammar is evident in the development of the doctrine of the parts of speech from Plato down to Dionysius Thrax.[1] What began as an analysis of the sentence with respect to its illocutionary function of making an assertion (hence a simple division into the two parts ὄνομα and ῥῆμα, corresponding to that of which something is asserted, and what is asserted of it) has by the first century B.C. ended up as a heterogeneous classification, in which the eight divisions recognised are determined by a mixture of formal, semantic and syntactic criteria.[2] This development reflects the supersession of the question 'What are the parts of the sentence for?' by the more practical pedagogic question 'How do we identify different types of word?' In turn, the answer to why one needs to be able to identify them at all is provided by Priscian's catechism. A school curriculum based on word-by-word analysis of literary texts demands an accepted systematisation which will both incorporate the most immediately obvious differentiae of words, and also facilitate the formulation of simple rules for putting them together in approved ways. From a contractualist point of view, there could be no other reason for setting up a classification at all.

At the same time, Priscian's catechism illustrates why, as far as a writer like Quintilian is concerned, the very contractualism of grammar makes it inferior, as a study, to rhetoric. For rhetoric requires a constant appraisal not of correctness, which may be taken for granted, but of communicational effectiveness. This modest assessment of the place of grammar (shared by Dionysius Thrax, who classed it as concerned merely with 'practical knowledge')[3] is a natural concomitant of the contractualist view that all

[1] R. H. Robins, *A Short History of Linguistics*, London 1967, pp. 26–36.

[2] For example, while the 'noun-adjective' (ὄνομα) is defined on a morphological-cum-semantic basis as 'a part of speech with case inflexion, signifying a person or thing', the 'article-relative' (ἄρθρον) is defined on a morphological-cum-syntactic basis as 'a part of speech inflected for case and preposed or postposed to nouns', and the 'prefix-preposition' (πρόθεσις) is defined distributionally as 'a part of speech placed before other words in composition and in syntax'.

[3] Robins, op. cit., p. 31.

that is involved is learning what the linguistic contract operative in a given community is, and how to abide by it. Quintilian does not deny that there are grammatical topics which may be pursued for their own sake, but the pursuit will be an academic pastime rather than a matter of serious import. One may pursue such pastimes, provided one does not get bogged down in them (*haerere*). After all, he observes, Caesar once wrote a treatise on analogy, but it seems to have done no harm to his eloquence.[1]

It is not by chance that contractualism has remained associated with the notion of 'rules' for language-using throughout the history of Western thought. Those contractualists who dislike the authoritarian implications of that notion have often tried to distinguish between prescriptive linguistic rules and descriptive linguistic rules. The 'rather tiresome analogy with games', as it has been called,[2] (although what is objectionable is not its tiresomeness so much as its trivialising character) is another facet of the attempt to retain the notion of rules but rid it of prescriptive overtones. What metaphor the modern contractualist could clutch at in a civilisation without games of any kind offers an interesting topic for speculation. (Even the contract metaphor will hardly do for the ultra-contractualism represented by the *Philosophical Investigations*, since contracts normally presuppose prior objectives related to the specific terms of the contract.) But the rules of games have to be interpretable as imperatives, addressed to potential players: otherwise it is difficult to see in what sense they would stipulate conditions for playing. The 'l-b-w' law of cricket can hardly be taken just as descriptive of certain things batsmen avoid doing; for at least two reasons. One is that batsmen all too frequently fail, at least in the opinion of umpires, to avoid doing precisely those things the 'l-b-w' law alludes to (although perhaps not frequently enough in the opinion of bowlers). The other is that there are many other things that batsmen avoid doing, e.g. batting blindfold, which are none the less not the subject-matter of laws of cricket. However the notion of a linguistic

---

[1] *Institutio Oratoria* I. vii. 34.

[2] J. R. Searle, 'What is a speech act?', in *The Philosophy of Language*, ed. J. R. Searle, Oxford 1971, p. 52. Searle distinguishes 'regulative rules' from 'constitutive rules', the latter being those of the kind which govern games like football. In Searle's view, there are constitutive rules which are not imperative in character: they are rules of the form 'X counts as Y'. (But this is no more than a matter of drafting. For 'X counts as Y' it will always be possible to substitute 'Count X as Y'.)

rule is interpreted or justified, it must be doubtful whether there would have been any temptation to think of language-using in terms of rule-following at all, but for the cultural conditioning imposed by a long pedagogic tradition of rule-giving. In this sense, the notion of a 'descriptive linguistic rule' remains intrinsically parasitic upon its prescriptive counterpart.

If only for this reason, the contractualist may prefer to avoid speaking of linguistic rules altogether, and keep instead to speaking of linguistic conventions. If pressed to supply some further account of a linguistic convention, he will tend to react in one or other of two ways. One is to say that anyone who insists on trying to provide too rigorously rational an explanation of why conventions take one form rather than another overlooks the fact that in many cases it does not much matter what the convention is provided that people keep to it. The fact that there is apparently little to choose between one convention and a possible alternative is itself part of the arbitrariness of conventions, and to suppose that if we look carefully enough we shall always be able to find some advantage which attaches to one convention over its possible rivals, and thus explains why it became established, is simply to be under a misconception about the nature of social conventions. It makes little difference whether the English drive on the right or on the left: what matters is that they should agree which, not why or how they maintain this agreement. At the same time, the contractualist will point out that a convention, once established, automatically tends to be maintained as part of a complex of related social practices both conventional and non-conventional, so long as it continues to serve its social purpose adequately. In the case of explaining why the English drive on the left, it would be legitimate to point out that it would be rather surprising if they drove on the right, given that their motor cars, their traffic signals, their road markings and their bye-laws are all adapted to driving on the left. Thus the contractualist will be disposed to emphasise that just because a convention is arbitrary, it does not follow that it can be arbitrarily altered. For although arbitrary in itself the convention may none the less be part of a system of practices interconnected in ways which are ultimately not arbitrary. The convention about driving on the left relates ultimately to the fact that uniformity of practice is necessary in order to ensure the unhindered flow of traffic and the prevention of accidents.

The other kind of account of linguistic conventions which the contractualist will be disposed to favour is an evolutionary account. The linguistic practices of one generation he will relate to the linguistic practices of a previous generation. The non-linguistic analogy here would be to answer the question as to why the English drive on the left by giving the history of relevant road conventions since the introduction of wheeled traffic in England.

In brief, the typically contractualist explanation of both the maintenance and change of linguistic conventions will be a sociolinguistic explanation.

In this connexion, it is relevant to note the natural link in the Western tradition between contractualism and the study of the history of a language. In antiquity, etymology and reference to the usage of previous generations were invoked to support the pedagogical contractualism of the grammarian. In more recent times, on the contrary, historical considerations have been used to question the validity of the grammarian's pedagogical position. But the link between contractualism and language-history survives.

If one asks why in present-day English people call a certain item of furniture by the term *chair*, or why plural morphs are suffixed and not prefixed, and one is told that the reason is not for any special appropriateness of the sounds or letters or their arrangement, but simply because English people's fathers, grandfathers and great-grandfathers did likewise, the urge to seek for some further explanation is singularly diminished. For it becomes obvious that if a similar question is posed concerning the usage of great-grandfather's generation, a similar answer and a similar historical regression will be forthcoming. The only occasion for further explanation seems to arise in cases where, at some point in the historical chain, the fathers, grandfathers or great-grandfathers apparently did something different. Thus changes in the linguistic contract may come to be seen as all a science of linguistics needs to account for. The maintenance of the contract unchanged needs no special justification. It is just part of the natural order of things.

That does not explain, nor is it intended to explain, how the contract arose in the first place. But that may not be regarded as amenable to scientific investigation in any case. If it is, the basic questions concerning languages number two. One is the question of glottogenesis, and the other the question of linguistic change.

In the nineteenth century, the study of linguistic change appeared to offer convincing evidence that the contractualist was right. Languages were found to change in accordance with laws of which the speakers themselves were not aware, and could not be aware, since these were laws which operated over such large spans of time and such widespread communities that it was impossible to suppose that they were under the control of human decisions. The changes concerned were not convincingly correlatable either with changes in the physical environment, or with changes in human communicational objectives. The factors involved seemed to be partly physiological and partly psychological. Sound-change and analogy appeared to wage a constant tug-of-war, of which the outcome in any particular instance was unpredictable, but irreversible, and binding on the whole community.

If language-users were not free agents to direct the course of sound-change or the operations of analogy, but were simply implementing the fulfilment of historical processes they did not understand, it followed that it was idle for the grammarian or any other authority to claim to know what linguistic usage ought to be. For languages would change in accordance with their own laws, regardless of what the authorities said. Secondly, it followed that, apart from relatively minor innovations which merely proved the rule, such as inventing new words to designate novel artifacts, a linguistic community had in practice no option but to accept the linguistic contract it had collectively inherited from its forefathers, subject to the natural operation of laws of linguistic change which were in any case beyond its powers to interfere with.

Nineteenth-century historical linguistics was what contractualism was to become, once finally divested of its pedagogical role. The alternative to laying down the contractual law would turn out to be having no say in it at all.

5

*If Men by nature had been framed for Solitude, they had
never felt an Impulse to converse with one another.*

The emergence of surrogationalism, instrumentalism and contractualism as three main strands in the development of the Western
concept of a language cannot be understood except as part of a
European cultural pattern of much broader significance. This
pattern was originally moulded in Greece, and it reflects the specific
historical conditions under which Greek society evolved.

The first relevant point which must strike anyone who studies
the history of Greek thought is the relative absence of interest in
language as such in Archaic Greece. Marrou has drawn attention
to the fact that the ἀρχαία παιδεία, the old aristocratic education,
does not appear to have included reading and writing at all until the
eve of the Classical period.[1] Nor do the earliest Greek thinkers
seem to have found any linguistic topics worthy of serious reflection.
While the survival of the Homeric poems attests the existence of
oral poetic traditions[2] in pre-Classical times, the borrowing of the
alphabet from the Phoenicians strongly suggests that after the dis-
appearance of writing during the Dark Age a new demand for written
records arose initially in connexion with trade.[3] These indications

[1] H. I. Marrou, *A History of Education in Antiquity* (tr. G. Lamb), 1956, ch. 4.

[2] Strong enough, it has been suggested, to make it unnecessary to commit the Homeric
poems to writing. The first written text alleged by tradition to have been made by order
of Pisistratus in the middle of the sixth century may have been to provide an official copy
of the poems to be recited at the Panathenaea (L. D. Reynolds and N. G. Wilson,
Scribes and Scholars, 2nd ed., Oxford 1974, p. 1).

[3] L. H. Jeffery (*Archaic Greece*, London 1976, p. 26) makes the point that casual
trading contacts of the kind described by Homer or Herodotus would not have sufficed.
The transference of a script between spoken languages as different as Greek and

point to a pre-Classical phase in the linguistic ethnography of Greek civilisation which has its parallels in the development of other societies: a phase in which verbal skills of a specialised kind are restricted to two main classes of activity, festal and clerical. This presupposes a social and economic structure which generates no demand for linguistic accomplishments other than those which can be satisfied by the separate vocational training of quite small classes of specialist, and no demand either for expansion in their numbers.

This state of affairs was to change very radically and very swiftly in the Classical period, in the course of what has been described as an 'evolution from a warrior to a scribe culture'.[1] It can be argued that the institution of ostracism by Cleisthenes at the end of the sixth century already implies that most of the citizens could write;[2] but the ballot is not a procedure which is altogether convincing evidence of literacy. Perhaps more significant is the fact that after an age of total neglect by the earlier pre-Socratic philosophers, words begin to emerge as a topic of interest towards the middle of the fifth century. Protagoras discusses the gender of Greek nouns. Socrates argues about etymologies. One may ask how and why this new interest has come to the fore, and what it signifies.

Discussing the origins of Greek science, G. E. R. Lloyd points to an interesting connexion between science and politics. The specu- lations of Thales and the constitutional reforms of his contem- porary, Solon, have in common at least two things: a rejection of any supernatural authority for the new ideas they propose, and an acceptance of the legitimacy of criticism and argument on the basis of available information. The new critical attitude towards the world of nature which emerges in the work of the Milesian philo- sophers can be seen as 'a counterpart to, and offshoot of, the con- temporary development of the practice of free debate and open dis- cussion in the context of politics and law throughout the Greek world'.[3]

A parallel and perhaps closer connexion with politics might be suggested in the case of Greek linguistic inquiry; for here the

---

Phoenician implies bilingual trading communities of the kind that doubtless existed in Greek settlements like that at Al Mina on the north coast of Syria, or Semitic settle- ments in Crete.

[1] Marrou, op. cit., p. 36.
[2] ibid., p. 43.
[3] G. E. R. Lloyd, *Early Greek Science: Thales to Aristotle*, London 1970, p. 15.

connexion would extend not only to similarities of approach but also to content. It is no accident that linguistic topics begin to come to the fore during a period in which the Classical city-state reaches its zenith, for the new interest in such matters is connected with the growing maturity of the city-state's political and educational institutions. Specifically, the connexion is seen both in the form which the attention to language takes, and also in the source of its propagation. The form is the development of an explicit art of speaking, and the source is the educational movement initiated by the Sophists.

The transition from early monarchical and oligarchical forms of government to a participatory democracy of the type represented by Athens in the fifth century was bound to prove a severe test for the traditional forms of Greek education. The slow development of the ἀρχαία παιδεία meant that even Athenians of the generation of Pericles had a formal education which hardly went beyond what is taught in a modern elementary school.[1] Such an education could not for long be expected to prove equal to the demands of a social and political system in which every adult male citizen was entitled and expected to take a part in public life; a system under which members of the Council and state officials were chosen annually by lot, and were responsible not to other officials but directly to the Assembly. The Assembly comprised in principle the totality of their fellow citizens, and alone decided matters of war, peace, taxation, and all questions of external and internal policy. Last but not least, it was a system which was expected to function without any permanent civil service. It is small wonder that in these circumstances there should have arisen a demand for a broader education, of a kind which could fit a man to play a role in public affairs; and it was for this demand that the Sophists catered.[2]

The bad name which the Sophists eventually acquired was due partly to the attacks upon them by Socrates and his followers, and partly to the fact that they made a great deal of money. (Protagoras amassed a fortune. Hippias boasted of having taken 150 minae,

[1] Marrou, op. cit., p. 46.
[2] Discussing the success of the Sophists, J. B. Bury observes that 'with the growth of democracies in so many cities, ability to speak in public and persuade your audience, whether in a court of law or in meetings of the Assembly or the Council or of a political club, was every year becoming more necessary for the man who wished to take part in public life, and desirable as a weapon of self-defence even for those who had no such ambitions' (*Cambridge Ancient History*, 1953, vol. v, p. 378).

perhaps the equivalent of £3,000, on a single lecture tour of Sicily.)[1]
But the very extent of their financial success as itinerant free-lance
educators, and the fact that the basis of their system was instruction
in the skills of speaking and debate, demonstrates beyond reasonable
doubt that, not merely in Athens but all over the Greek-speaking
world, there was a sudden focus of interest on language, related to
a new importance which the spoken word had acquired in public
life. This is corroborated by the old tradition, reported by Cicero,[2]
that the art of rhetoric was founded by Corax and Tisias to teach
citizens dispossessed by the tyrants how to plead in court for the
recovery of their property, when Syracuse became a democracy in
467 B.C. Similar needs explain the rise of the professional λογογράφος,
of whom Antiphon and Lysias are representative, and whose liveli-
hood depended on the fact that although Athenian law required
every citizen to speak for himself in court, whether in prosecution
or defence of a charge, it did not prohibit him from delivering a
speech composed for him by someone else.

Thus in the course of the fifth century, Greek society became
language-conscious in a way and to a degree hitherto unprecedented, as a direct result of the requirements imposed by the institutions of the democratic city-state.

This is the situation which provides the point of departure for the
next important development, which culminates in the Aristotelian
systematisation of logic. What is involved is the recognition and
separation of two perlocutionary functions of language-using:
securing agreement and discovering the truth. This distinction was
itself originally a subject of controversy. Objections were raised
against the Sophists on two points of principle. One was that their
teaching did not lead to true knowledge of linguistic skills, because
it was not properly analytic. This is the objection raised by Aristotle
when he likens Gorgias' method of teaching by example to the
claims of someone who says he can tell you how to avoid getting
sore feet; but then, instead of explaining how, simply offers you a
variety of footwear of all shapes and sizes.[3] The other objection was

---

[1] K. Freeman, *Companion to the Pre-Socratic Philosophers*, 2nd ed., Oxford 1966,
p. 345 fn.
[2] Cicero (*Brutus* xi. 46) says that although previously many had endeavoured to speak
carefully and with orderly arrangement, before Corax and Tisias no one had devised a
system or precepts (*artem et praecepta*).
[3] *De Sophisticis Elenchis* 183B36–184A.

that their teaching failed to distinguish between persuasive argument and correct argument. This is a recurrent theme of Socrates
in Plato's dialogues. In the *Gorgias*, rhetoric is compared dis-
paragingly to cookery, which merely seeks to flatter the appetite,
as opposed to medicine, which seeks to understand what food is
best for nutriment.[1]

Behind this, there lies more than just a quarrel between rival
schools of teachers in fifth-century Athens. Seen from one point of
view, it is an issue which puts the whole system of Greek democracy
on trial. For if the Sophists are right, democratic government re-
solves itself into a battle of persuasion, in which technical expertise
and astuteness must always win, regardless of truth or justice.
Protagoras, who is constantly under attack in the Platonic dialogues,
evidently took the position that the art of verbal persuasion is second
to none, since truth is an illusion; or rather, truth differs from one
observer to another, and in the end all opinions are equally true.
The Socratic answer to this insists on the validity of a distinction
between using words to persuade and using words to reason correctly. But this alone is not enough; since even if the laws of reason
are different from the laws of persuasion, some assurance is needed
that premisses can formulate assertions which are true independently
of anyone's opinion. The discussion of the connexions between
names and what they stand for which is conducted in *Cratylus* is
ultimately part of an inquiry into the philosophical basis of a political
system which relies intrinsically upon free discussion and argument
as the only way of arriving at the right course to follow.

Carried to one extreme, the Sophists' view is represented by
Gorgias' treatise *On Being*, in which it is argued that words can tell
us nothing about the nature of reality. If anything that exists can be
comprehended by man, it cannot be communicated; for speech is
by nature quite different from the objects of human perception.[2]
Scepticism of this order clearly presents a challenge to its critics.
Those who claim that truth is to be distinguished from mere opinion
are required to explain what the connexion is between words and
reality which can guarantee some assertions as truths, independently

---

[1] Socrates says rhetoric is to the soul 'what cookery is to the body', a form of flattery
(*Gorgias* 465E). Cookery assumes the semblance of medicine, and pretends to know
what food is best for the body. If children are the judges, cooks will be supposed to
know more about food than physicians (*Gorgias* 464D).

[2] Freeman, op. cit., pp. 360–1.

of what anyone may think. This is the background against which the arguments about the 'correctness' of names in *Cratylus* must be seen. Unless it is possible for words to give us accurate information—at least sometimes—about real states of affairs, then it might seem that the pursuit of truth rather than persuasion is not so much an unattainable goal as an incoherent one. Hence the importance of the doctrine that words are not just sounds, but stand for things.

Surrogationalism thus emerges originally as part of a natural alliance with logic, against the claims of rhetoric to be the supreme art of man: a claim which only makes sense in the first place in a political and social context in which, literally, verbal persuasion does decide the conduct of human affairs. It was an alliance which was to survive more than two thousand years of political and intellectual change. So long as logic remained wedded to the syllogism, it needed surrogationalism to explain what the difference was between a valid inference and an invalid one; for without that distinction, logic had no justification for claiming independence from rhetoric.

With respect to the conflict between the rival claims of rhetoric and logic, grammar initially plays no role; for rhetorician and logician alike take for granted what Locke was later to call the 'civil' use of words.[1] It is relevant to note, however, that the contractualism with which grammar eventually comes to be associated can be foreseen as the only position of neutrality available between the rhetorician's instrumentalism, on the one hand, and the logician's surrogationalism on the other. But this neutrality was bound to remain without wider implications until a situation arose in which membership of a particular community of language-users could be seen not only as important in itself, but even more important than oratorical or logical expertise in language-using.

Grammar does not assert its independence as against both rhetoric and logic until a later stage in the evolution of Greek linguistic ethnography. Grammar is essentially the creation not of the Classical but of the Hellenistic period. Its emergence as a separate subject reflects the profound difference in linguistic orientation between the Greek world of the small city-state and the Greek world of the Empire.

---

[1] i.e. everyday communicational competence: 'such a communication of thoughts and ideas by words as may serve for the upholding common conversation and commerce, about the ordinary affairs and conveniences of civil life, in the societies of men, one amongst another' (*An Essay Concerning Human Understanding*, III. ix. 3).

After Alexander's conquests, for the first time Greek became a language which large numbers of non-Greek speakers needed to learn, and administrative needs generated a pressing demand for a large secretarial class who could read and write. Their writing did not need to achieve effectiveness in the rhetorician's sense, nor dialectic skill; since for the most part they would only be writing what others dictated. It simply needed to achieve a certain standard of correctness. Thus grammar, as Max Müller observed, 'owes its origin, like all other sciences, to a very natural and practical want'.[1] Since it was a want more elementary than that for which the training provided by the Sophists had catered, the grammarian naturally acquired a status inferior to that of the rhetorician in the educational hierarchy of antiquity. In order to stake any claim to academic prestige at all, he had to base his teaching on a specialised knowledge of the language of the ancient authors. The long-lived association between literary studies and grammar was no fortuitous product of Alexandrian scholarship under the Ptolemies, but a reflection of the fact that the grammarian, arriving late on the scene, had no other field of expertise to turn to which was not already marked out as the province of the rhetorician or the logician. The 'classical fallacy' was his professional charter. By the same token, contractualism became his professional creed, because it denied the rhetorician and the logician any right to tell the grammarian what correct usage 'ought' to be.

The system of grammatical analysis which was to provide Europe's scholars with their basic model for the next two thousand years took a form determined by the particular educational context for which it was originally designed. To see that this is so, it suffices to compare the kind of grammar which the tradition of Dionysius Thrax, Donatus and Priscian produced, with the quite different kind of grammar formulated for Sanskrit by Pāṇini some centuries earlier.[2] Arguably, part of the difference may be due to structural divergences between Sanskrit on the one hand, and Greek and Latin on the other. But this is not a completely satisfactory explanation. In principle, Sanskrit could perfectly well be described in more or less the way Greek and Latin are dealt with by Dionysius Thrax, Donatus and Priscian. Likewise, Greek and Latin could equally well be

---

[1] *Lectures on the Science of Language*, London 1861, p. 80.
[2] Ed. O. Boehtlingk, Leipzig 1887.

The Language-Makers

described in more or less the way Pāṇini describes Sanskrit. The reason for the adoption of different descriptive systems lies elsewhere.

A teacher who, like Pāṇini, can provide context-sensitive rules for the derivation of forms, order his rules in such a way that there is an agreed procedure for determining which take precedence over which, and increase their efficacy by postulating 'dummy' elements subsequently deleted or replaced, is clearly thinking about the language he is describing in quite a different way from the Graeco-Roman grammarians. The Pāṇinian approach presupposes that surface forms are the final products of operations on latent forms underlying them. The Graeco-Roman approach, on the contrary, proceeds by comparing surface forms in order to construct a classification of them. Dionysius Thrax would not have understood the point of a Pāṇinian rule.[1] Pāṇini would not have seen the virtues of setting up a crude and somewhat arbitrary system of parts of speech.

None the less, each method of analysis is well suited to the purpose it was intended to serve. Pāṇinian rules would have been of very little practical use to the Greek or Roman schoolboy called upon to stand up in class and parse a line of Homer or Vergil in the manner so graphically captured in Priscian's catechism. In order to stand a chance of being widely adopted in Graeco-Roman antiquity, any system of grammar that might be devised had to fit into an educational programme of which both the starting point and the ultimate objective were already fixed. It had to bridge the gap between the rote learning of the letters and syllables, which invariably commenced primary education,[2] and the lessons of the rhetorician, to whom the pupil would eventually be handed on. Thus,

---

[1] Literal translation of individual rules is not viable as a means of exemplification, for reasons which may be illustrated by citing part of Staal's account of Pāṇini 7.3.102, the rule *supi ca*: '*ca* means "and" and *supi* is *sup* followed by the Locative ending; *sup* itself denotes any case ending, in accordance with a principle of abbreviation laid down elsewhere in the grammar. Since in this rule no Nominative or Genitive occurs, and the rule is ordered immediately after the previous one, the substitute, the substituendum and the limiting context from the previous rule carry over . . . But since the . . . rule speaks of case endings, it can no longer apply to verbal stems. The . . . rule therefore expresses that final short *a* of a nominal stem is lengthened whenever a case ending beginning with any of the sounds *y v r l ñ m ṅ ṇ n jh bh* follows.' (J. F. Staal, 'The origin and development of linguistics in India'; in *Studies in the History of Linguistics*, ed. D. Hymes, Bloomington 1974, pp. 67–8.)

[2] Marrou, op. cit., pp. 150–2.

from syllable to sentence by the shortest route was the brief that the educational programme imposed on anyone who set out to devise a system of grammatical analysis, and Dionysius Thrax fulfilled that brief admirably. His word-class system was an ugly theoretical hotchpotch, but that did not matter. (Varro advocated a theoretically much more elegant system, but its pedagogical utility would have been much more restricted, and it never caught on).[1] The absence of word-form rules did not matter either, when it was simpler and more effective to get the class to learn the paradigms off by heart.

The cultural context of Pāṇini's grammar is totally different. It belongs to a tradition with a primarily religious background. Grammar in ancient India was one of the 'six limbs of the Veda'. Its study was held to be necessary for a full understanding of the mantras, and the correct performance of ceremonies; and 'it was of the utmost ritual significance that every word used in the recitals at the sacrifices should be pronounced absolutely correctly'.[2] There was an obligation to ensure the faithful transmission of the sacred texts, free from corruption or misinterpretation. In particular, the system of description which Pāṇini employs seems to have its origin in comparison between *pada* (word-by-word) and *saṃhitā* (continuous) versions of the same Vedic texts. Since the *saṃhitā* versions were held to be of divine origin, and hence unalterable, a natural form of comparison would be to devise rules systematically linking the *saṃhitā* forms with the corresponding *pada* forms.[3] Here doubtless is to be found the underlying reason for the adoption of a basic type of rule formulation which is quite alien to Graeco-Roman grammar. Pedagogically useless,[4] it would give an excellent system for verifying textual accuracy. Its adoption suggests an orientation towards exactness of linguistic detail, rather than simplicity of expository teaching. The religious background probably also accounts for the

---

[1] *De Lingua Latina* viii. 44.

[2] T. Burrow, *The Sanskrit Language*, London 2nd ed., 1965, p. 47.

[3] *Pada* texts presumably originated as simplified versions when the language of the original *saṃhitā* texts was no longer easy to understand. This seems to be indicated by the artificial way in which *pada* texts give the words in their uncombined forms, and resolve compounds into their elements.

[4] In Pāṇini's case, the intricate interdependence of the rules presents what has been described as 'unsurmountable difficulty in application' unless one is already thoroughly familiar with the complexities of the rule system (V. N. Misra, *The Descriptive Technique of Pāṇini*, The Hague 1966, p. 36).

5

significance of various issues in Indian linguistic theorising which would have baffled Dionysius Thrax or Priscian; such as the principle of the 'eternity' or 'permanence' of words, and the question whether a word has a meaning in isolation from its context.

The Graeco-Roman concern to have a grammar which would suit a particular educational programme perhaps also explains certain features which are otherwise difficult to account for. If one compares the system which Dionysius Thrax first codified at the end of the second century B.C. with earlier Greek analyses of the parts of speech, it seems clear that there is a break in the tradition. The Stoic system of Diogenes of Babylon had recognised only five word-classes, distinguished as follows:

> A common noun or appellative is defined by Diogenes as part of a sentence signifying a common quality, e.g. man, horse; whereas a name is a part of speech expressing a quality peculiar to an individual, e.g. Diogenes, Socrates. A verb is, according to Diogenes, a part of speech signifying an isolated predicate, or, as others define it, an undeclined part of a sentence, signifying something that can be attached to one or more subjects, e.g. 'I write', 'I speak'. A conjunction is an indeclinable part of speech, binding the various parts of a statement together; and an article is a declinable part of speech, distinguishing the genders and numbers of nouns.[1]

This system of Diogenes is manifestly an expansion of the simpler Aristotelian tri-partite system, which did not recognise the article, nor Diogenes' distinction between common noun and proper name. Earlier still, in Plato, we find simply a distinction between two parts of the sentence ὄνομα and ῥῆμα. Thus there is a common thread running through from Plato to Diogenes of Babylon. But it does not continue on to Dionysius Thrax. The earlier system is too closely tied to the interests of the logician. Dionysius refuses to recognise a major grammatical distinction between common noun and proper name, but he does distinguish pronouns from nouns, adverbs from verbs, prepositions from conjunctions, and participles from both nouns and verbs. Unlike Aristotle and Diogenes, he is not concerned principally with the different ways in which a proposition may be expressed in words, but rather with the ways in which the individual verbal components of any phrase or sentence compare

[1] Diogenes Laertius, vii. 58, tr. R. D. Hicks (Loeb Classical Library edition).

and contrast with one another. From the point of view of the logician such distinctions as Dionysius introduces are trivial; but from the point of view of someone who simply has to learn how to construct a Greek phrase or sentence, they are important. In short, instead of working from the proposition downwards, the system codified by Dionysius is the first to work in the opposite direction, from word-forms upwards. Furthermore, although the system is originally presented as a description of Greek, it is difficult to believe that whoever elaborated it was not perfectly well aware of its applicability to Latin. Otherwise it would be by a quite remarkable chance that the degree of generality with which its definitions are formulated is such as to allow them to be transferred without difficulty for the identification of the corresponding word-classes in Latin. One might even hazard a guess that the system had been worked out by maximising the similarities between Greek and Latin morphology, and minimising the differences.

From well before the time of Dionysius Thrax, Roman education had turned to Greek sources, and by the Classical period was normally a bilingual education.[1] Quintilian even warns that concentration on Greek at an early age, necessary as it is, may lead to acquisition of faulty Latin.[2] Earlier, Greek influence had been much deplored by conservatives like the elder Cato (who none the less eventually decided to learn Greek in his old age). Lessons in Greek had been available in Rome, for anyone who could afford to pay for them, since the third century B.C., long before there is any mention of *grammatici latini*.[3] Greek rhetoric and Greek philosophy were also taught in Rome in the second century; so successfully that in 161 B.C. all rhetoricians and philosophers were banished. What is significant is that although the Romans had had this long acquaintance with Greek educational models, indigenous Latin grammar does not emerge until a stage in Rome's political evolution when citizenship had been extended in Italy to the point where native speakers of Latin were themselves in the minority. Once the lesson of the Social War had been learned, the promotion of Latin became part of a political policy aimed at the unification of the peninsula under Roman rule. This situation alone would have sufficed to motivate the codification of Latin grammar. But at the

[1] Marrou, op. cit., p. 255 et seq.   [2] *Institutio Oratoria* I. i. 13–14.
[3] Marrou, op. cit., pp. 251–2.

same time the administration of the provinces was creating a growing demand for a literate secretarial class, in exactly the same way
as Greek imperial expansion had done. As Rome's frontiers continued to advance during the first and second centuries A.D., absorb-
ing an ever greater number of diverse populations, knowledge of
Latin came to play an even more crucial role in the social, political
and administrative architecture of the Roman world. By the time
provinces like Gaul had outstripped Italy in their zeal for learning
Latin, the grammarian was no longer just a school teacher; he had
become one of the constructional engineers of the *pax Romana*.

By that time too, the Roman concept of a language was established as part of a philosophy of civic man, and the relationship
between grammar, rhetoric and logic fixed accordingly. Behind the
rhetorical treatises of Cicero and Quintilian there is clearly a doctrine of civic virtues which differs in emphasis from anything we
find in Aristotle, even though there is almost no individual point
they make which cannot be traced back to Greek sources. But in
everything that Cicero and Quintilian say on this subject, there is
an awareness that they are shaping the education of a governing
class destined to rule the world. The concept of a language implicit
in their writings is part of a very Roman theory of what life is about:
it is about leadership.

Leadership resides in natural superiority, and to exercise it is the
duty of those thus gifted (a fact too obvious for the subtle Greek
mind to be content with). But to be worthy to lead calls for the
assiduous cultivation of those natural excellences on which leadership is based. Foremost among these is the art of speaking. For man
is naturally superior to other animals by having the faculty of language and rationality. Logic provides a training for the exercise of
this rationality as manifested in the use of words. Among the races
of men, some peoples are naturally superior to others, and the
superior peoples will impose their laws upon the inferior. Grammar
is the codification of a people's linguistic laws. Among a given
people, some individuals are naturally superior to others, and one
way in which this superiority will manifest itself is in respect of the
distinctive human faculty of language. It is the duty of the gifted
individual to learn to cultivate skill in public speaking, so that he
may thereby provide leadership in public life. Rhetoric is the art of
exercising this skill. Just as Rome provides natural political leader-

ship, so the language of Rome is naturally pre-eminent. The orator who is not a native of Rome, says Cicero,[1] naturally labours under a disadvantage. However skilled he may be, his speaking will lack the authentic *urbanitas*. The basis of oratory is impeccable Latin pronunciation; but whereas this used to be common, the language of Rome itself is now so debased by the intrusion of outside influences that it needs the grammarian to say what is correct.[2] Since effective public speaking is the way in which the gifted individual manifests this characteristically human superiority, rhetoric calls for the cultivation of all the highest qualities. It is in Cicero and Quintilian that we find the clearest equation of the ideal orator with the ideal leader of men. It was an equation in which Cicero himself patently believed: as the outstanding orator of his age, he clearly saw himself as fitted for the highest public office. Quintilian, personally more modest, none the less does not hesitate to subsume the whole of formal education and character formation as part of the training of the orator. For him, excellence in speaking even takes on something of a mystical quality, for he disdains to judge it merely by success in persuasion: to train the perfect orator involves the whole of education, and simply to speak well (*bene dicere*) is the highest aim of rhetoric.[3] In short, according to Cicero and Quintilian, to speak Latin with the skill of a consummate Roman orator is the summit of human ambition: it is to be one of the outstanding individuals among the élite of the world's natural leaders. The status of Latin had become simultaneously part of the theory, practice and propaganda of Rome's supremacy.

*   *   *

It might seem almost impossible that anything of this complex of moral, vocational and linguistic ideals should survive the destruction of the political and social system on which it was based. Yet it did. Even the complete military collapse of the Roman empire did not seriously undermine the pre-eminence of Latin. Paradoxically, it was strengthened. For clinging to Latin, in whatever form, became the only effective resistance available in Western Europe against the barbarian invasions. But clinging to Latin *per se* might not have been enough, had it not also meant clinging to a religion. It is

[1] *Brutus* xlvi. 170 et seq.   [2] *ibid.* lxxiv. 258 et seq.   [3] *Institutio Oratoria* II. xv. 38.

difficult to say whether the Vulgate saved Europe for Latin, or whether Latin saved Europe for Christianity. In all probability, neither would have survived if the language of the New Testament had still been Greek when Alaric sacked Rome. As it was, Latin conquered the barbarians not once but twice. In its colloquial form, it eventually split up, under pressures for regional differentiation, into the various Romance languages. But it also survived in a more conservative form as the official language of established religion, of law, and of secular government. So the price the barbarians—or their descendants—ultimately paid for wrecking the Roman empire was having two varieties of Latin to learn instead of one.

The official Latin of the European Dark Ages, however, was a language increasingly incomprehensible to the masses of the population, revered though it might be. Its very incomprehensibility acted as an important social barrier, a restriction of access to privileged positions, and necessitated the maintenance of a Latin-based educational system, which would provide for the needs of secular and religious administration. During the medieval period, a mastery of this official form of spoken and written Latin continued to be a practical necessity for anyone who aspired to 'no matter how humble a position in the republic of learning or in the hierarchy of the Church'.[1] Without the political reality of Roman supremacy, it was this new social role of Latin throughout the Middle Ages which ensured the unbroken continuity of the Western grammatical tradition. So long as Latin maintained this role, Priscian was still the key to a career, even though there might be a rather hollow ring to much of what Cicero and Quintilian had said. What the great men of Rome had said remained authoritative none the less, at least in linguistic matters, simply because a Latin-based educational system had no alternative source of authority to turn to.

Thus, with the establishment of rhetoric, dialectic and grammar as the components of the medieval trivium, what had begun as a differentiation of responses to the role of language, prompted by a series of historically interconnected social and political situations in antiquity, became finally institutionalised as the permanent structure of a system of higher education. It put the intellectual development of Europe into a straitjacket from which the concept of a language has yet to struggle free.

[1] O. Jespersen, *Language, its Nature, Development and Origin*, London 1922, p. 24.

6

Be the Language upon the whole ever so perfect, much must be left, in defiance of all analogy, to the harsh laws of mere authority and chance.

In linguistic studies, medieval scholarship inherited a basic weakness where vocabulary was concerned. A systematic treatment of the meanings of words posed a problem of which the intrinsic difficulty may be measured by the fact that throughout antiquity it was never clearly formulated, much less satisfactorily tackled. No scholar of Greece or Rome devised any general method for distinguishing and characterising all the diverse human purposes which, on the instrumentalist view at least, must be presumed to underlie the significantly different meaningful uses of words. Direct acquaintance with those purposes through experience and observation (as in Augustine's account of language-learning) was assumed to be required.

The solution to this problem, when eventually it was found, had the unmistakable simplicity and generality of all great advances in thinking. It lay in recognition of the principle of intralingual definition, and the systematic application of that principle to the construction of a monolingual dictionary. The communicational function of any word could be expressed in terms of other words of the same language. The very familiarity of the word-book in modern European culture is apt to disguise from us the fact that it represents a landmark in human evolution no less significant than the wheel, the steam engine, or the computer. Like many another major intellectual step, it appears in retrospect so obvious and so long anticipated that one is puzzled to understand why no one had taken it before. Yet the very fact that it was not taken sooner, and the role which the dictionary rapidly acquired once it had been taken, combine to tell us more about the Western concept of a language than all the explicit philosophical discussions of linguistic topics from Plato down to Wittgenstein.

The indefatigable and plagiaristic compilers who thrived throughout antiquity and the Middle Ages could produce everything a literate civilisation might require: from encyclopaedic works of reference on all subjects, to bilingual glossaries and lists of archaisms, barbarisms, misspellings, dialect words, etymologies, culinary terms, botanical terms and medical terms, not to mention glossaries of Homer, Plato, Hippocrates, the tragic poets, the comic poets, the orators and the Bible. Yet, mysteriously, they managed not to produce the lexicographical equivalents of the modern *Petit Larousse* or the *Concise Oxford Dictionary*. It was not lack of industry or want of method that prevented them, but considerations of a quite different order. Itemising and defining the total word-stock of a language had not for them the significance it was to have for later medieval and post-medieval Europe. For one thing, Greek and Latin already had what the emergent modern European languages as yet lacked: the repository of authoritative and exemplary usage represented by the works of acknowledged authors of the first rank. But this was only one aspect of the question. More important, the vernacular dictionary, when it eventually appeared in Europe, was essentially a product of the rise of nationalism, which gave birth also to the serious study of the grammar of the modern European languages.[1] It was no accident that vernacular lexicography eventually came to be placed under the tutelage of such bodies as the Accademia della Crusca and the Académie Française. The lexical compilations of a Julius Pollux, an Isidore, or a John of Garland, had been simple aids to erudition, not monuments to nationhood.

---

[1] Earlier medieval treatises relating to languages other than Latin (such as that on Icelandic by the so-called 'First Grammarian', or the Irish *Auraicept na n-Éces*) remain sporadic and do not appear to herald any widespread development of interest in codifying the vernaculars. An exception is the case of Provençal, where in the thirteenth and fourteenth centuries interest in grammar was closely linked to the popularity of troubadour poetry and the intricacies of its composition, before the extinction of Provençal culture as a result of the Albigensian war. French also occupies a rather special position in that the earliest works on French grammar were written in England in the fourteenth century, and were evidently prompted by the decline there of Anglo-Norman in face of competition from English.

During the sixteenth century, instrumentalism was called upon to act as midwife at the birth of a new development in the Western concept of a language; a development which was to surpass in importance instrumentalism itself. Its outward manifestation was the overthrow of the linguistic hegemony of Latin in Europe; but this was the product of a unique concurrence of trends, in different social, political, literary and religious movements, to reject what the hegemony of Latin stood for.

An instrumentalist approach to language was naturally suited to the linguistic self-consciousness of nascent nationalism. Unlike surrogationalism, which tends to support the view that the language-user has no option but to accept an established connexion between words and their surrogates, instrumentalism is favourable to the opposite view: that languages are open to manipulation and modification to suit changing needs. Hence it is no surprise to find that a Renaissance writer like du Bellay, upholding the cause of the French vernacular,[1] insists that there are no criteria of adequacy for languages other than fulfilment of the needs of their users, and that these needs vary from one society to another. Were it otherwise, he argues,[2] the pursuit of common needs would have prevented the proliferation of so many different languages.[3] The same argument is put forward in Italy by the Paduan poet and philosopher Speroni.[4] The importance of this point for the Renaissance champions[5] of the European vernaculars is that in one move it destroys the basis for the arguments of the conservative opposition, i.e. the upholders of the Classical languages as models of perfection, by comparison with which French or Italian are seen as corrupt and impoverished. The comparison is shown to be invalid, because one cannot judge a language except on the basis of the requirements of its own users. There is nothing intrinsic to the nature of languages which makes

[1] *Deffence et Illustration de la Langue Francoyse*, 1549.

[2] Thus by implication rejecting the Babel story as an authentic explanation of the diversity of languages.

[3] op. cit., ed. H. Chamard, Paris 1948, p. 12.

[4] From whom du Bellay borrowed it. The relevant passage from Speroni's *Dialogo delle lingue*, probably written between 1530 and 1535, is cited by Chamard, loc. cit., p. 13, fn. 2.

[5] Of whom the great precursor was Dante, whose *De vulgari eloquentia* had praised the vernaculars acquired 'naturally', as against the Latin acquired 'artificially' at school, and pleaded the case for a common vernacular which would unify Italy linguistically.

one 'inferior' to another, or incapable of adaptation to whatever new purposes its users may require of it. Instrumentalism also provided naturally for the phenomena of linguistic change, which increasingly attracted the attention of Renaissance thinkers, in particular in connexion with the Renaissance concept of historical evolution.[1] Furthermore, instrumentalism fitted in admirably with the rejection of medieval scholastic philosophy, by offering an alternative to the rigid surrogationalism of the modistic grammarians. It was sufficiently flexible to accommodate the influx of knowledge about non-European languages, resulting from the Renaissance 'voyages of discovery'.[2] In short, instrumentalism became pivotal to Renaissance philosophy of language, which was itself the product of a new social evaluation of the role of Latin and of learning,[3] and of the new political context provided by Renaissance nationalism.

It was ironical that the monolingual dictionary, predestined to be the visible symbol of a nation's linguistic independence from Latin, prepared by an instrumentalist philosophy of language which vindicated the claims of growth and adaptability against an outmoded ideal of static perfection, should turn out to be the most powerful instrument men could have devised to ensure the eventual imposition of a new version of the 'classical fallacy'. In part this was due to a reaction against the linguistic exuberance and innovation of the Renaissance, and consciousness of a need to 'fix' and stabilise the vernaculars as literary media. To this, the nationalistic ideal of a single, unified language added no small contribution. In part also it was the foreseeable consequence of the authority attributed to works compiled by 'language experts', backed by the prestige which the endemic scriptism of literate societies accords to the permanence of written records. This was newly reinforced in the case of Renaissance Europe by the invention of printing. How the replacement of the manuscript by the printed book adds to the unchallengeable impersonality of what is contained therein can hardly be overestimated. The manuscript page is a constant reminder that what

---

[1] R. A. Hall, 'Linguistic theory in the Italian Renaissance', *Language*, vol. 13, 1936, pp. 96–107; R. Simone, 'Sperone Speroni et l'idée de diachronie dans la linguistique de la Renaissance italienne', in *History of Linguistic Thought and Contemporary Linguistics*, ed. H. Parret, Berlin/New York 1976, pp. 302–16.

[2] R. H. Robins, *A Short History of Linguistics*, London 1967, p. 103 et seq.

[3] Simone, op. cit., p. 305.

we are dealing with is in the last resort communication from human being to human being; whereas the printed page invites us to inspect a visual representation of ideas nobody owns. Their independence and capacity for survival in limitless, identical copies seems guaranteed by the very hallmarks of mechanical production. How much more so when the printed page is one presenting columns of entries in which words are simply juxtaposed without, for the most part, comment of any kind. By the time the presses of Europe could provide every scholar with his own copy, it was inevitable that the monolingual dictionary should not only provide the lexical inventory of the language, but at the same time set the standard, from which any departure invited a query, if not a charge of idiosyncrasy, or ignorance, or error. The difference in linguistic psychology between pre-dictionary and post-dictionary Europe must have been rather like the difference in commercial psychology before and after the introduction of standard national currencies.

Although seventeenth-century rationalism rehabilitated surrogationalism in the field of grammar (as exemplified by the Port Royal grammar of 1660), it was powerless either to reverse the movement towards the codification of standard national languages, or to neutralise its consequences; and in any case it had no contribution to offer which would have affected the theory or practice of vernacular lexicography. The production of dictionaries of one's native language gathered momentum as a scholarly activity throughout the seventeenth century,[1] and in the end what the dictionaries did neither Descartes nor Port Royal could undo. The new dictionary-based orthological dogma lacked that profound linguistic respect for one's ancestors which had characterised the earlier 'classical fallacy'. (The language of the *Chanson de Roland* was nothing held in high esteem by the Pléiade's audience, and even less by Racine's

---

[1] By 1700, English had the very incomplete dictionaries of Bullokar, Cockeram, Blount and Phillips: Italian the *Vocabolario* of the Accademia della Crusca; French the dictionary of the Académie Française, besides two other major monolingual dictionaries by Furetière and Richelet, which had been published abroad so as not to infringe the monopoly of the Académie: and Spanish the *Tesoro de la lengua castellana* of Cobarruvias Orozco. National pride is clearly an important motivation. Edward Phillips (1658) says of English: 'For elegance, for fluency, and happiness of expression, I am perswaded it gives not place to any Modern Language, spoken in Europe; scarcely to the Latin and Greek themselves.' Cobarruvias Orozco (1611) says that a language like Spanish must have its own dictionary if it is not to be counted 'entre las barbaras', but to be seen to be equal with Latin and Greek.

or Molière's.) Essentially synchronic in orientation it was to be no less influential than its precursor in antiquity, and for a variety of reasons.

In the first place, it both supported and received support from the prevailing scriptism of Renaissance and post-Renaissance attitudes to knowledge, a scriptism enhanced by the new possibilities of dissemination inherent in the invention of printing. From Gutenberg onwards, the book held the key to education as never before in the history of Europe, and universal literacy could become a remote but realisable objective. By the same token, the printed word became a potential political and religious weapon of unprecedented power. From all this the dictionary, as the rule-book of the printed word, could not fail to acquire a status as a cultural instrument without parallel in antiquity. In turn, the dictionary reinforced the scriptism on which it thrived, by setting up literary rather than colloquial usage as the standard representing the national language. In so doing, it bypassed the major dialect differences which still divided speech, and thus contributed simultaneously to the ideal and to the reality of national linguistic unity. Furthermore, once printing had ensured its ubiquitous accessibility as a work of reference, the dictionary could not fail—for reasons of purely practical convenience —to become accepted as a final court of appeal to which any disputes about diversity of practice, or 'correctness', could be referred. It is not only in linguistic matters that most people, when in doubt, prefer to accept—even with grave misgivings—a ruling clearly laid down by some authority, rather than let disagreement continue indefinitely, or settle it by the toss of a coin. The more is this so if the ruling in question is envisaged as applying without discrimination to the entire community.

The new orthology thus became an integral part of an equation between linguistic unity and socio-political unity which had not obtained generally in Europe since the barbarian invasions. It also influenced the development of the Western concept of a language in ways its counterpart of antiquity could never have done.

Since the dictionary presented an extensive coverage of vocabulary, it was but a short step to the assumption that it presented a complete coverage.[1] This easily gave rise to the view that any word

[1] A very selective compilation such as Bullokar's *English Expositour* (1616) could none the less misleadingly call itself a 'Compleat Dictionary'.

not in the dictionary did not genuinely belong to the language.[1] 'There is no such word' came to be a criticism which meant in effect 'It is not in the dictionary'. Thus the very 'existence' of words eventually depended not on their being current, but on their being registered by the lexicographer.[2] Words widely used might none the less officially not 'exist'; while a word could 'exist' even though no one used it, simply by virtue of having a place in the dictionary. The lexicographer performed for the word the same service as God for the tree in the quad. What ensured that the word continued to be was the permanent, quasi-divine surveillance provided by lexicography.

So, by exhibiting each word as an established item with its own identity, the dictionary effectively discouraged its users from seeing a language as consisting in a form of continuous activity. It gave visible embodiment to a distinction between the word and its use. Words were units somehow having their own static and separate existence from the ongoing course of human affairs, and the columns of the dictionary provided a physical location for this separate existence.

No less important, by excluding 'dubious' items (on whatever grounds) the dictionary encouraged the view that 'the language' was a specific, identifiable system of words, and moreover that it was a closed system. The consequences of this for later linguistic theorising were profound. The possibility was not ruled out that the closed system might, from time to time, 'open' to admit new words; but the newcomers, once admitted, also belong to the closed system, as the metaphor of 'admission' itself implies. A language thus came to be seen as constituting, in principle, a finite system of elements at any given time, and the psychological foundation was laid for all modern forms of structuralism.

By listing the vocabulary in alphabetical order, rather than by any other system of arrangement, the dictionary both buttressed the

[1] Even what nearly became the classic blunder of European lexicography, when the Académie Française, drawing up their list of entries beginning with 'A', at first by oversight omitted the word *académie*, may, although illustrating the fallibility of compilers, none the less be seen as a blunder only on the assumption that the omission of a word implies that its credentials are dubious.

[2] Nowadays a writer can, apparently without any sense of paradox, use a word and also in the same breath deny that it exists, as in the following example from a recent contributor to *The Field*: 'A cricketer is a great reminiscer (the word is non-existent but is easily understood).'

view that orthographic form is in some way more basic than phonetic form, and, simultaneously, refused to single out special groups
of words for privileged treatment, or to recognise any grammatical
or semantic relations as affording a natural basis for lexicological
classification. It thereby introduced a kind of lexical egalitarianism,
which sees each word as being as important and as independent
as the next. (The implied lexical elitism of Plato's theory of Forms
suffices to tell us that its author lived in a civilisation without
dictionaries.) But at the same time, by lining up words for alphabetical inspection, like troops on the parade ground, the dictionary
disguises from us the extent to which their apparent individuality
and independence are the result of unstated processes of analysis.

Another important consequence was that in representing the vocabulary by a single set of discrete entities, the dictionary appeared
to accord canonical status to what was later recognised, to use the
terminology introduced by Peirce, as the 'type-token' distinction.[1]
A language is thus not merely characterised in terms of a set of
lexical types, but it appears to be taken for granted that there is only
one possible or correct set of such types. (Otherwise, presumably,
there would be alternative or overlapping lexical entries.) Whether
there might not be a number of different ways of setting up the
lexical inventory is a question the lexicographer never allows to
obtrude, and quite reasonably. But the result is that his compilation
can be interpreted as defining the sum total of lexical possibilities
in discourse: that is to say, speaking or writing—at least in their
lexical aspects—become interpretable simply as the serial production of tokens of the listed types. Thus the potentialities of discourse
are fixed in advance. The meaning of any word-token we use is
already supplied by the word-type it instantiates.

This cluster of dictionary-based assumptions has been an unfail-
ing source of theoretical entanglements in modern linguistics. The
thesis that discourse comprises just instantiation of linguistic types
is implicit in Saussure's view of the relation between *langue* and
parole, and is made an explicit tenet of theoretical linguistics by
Bloomfield as 'Assumption 2' of his 'Set of Postulates for the
Science of Language',[2] where it appears as: 'Every utterance is

[1] C. S. Peirce, *Collected Papers*, ed. C. Hartshorne & P. Weiss, Harvard 1933, Vol. 4,
§537.
   [2] *Language*, vol. 2, 1926, pp. 153–64.

made up wholly of forms'.[1] Consequently, it has often been assumed that it is incumbent upon linguistic theorists to specify a set of necessary and sufficient conditions governing the type-token relationship, even though it is conceded that, as one recent understatement puts it, 'great difficulty has been experienced'.[2] This is doubtless because great difficulty regularly accompanies attempting the impossible. What is of interest concerning attempts to do the impossible is not their failure, but how they come to be thought necessary in the first place.

A clue to this is provided in the present case by the fact that the linguist's problem is usually regarded as arising from the question 'How similar do two tokens have to be in order to be tokens of the same type?' When an effort is made to spell out the limits of phonic or graphic similarity within which the similarities between two tokens of the same type must fall, their being of the same type proves to be unaccountably elusive. On the other hand, if recourse is had to saying merely that their sameness of type consists in their having the same linguistic function, this appears to provide no safeguard against the possibility that tokens of different types might have the same linguistic function; unless, that is, a way could be found of defining linguistic functions so that sameness of function guaranteed absence of phonic or graphic dissimilarity great enough to differentiate tokens of one type from tokens of another. It is difficult to see how this guarantee could be obtained. However, unless it can be obtained, so the argument runs, how will the linguist ever be in a position to justify even the simplest kind of identity statement that his science calls for, e.g. that two people, X and Y, both uttered 'the same word' or 'the same sentence'? Thus a chicken-and-egg conundrum is conjured up out of Peirce's types and tokens.

All that Peirce discovered was the unsurprising fact that the words of printed texts may be put, roughly speaking, in many-one correspondence with the lemmata of a dictionary. The fact is unsurprising, since dictionaries are designed so as to facilitate this. In other words, the system of itemisation they employ is such that an ability to read, together with a grasp of the principle of alphabetical ordering, is all one requires in order to be able to look up in the

---

[1] A form is defined as 'the vocal features common to same or partly same utterances' (ibid., p. 155).

[2] J. Lyons, *Semantics*, Cambridge 1977, vol. 1, p. 17.

dictionary any word one encounters in a book. Now what reading
ability is is a different and complex empirical question; but unfortunately one that modern linguistics, with its professional anti-
scriptism, has shown barely any interest in. Reading ability certainly involves prolonged training in visual pattern recognition, and
varies from individual to individual. But whatever it involves need
not pose any general theoretical problems for the linguist until he is
rash enough to extrapolate from the quite unmysterious connexion
between dictionary lemmata and words in a book, and insist on reading into it the model of a postulated relationship between all theoretically defined units of the language and all actually occurring
items in discourse. Only thus is he led to envisage 'the language' as
some fixed set of idealised simulacra, conformity to one or other of
which is required of every single item in speech or writing if it is to
be counted as part of linguistic discourse at all. Having once made
this extrapolation, although not necessarily aware of having done
so, he may well then be puzzled to know how to state exactly in
what respects items must, in general, 'conform' to their postulated
simulacra in order that one may group them together for purposes
of descriptive linguistics with anything like the same assurance as
that with which we can detect in a printed book the recurrence of
words answering to the same lemma in the dictionary. His very
perplexity is a measure of the extent to which the dictionary, like
all great cultural institutions, has unobtrusively become a symbolic
paradigm for the interpretation of that part of social life it was
originally intended to serve. The linguist no longer asks himself
where the 'type-token' distinction comes from; or, if he does, why
it should be so unproblematic in its original context, and so fraught
with difficulty once an attempt is made to generalise it.

On a quite different level, the status acquired by the dictionary
made it inevitable that henceforward the division between lexicon
and grammar should be seen as fundamental to linguistic structure,
in a way that it could never quite have been under the auspices of
the pre-dictionary doctrine of parts of speech. The Classical doctrine of the parts of speech had set up word-classes based partly
on morphological, partly on syntactic, and partly on semantic
criteria. This hybridism necessarily failed to focus attention on the
individuation of each word as a unique formal and semantic entity.
With the advent of the dictionary, however, it became natural not

only to treat a language as falling into two parts, but also to define each part by reference to the other. Given the lexicon as a set of individual words, grammar will be defined as rules for putting the words together. Or, given grammar as a set of combinatorial rules, the lexicon will be defined as the set of elements on which the rules operate.

This too provided modern linguistics with a quota of theoretical problems. What exactly was the basis of the division between grammar and lexicon? According to Jespersen, developing a position taken by Sweet, the grammarian has to deal with the general facts concerning a language, whilst the lexicographer deals with particular facts.[1] Particular facts, on this interpretation, are facts such as that the word *cat* designates a particular type of four-legged animal. For this is a fact pertinent to the word *cat* alone. General facts, on the other hand, are facts such as that the word *cat* forms its plural by adding -*s*. This is a general fact because many other words, e.g. *rat*, *hat*, *mat*, also form their plural by adding -*s*. Thus the meaning of *cat* belongs to the dictionary, whereas its plural formation goes in the grammar book.

Formulated in the above way, however, the reasoning is hardly convincing. The fact that *cat* forms its plural by adding -*s* is no less a particular fact about the word *cat* than the fact that it designates a particular type of four-legged animal. It might, after all, have had an irregular plural, or even no plural at all. We could not predict from the singular form *cat* that its plural would be *cats*, even though we knew that *rat*, *hat* and *mat* had *rats*, *hats* and *mats* as their plurals. Furthermore, as Jespersen himself concedes, if the line is to be drawn strictly between the general and the particular, the plural form *oxen* must belong in the dictionary, not in the grammar book, since no other English noun forms its plural exactly in that fashion. But if that is so, it appears that we must resign ourselves to splitting the facts of morphology between the grammar book and the dictionary, since it is probable that in most languages some morphological facts will be general and others particular. An echo of the resultant doubt about the position of morphology survives in more recent treatments of morphological questions. For instance, one encounters refusals to recognise the -*en* of *oxen* as an allomorph of the English plural morpheme, on the ground that its occurrence is

[1] O. Jespersen, *The Philosophy of Grammar*, London 1924, pp. 31–5.

not determined either by the phonology of the morpheme *ox*, nor by any other feature 'which can be brought within the scope of any general statement about the structure of English'.[1]

Jespersen's solution to the morphology problem was to point out that in one sense even an irregularity like *oxen* belongs among the 'general facts' of a language, since it serves to delimit the extent of application of a general rule of plural formation: without mention of *oxen*, therefore, the general rule cannot be accurately stated. He concluded from this that in some respects grammar and dictionary 'overlap and deal with the same facts'. But the compromise is an awkward one, since once it is made on these grounds, as Jespersen saw, it looks as though the grammar ought to take over a class of facts which no traditional grammar includes: namely, general facts concerning the meanings of words. For the dictionary deals with each word as an individual item, but makes no attempt to synthesize this information or formulate rules concerning word meanings.[2] Thus the prospect of a theoretical justification along these lines for the division between grammar and dictionary seems unpromising.

A possible alternative strategy, although one which conflicts with traditional practice, would be to treat grammar as dealing with words as non-meaningful elements, leaving the dictionary to deal with words as meaningful elements. A rational and systematic coverage of the whole range of linguistic facts could then be achieved simply by supplementing the dictionary with a set of semantic generalisations. This is basically the strategy adopted in early versions of transformational grammar.[3] But it is a strategy which is based, just as much as Jespersen's, upon leaving the dictionary where it is, and trying to fit the other components of linguistic analysis round it. This is also reflected in the treatment of the level of grammatical 'deep structure' as the level at which lexical 'insertion rules' insert the words into the underlying grammatical frames of

---

[1] J. Lyons, *Introduction to Theoretical Linguistics*, Cambridge 1968, p. 186.

[2] For example, combinations like *blue smell* and *green sound* may be envisaged as prohibited by a semantic rule which applies generally to colour words in English.

[3] 'Semantics' was defined explicitly as 'linguistic description minus grammar', and a 'semantic theory' of a language was envisaged as comprising two components: (i) 'a dictionary of the lexical items of the language', and (ii) 'a system of rules ... which operates on full grammatical descriptions of sentences and on dictionary entries to produce semantic interpretations for every sentence of the language' (J. J. Katz & J. A. Fodor, 'The structure of a semantic theory', in *The Structure of Language*, ed. J. A. Fodor & J. J. Katz, Englewood Cliffs 1964, pp. 479–518).

sentences. Not until some transformational grammarians began to question the position of lexical insertions, and to treat individual words as lexically decomposable items and not as basic units at all,[1] did any serious threat appear to the dictionary's dominating influence over the organisation of linguistic analysis.

However the division between dictionaries and grammars is interpreted, their coexistence as separate sources of information about a language must necessarily confer importance upon the general distinction between lists of linguistic units and lists of linguistic rules. This distinction, it may be noted, is the basic concept underlying the development of two influential models of grammatical description, known as 'item and process' and 'item and arrangement'.[2] The essential difference between the two models concerns the types of rules that are admissible; but a 'list of items' is basic to both. By post-Bloomfieldian distributionalists in particular, linguistic analysis was envisaged as depending on a series of operations which, applied to a representative corpus of linguistic material, would yield listable 'sets of linguistic elements' of various orders of magnitude.[3] The combination rules for each such set of elements would be stated separately. Thus the role of the dictionary as a descriptive model, and the implications of that model, are by no means confined to the field of lexicography as such.

Lastly, the most pervasive effect of the advent of the monolingual dictionary lay in its direct influence upon the concept of meaning. The lexicographer, by concentrating narrowly on the project of specifying and defining the vocabulary of one language, had outflanked both the surrogationalist and instrumentalist positions on meaning. He had shown, in effect, that semantics did not require anchorage in a theory of non-verbal surrogates, nor in the prior analysis of communicational intentions. What the lexicographer had succeeded in doing—for all words, not just for some—might

[1] Even then, the type of lexical analysis proposed (e.g. treating the verb *kill* as transformationally derived from an underlying 'CAUSE TO DIE') was essentially an adaptation of the traditional lexicographer's technique of word definitions.

[2] C. F. Hockett, 'Two models of grammatical description', *Word*, vol. 10, 1954, pp. 210–34.

[3] 'Some of these sets of elements are relatively small, e.g. the list of phonemes and their chief members; such sets are listed in grammatical descriptions of a language. Other sets are very large, e.g. the list of morphemes or of particular constructions (such as words); such sets are listed in a morpheme class list . . . or dictionary' (Z. S. Harris, *Methods in Structural Linguistics*, Chicago 1951, §20.13 fn.4.)

perhaps be regarded as a vindication of contractualism; but if so it showed contractualism in a new light. For by the systematic use of words to define other words in the same language, in such a way that no words are eventually left undefined, the monolingual dictionary demonstrated that meaning could be regarded as inherent in the language. No appeal to what lies outside is needed. The semantic values of words are seen to arise from their relations with other words, and can be expressed in terms of them.

The persuasiveness of this notion and the influence of the monolingual dictionary in promoting it are not denied even by those who believe it to be fundamentally erroneous. Consequently, they have sometimes sought to explain how it arises from a popular misconception of what a dictionary is. For instance, it is claimed that most dictionary users 'look upon a dictionary not as they look upon a book of history but rather as they look upon a book of mathematical tables'. The same writer continues:

> A table of square roots is not history. It is a table of eternal facts that were not made by men and cannot be unmade by them, but must be followed and respected if men are to succeed in their purposes. When we wish to infer the diameter of a circular floor from its area, we must either obey the table of square roots or get a false answer. As the square root of 1,369 is and always must be 37, no matter what any human may have thought or said or done, and this fact is pretty sure to be accurately stated in one's book of mathematical tables, so, men think, the meaning of a word is and always must be such and such, no matter how men have actually spoken and written, and this eternal and independent meaning is pretty sure to be accurately stated in one's dictionary. As the engineer who goes against the mathematical tables comes to grief, they think, the writer or speaker who goes against the dictionary comes to grief . . . Yet it is perfectly clear, when we reflect on the matter, that the meanings of words cannot possibly be independent of man as square roots are. A word is a man-made contrivance, and its meaning can only be what some man means by it.[1]

If most people do look upon dictionaries in this way, however, it is by no means clear that they are altogether wrong. Nor is it clear that a table of square roots differs so profoundly from a dictionary. While we may concede that it would be absurd to suppose that the

[1] R. Robinson, *Definition*, Oxford 1954, pp. 36–7.

square root of 1,369 might be different in a hundred years' time from what it is today, that is not quite the point at issue. It is certainly possible that in a hundred years' time the forms of words we now use, such as *eat* or *drink* or *happy* or *salary*, may still be used, but with different meanings. But this is equally the case with respect to symbols such as '1,369'. The table of square roots may, if we wish, be looked upon as a partial dictionary of such symbols, in which the meanings are defined in terms of one particular mathematical relation (i.e. 'square root of').[1] Although in a hundred years' time other patterns of relationship may obtain in the English vocabulary, or in sets of mathematical symbols, definitions which hold for any future systems will not in some way retrospectively render erroneous any of the definitions which hold for the systems we are now familiar with. The meaning of the Classical Latin word *tabula* has not changed because of anything that subsequently happened to its descendants in French or Italian: it is still what it always was, just as the form in question is still *tabula*, and not *table* or *tavola*. But to say that 'it is still what it always was' is perhaps itself a misleading way of speaking. For one thing, it invites the objection that we ought properly to describe the word *tabula* as no longer existing. It is difficult to see what this amounts to saying, other than that Classical Latin is no longer in common use. The fact that Classical Latin is a dead language, however, hardly prevents us here and now from formulating a correct definition of *tabula*. The irrevisability of the definition of Classical Latin *tabula* is in this sense parallel to the irrevisability of the truth that Caesar crossed the Rubicon. But the definition of *tabula* also has a quite different irrevisability, in that it may be seen as constituting one of the rules governing the use of Classical Latin, regardless of whether the users happen to be living in Caesar's day or in the year 2000 A.D.

If the above considerations have any validity, they are valid irrespective of whether the meaning of a word is regarded as being intralingually defined as in a monolingual dictionary, or by correlation with some extralinguistic object, or by reference to the intentions of its users. The relevant point about familiarity with dictionaries is not that people are liable to confuse them with other

---

[1] An analogous case for ordinary words would be, for example, a dictionary of antonyms, with each word defined in terms of its opposite (*hot: cold, tall: short, honest: dishonest*, etc.).

types of reference book, such as mathematical tables; but that this familiarity gives practical, experiential support to a way of looking at languages, of which the possibility would otherwise be grasped only dimly if at all.

The dictionary-based meaning of 'meaning' was to become central to a wide range of theoretical discussions, in a way which is hardly reflected by its inconspicuous position as one of the sixteen meanings of 'meaning' in the well-known list drawn up by Ogden and Richards.[1] These writers comment on the role of dictionaries in maintaining 'fixities in references' of words.[2] They describe the dictionary as 'a list of substitute symbols', and point out the implied context-dependence of its definitions. 'It says in effect: "This can be substituted for that in such and such circumstances." It can do this because in these circumstances and for suitable interpreters the references caused by the two symbols will be sufficiently alike.'[3] But by thus concentrating on how dictionaries are able to fulfil their definitional role, Ogden and Richards seem to miss the significance of what dictionaries treat meaning as. Relating words to other words is not just one among sixteen possibilities for the multiply ambiguous term *meaning*: it is one of only two types of procedure for identification of meanings.

Dictionary definition corresponds to the mode of intensional meaning distinguished by C. I. Lewis as 'linguistic meaning'.[4] Lewis illustrates this mode of meaning with the following example. We are invited to imagine the plight of someone who knows no French, but is trying to find out the meaning of a certain French word, with only a monolingual French dictionary to help him. He looks up the word in question; and then the words used in the definition of that word; and then the words used in those definitions; and so on. If this process, says Lewis, 'could, by some miracle, be carried to its logical limit, a person might thus come to grasp completely and with

[1] C. K. Ogden & I. A. Richards, *The Meaning of Meaning*, London 1923, pp. 186–7. No. III in their list is: 'The other words annexed to a word in the Dictionary.' This 'Dictionary meaning', which they also call 'philologist's signification' is, according to the authors, very widely used 'in spite of its comical appearance as formulated'.

[2] ibid., pp. 206–7.

[3] ibid., p. 207. The 'reference' is, for Ogden and Richards, the 'thought' in the interpreter's mind.

[4] C. I. Lewis, 'The modes of meaning', *Philosophy and Phenomenological Research*, vol. 4, 1944, pp. 236–49. For Lewis, the intension of a term 'is delimited by any correct definition of it' (ibid., p. 238).

complete accuracy the linguistic pattern relating a large body of foreign words'. He would then know what Lewis terms their 'linguistic meaning', although *ex hypothesi* he would be no better off than when he started if he had hoped to find somewhere a clue that would enable him to translate the original French word into English. In that sense, he would still not know the meaning of the word he had first looked up.

What Lewis calls 'linguistic meaning', but which might perhaps more specifically be termed 'intralinguistically defined meaning', is the mode of meaning which never goes outside the language to which the words in question belong. Precisely for this reason, intralinguistic definitions are sometimes said to be intrinsically circular; or, at least, would be if no other way of defining words were available.[1] This may have to be admitted; but it does not sound nearly so bad if for 'circular' we substitute the more fashionable term 'structural'.

The typical surrogationalist objections to structural semantics are either on the grounds of feasibility, or else on the grounds of vacuity. In the former case, it is questioned whether intralinguistic definition of all words is possible. In the latter case, the objection is closely related to the charge of circularity.

Locke claimed that no word which is the 'name of any simple idea' is 'capable of a definition',[2] and definition he regarded as 'making another understand by words what idea the term defined stands for'.[3] From this it would seem to follow that a dictionary must rely ultimately on prior understanding of certain basic terms which defy definition: e.g. *red, white, hot, cold, round.* The impression the dictionary gives us that all words can be explained by other words must thus be an illusion.

If an objection along these lines is well founded, it is interesting to consider why lexicographers are not forced to admit defeat on a certain range of basic terms. Why do we not find a blank, or 'Undefinable', opposite the lemma *red*, for example, in our dictionary? The answer is that neither a blank (which would presumably indicate that the word had no meaning), nor 'Undefinable' (which would presumably indicate that no definition analogous to those

[1] 'If . . . the meaning of all words were given only through other words, the meaning of all words would be circular' (R. Robinson, *Definition*, Oxford 1954, p. 121).
[2] *An Essay concerning Human Understanding*, III. iv. 14.   [3] ibid., III. iii. 10.

supplied for other words was available), would, from the lexicographer's point of view, be a correct account of the matter. He is not
concerned, *qua* lexicographer, with the Lockean problem of what
happens if the dictionary user has never had the experience of seeing
something red—as would be the case with someone blind from
birth. Patently it would be absurd to criticise the lexicographer on
the ground that his definitions were unhelpful to the blind, or the
deaf, or to any other class of handicapped user. It would be equally
misguided to think of the lexicographer as trying to convey the
meanings of words to some complete ignoramus. His definitions
are intended to show how a word fits in to the overall pattern of the
vocabulary, and they do this by identifying the lexical gap which
would be left by its hypothetical absence. Wherever possible, this is
done by indicating possible verbal alternatives (chosen for their
explanatory utility, not necessarily for their likelihood of occurrence). Where this is not possible, or potentially misleading, recourse is had to metalinguistic discussion and exemplification of the
word's function. Sometimes both methods are combined. Now
there are all kinds of pertinent criticisms that can be levelled at
lexicographers' methods and practice. But it is simply misguided to
criticise them on the ground that what they do cannot be done. It is
equally misguided to criticise them on the assumption that they are
trying to do what they are not trying to do. For in no way is the
lexicographer's primary aim to link up language with what lies
outside language. The critic who supposes otherwise is confusing
the dictionary with the encyclopedia.

The objection that structural semantics, although feasible, is a
vacuous enterprise is different. It is stated particularly forcefully
by Evans and McDowell,[1] who point out that the semantic descriptions of natural languages provided in contemporary linguistics in
many cases go no further than setting up 'translation rules', which
enable the meanings of expressions to be rendered in a chosen
metalanguage. Since the chosen metalanguage may, in principle,
also be the language under description, there would be nothing to
prevent the production of totally trivial semantic descriptions (comprising, e.g., statements to the effect that *Snow is white* means 'Snow
is white'), were it not agreed that certain restrictions must be placed

---

[1] *Truth and Meaning*, ed. G. Evans & J. McDowell, Oxford 1976; Introduction,
pp. vi–xxiii.

upon the translations. These restrictions are usually aimed at, for instance, indicating ambiguities, indicating meaningless combinations of words, and indicating entailment relations. But the pursuit of such objectives does not, according to Evans and McDowell, in any way alter the basic fact that 'translational semantics', whatever the metalanguage and whatever the restrictions imposed upon the metalanguage, ultimately leads nowhere. For in order to understand the semantic description, we need to know what the expressions of the metalanguage mean: 'but this is knowledge of precisely the kind that was to be accounted for in the first place.' The satisfaction of linguists with 'translational semantics' is presumably to be accounted for by their belief that it is simply impossible 'to get outside the circle of language'. None the less, it is no excuse for the failure of 'translational semantics' to give an account of the meanings of sentences by 'stating something such that, if someone knew it, he would be able to speak and understand the language'. The 'objection which devastates translational semantics' is that knowledge of the metalinguistic translation is entirely compatible with not understanding the language translated. Thus, for example, Pierre could know the translation correlation between the French word *chauve* and the English word *bald* 'without knowing what either meant'.

In order to support a rejection of 'translational semantics' lock, stock and barrel, this last point has to be generalisable. In other words, it has to be claimed that one could know indefinitely many translation correlations (whether interlingual, as between *bald* and *chauve*; or intralingual, as between *bald* and *hairless*) without knowing what any of the words involved meant. In the process of generalisation, however, the contention rapidly loses the plausibility which it has when only single examples are considered. We shall need to consider the case of someone who can supply equivalents not merely for *bald*, but also for *hairless, hair, head, baldness, bald-headed, pate, coot, tonsure, alopecia*, etc.; in short, for the whole series of interlocking lexical subsystems to which *bald* belongs. The point is that the more exhaustively and accurately a person can produce equivalents not merely for one word, but for closely connected sets of words, the odder it sounds to maintain that he still might not know what the words mean. For precisely such skills of inter-verbal correlation are what we normally take to be a sign of how well a person knows a language or languages. The extreme case would be that of the individual in Lewis's example, who, although he does not understand French, has *ex hypothesi* mastered the entire pattern of correlations presented by a monolingual French dictionary. Lewis on that score credits him at least with knowing the 'linguistic meaning' of French words; whereas Evans and McDowell would presumably deny that he had any semantic knowledge of French at all. The reason why this denial is unconvincing is that if Lewis's man, having digested the contents of the *Petit Larousse*, then gets hold of a copy of Harrap's *French-English Dictionary*, he will find, if his native language is English, that it is not necessary for him to look up in Harrap the English translation of every single French world that the *Petit Larousse* contains. There soon comes a point when constant reference to Harrap is no longer required, for whole areas of French vocabulary fall into place once the role of certain key terms has been grasped. This is because Lewis's learner already knew a class of very important facts, namely facts about the semantic structure of French. To insist that he had no semantic knowledge of French at all before acquiring his copy of Harrap would be rather like claiming that although a house has a fully wired system which connects power points, lights, fuses, etc., it lacks an electrical installation altogether until the electrician comes along and connects it to the mains.

The dictionary-based concept of meaning is also an important underpinning of what has been described as one of the two main philosophical 'dogmas of empiricism'. This is 'a belief in some fundamental cleavage between truths which are *analytic*, or grounded in meanings independently of matters of fact, and truths which are *synthetic*, or grounded in fact'.[1] In the philosophical tradition from Kant onwards, analytic truths are invariably envisaged as couched in sentences which might have been constructed simply on the basis of dictionary equivalences, in such a way that to deny what is asserted seems to be tantamount to denying that the words used mean what they do. Thus one possible reaction to a person who claims that *No bachelor is married* is false, is to say that all this shows is that he does not know the meaning of the word *bachelor*; or, at least, that he does not know the semantic relation between the words

[1] W. V. O. Quine, *From a Logical Point of View*, rev. ed., Cambridge, Mass. 1961, p. 20.

bachelor and *married*. Although mid-twentieth-century philosophy has come to be sceptical about the synthetic-analytic distinction, it is still often taken for granted in linguistics that one of the aims of the semantic description of a language must be to distinguish the analytic sentences from the non-analytic sentences. The distinction is held to be part of the linguistic knowledge of a competent speaker of the language, and a semantic description must systematically reflect this knowledge.[1] For some philosophers, on the other hand, attempts by linguists to do this provide just one more piece of evidence that linguists do not properly understand what semantic knowledge is.[2]

In his influential attack upon the synthetic-analytic distinction, Quine raises the question of what it means to say, e.g., that the word *bachelor* is '*defined* as "unmarried man" '. One answer might be that it appears thus in the dictionary. But Quine has little patience with this answer; for, he argues, it is not the lexicographer who was responsible for the definition. To accept the dictionary's formulation would be to put the cart before the horse. 'The lexicographer is an empirical scientist, whose business is the recording of antecedent facts; and if he glosses "bachelor" as "unmarried man" it is because of his belief that there is a relation of synonymy between these two forms, implicit in general or preferred usage prior to his own work'.[3]

Although in much, if not all, lexicography there is an inseparable —and unavoidable—blend of prescription with description, we may grant that what Quine says is right, as least as far as the descriptive element goes. But we may still ask whether, given that—inasmuch as it is not his fault that words mean what they do—the lexicographer is not responsible for definitions, there is none the less not a sense in which lexicography is responsible for definitions? Not perhaps for all definitions. Geometry has always required, and always will, answering questions like 'How do you define *triangle*?' But without lexicography, what would one make of 'How do you define *banana*?'? It may well be doubted whether, without the advent of the monolingual dictionary, the question of definitions would have taken quite the form with which we are now familiar, or come to play quite the role it does in our thinking. What might we mean by

---

[1] J. J. Katz, 'Analyticity and contradiction in natural language', in Fodor & Katz, op. cit., pp. 519–43.
[2] G. Evans & J. McDowell, op. cit., p. ix.   [3] Quine, op. cit., p. 24.

'definition' if we did not have the model of the dictionary constantly before us? We can guess easily enough: for the likely answer is already provided by the Greek search for definitions. As Quine's comment on the Aristotelian doctrine of essence puts it: 'Meaning is what essence becomes when it is divorced from the object of reference and wedded to the word.'[1] All there is to add is that, for the modern world, the dictionary solemnised the marriage.

---

[1] Quine, op. cit., p. 22.

7

As far as peculiar species of Substance occur in different regions; and much more, as far as the positive Institutions of religious and civil Politics are everywhere different; so far each Language has its peculiar Diversity.

The importance of the new dictionary-based orthology tends to be obscured for the historian of linguistics by the fact that it produced no immediate revolution in linguistic theorising. For generations after Europe had been amply provided with dictionaries, grammarians continued to discuss much the same linguistic topics as before, using much the same arguments as before. Centuries were to elapse before any new linguistic theory at last caught up with the semantics already implied in the existence of monolingual dictionaries. None the less, it was during those centuries that the dictionary became so firmly established as an authoritative guide to linguistic usage that, when such a theory eventually appeared, it was immediately accepted as capturing a fundamental truth about languages. The theory in question was Saussurean structuralism.

Saussure himself saw his theory primarily as marking a break with the historical bias of nineteenth-century linguistic studies. Trained as an Indo-European philologist, he did not deny the great linguistic achievement of the nineteenth century, which had been to take up successfully the challenge implicitly issued in 1786 by Sir William Jones's observations on Sanskrit:

> The Sanskrit language, whatever be its antiquity, is of a wonderful structure; more perfect than the Greek, more copious than the Latin and more exquisitely refined than either; yet bearing to both of them a stronger affinity, both in the roots of verbs and in the forms of

grammar, than could possibly have been produced by accident; so strong, indeed, that no philologer could examine them all three without believing them to have sprung from some common source . . .[1]

But believing in a common source was one thing. Being able to demonstrate in detail the feasibility of differentiation from a common source was another. Between the two lay many years of painstaking comparative work, as Darwin was to discover in the case of living species.

Establishing the comparative method and piecing together on the basis of very scanty evidence the sound changes by which, over the course of millennia, one language splits up into different dialects, and these in turn evolve into separate languages, was a labour of linguistic palaeontology which occupied three generations of nineteenth-century philologists.[2] Necessarily it led, as in Darwin's case, to the supremacy of an evolutionary view, which treats change and the processes of change as alone throwing light on the nature of the phenomena observable. Once an evolutionary perspective is adopted in any science, apparent stability will come to be regarded as a kind of illusion fostered by the very gradualness of change; just as the hands of a clock appear at a glance to be stationary, even though they are in reality moving all the time.

From a Darwinian point of view, the apparent stability of natural forms was the illusion which had for many centuries supported the thesis that each species was the product of a separate act of divine creation. This brought Darwinism into conflict with religious orthodoxy. In the case of languages, however, the corresponding battle had already been fought out in the eighteenth century, and there was no remaining obstacle to a sweeping acceptance of the evolutionary view. The *philosophes* had prepared the ground for Bopp and Grimm by discrediting the Biblical Tower of Babel explanation for the diversity of languages. Those who wanted to reconcile the Biblical account with a theory of linguistic evolution could adopt the compromise outlined by Beauzée.[3] This compromise accepted

[1] J. E. Sandys, *History of Classical Scholarship*, 3rd ed., Cambridge 1921, vol. 2, pp. 438-9.
[2] In Saussure's view, it was not until about 1870 that the comparative method was recognised as being a method for the reconstruction of the facts of historical linguistics (*Cours de linguistique générale*, 2nd ed., pp. 17-18).
[3] *Encyclopédie*, art. 'Langue'.

the historicity of the Tower of Babel, but regarded God's action on that occasion as a dramatic acceleration of a process which would in any case have occurred gradually in the course of time as part of the divine plan for man.

Thus Darwin was able to make tacit appeal to the theological and academic respectability which the idea of evolutionary differentiation had acquired in linguistics, in order to support analogous conclusions in the biological field. In *The Descent of Man* he argued:

> If two languages were found to resemble each other in a multitude of words and points of construction, they would be universally recognized as having sprung from a common source, not withstanding that they differed greatly in some few words or points of construction.[1]

For the nineteenth-century Indo-European philologists, it was not the idea that languages had been 'fixed' by divine intervention which stood as the alternative contrasting with evolution, but the idea that languages could be 'fixed' at all, e.g. by the decree of the grammarian. Thus any view of languages as given, immutable systems came to be branded as 'unscientific' and associated with a normative or merely pedagogical appraisal of linguistic facts. The pejorative overtones that the term 'grammarian' still has for many people, and the concomitant repugnance for laying down prescriptive rules in matters of linguistic usage, date mainly from the nineteenth-century insistence that the only scientific approach to language is a historical one. Thus any possibility of a valid non-evolutionary study of languages seemed for a long time to be ruled out.

This quite artificial opposition between the evolutionary and the prescriptive had long-lasting consequences which continue to affect the development of twentieth-century linguistics, even though since Saussure the primacy of the historical approach has been 'officially' denied by all the major schools of linguistic theory. In fact, there is no reason why prescriptive linguistics should not be 'scientific', just as there is no reason why prescriptive medicine should not be. But twentieth-century linguists, anxious to claim 'scientific' status for their new synchronic discipline, were glad

[1] *The Descent of Man*, London 1871, ch. 6, pp. 188-9.

enough to retain the old nineteenth-century whipping-boy of pre-scriptivism, in order thereby to distinguish their own concerns as 'descriptive', not 'prescriptive'. When the history of twentieth-century linguistics comes to be written, a naïve, unquestioning faith in the validity of this distinction will doubtless be seen as one of the main factors in the academic sociology of the subject.

To avoid being tarred with the prescriptivist brush, lexicography during the nineteenth century hastened to acquire its own historical credentials. A 'new' theory of the dictionary was propounded to replace the 'old' theory. 'The older view of the matter was that the lexicographer should furnish a standard of usage . . . his chief duty was conceived to be to sift and refine, to decide authoritatively questions with regard to good usage, and thus to fix the language as completely as might be possible within the limits determined by the literary taste of his time.'[1] This was contrasted with a 'new' view of lexicography, first put into practice in Germany by the brothers Grimm, but not clearly stated in England until 1857 by Trench in a paper to the Philological Society on 'Some deficiencies in existing English dictionaries'. The essential difference between the 'old' and the 'new' views is summarised in Trench's words: the lexicographer is 'an historian . . . not a critic'. The eventual outcome of Trench's address to the Philological Society was the publication in 1884 of the first volume of what stands, by any criteria, as the greatest single monument to nineteenth-century linguistic scholarship—and, arguably, to modern scholarship *simpliciter*: the Oxford *New English Dictionary on Historical Principles*. The title itself proclaims the new order. This dictionary, together with those of the brothers Grimm in Germany and Littré in France, left no room for doubt as to the complete triumph of the evolutionary approach in all fields of language study.

In the circumstances, it would have been a disaster for Saussure to try to reject the prevalent historicism of his generation by appeal to an older approach now irrevocably smeared as 'prescriptivist'. At the same time, he clearly saw that, prescriptivist or not, the concept of a language underlying the teaching of the old-fashioned gram-marian had more psychological validity than the 'scientific' concept of a language currently proclaimed by the historical philologists.

[1] *Encyclopaedia Britannica*, 11th ed., 1911, art. 'Dictionary', vol. 8, p. 187.

His problem, essentially, was how to recover a lost perspective without appearing to be a reactionary. The problem was to be solved, as so often, by posing as a revolutionary.

Saussure's first astuteness as a tactician of linguistic theory lay in seeing the opportunity of hoisting the historical philologists with their own petard. This could be done by exploiting a version of the Achilles paradox against them. If they claimed descriptive veracity for their approach to linguistic facts (as against the prescriptivists') by considering change over a recorded span of time, how could they refuse descriptive veracity to an approach which simply reduced the span of time in question to one during which no changes were observable? Must not any span of time long enough to yield observable linguistic change be composed of shorter periods without observable linguistic change? Ultimately, must not linguistic change itself be what we observe by noting the contrast between two different linguistic states? But then, how would the description of linguistic change be possible without presupposing the prior possibility of describing an unchanging state?

Saussure's second—and greater—astuteness as a tactician of linguistic theory resided in not laying out the argument in its above form (where its vulnerability is obvious); but invoking it obliquely and metaphorically, by appeal to images such as cutting through the stem of a plant to observe the structure of the exposed section,[1] or by pointing out the absurdity of trying to draw a panorama of the Alps simultaneously from different mountain summits in the Jura.[2] If the *Cours de linguistique générale* is aptly described as the New Testament of modern linguistics, it is not least because its teaching relies so much on parables.

By these tactics, Saussure could get away with such sacrilegious statements (from an evolutionist point of view) as: 'Classical grammar has been reproached for not being scientific; and yet its basis is less open to criticism and its objective better defined than is the case for the linguistics inaugurated by Bopp.'[3] He could get away with them because, on the one hand, he was careful not to expose an explicit line of argument which would be open to attack, and on the other he could claim to be agreeing with his opponents by espousing a descriptivism even more rigorous than theirs. His success can be measured by the fact that subsequently, for many of

---

[1] Saussure, op. cit., p. 125.   [2] ibid., p. 117.   [3] ibid., p. 118.

his followers, the terms 'synchronic' and 'descriptive' came to be more or less interchangeable, both being opposed to 'historical'.

When Saussure described a language as a system 'existing virtually inside everyone's head',[1] he was insisting on the validity of a different concept of a language from that which the founders of nineteenth-century historical philology had proclaimed. The grammar which Saussure envisaged the language-user as having available in his head was not a historical grammar; nor was the dictionary a historical or etymological dictionary. The language-user is not concerned with the past but with the present. Although the language he uses may be the product of a long process of antecedent evolution, it is the product and not the process which matters for the purposes of everyday communication.

By championing the independence of a synchronic concept of languages, Saussurean linguistics both appealed and contributed to the profound anti-historicism of twentieth-century Western culture. In politics, music, literature and the visual arts, a deliberate rejection of tradition and a conscious commitment to breaking with the past had been gathering momentum since the latter decades of the nineteenth century. Both in step and in tune with this movement, the timing and the spirit of Saussure's work in theoretical linguistics could hardly have been better calculated to ensure immediate success.

However, had his teaching relied solely on negative virtues, had it merely demonstrated the irrelevance of a historical viewpoint to the analysis of languages as grasped by their users, Saussure's name would never have become as widely known as it did, not merely among linguists, but in such fields as literary criticism and social anthropology. On the positive side as well, Saussure's claims concerning the nature of language systems fitted in with a variety of modern developments in academic disciplines as far removed from language studies as mathematics and physics, all manifesting comparable features.[2] Structuralism, as a modern intellectual movement, cannot be accounted for as a chain of influences emanating from one particular source. Rather, given structuralism as a powerful current in twentieth-century thought, it is difficult to see how the study of languages could for long have remained unaffected by it. If

---

[1] ibid., p. 30. [2] Jean Piaget, *Le Structuralisme*, Paris 1968.

Saussure had not existed, it would have been necessary to invent him.[1]

For all its apparent modernity, the Saussurean concept of a syn-chronic language system remains a projection from the linguistics of an earlier age. Its basis is provided by the contents of an idealised non-historical monolingual dictionary (but a dictionary of the spoken rather than the written word). Its five essential features are: (i) cen-trality of the sign as a unit, (ii) strict bi-planarity, (iii) self-contain-ment, (iv) finite, unique itemisation, and (v) supra-individuality.

The first of these five features was to mark a major difference of emphasis between Saussurean structuralism and some of its later progeny. For Saussure, it is the individual sign, not the sentence, which is seen as the key unit of linguistic structure. There is even some doubt about whether Saussure proposed to recognise the sentence, *qua* sentence, as a constructional unit of the language system at all.[2] Be that as it may, sentences were evidently for Saus-sure produced by the arrangement of independently existing signs. Thus the signs are primary, and their possible arrangements secondary. To this extent at least, Saussure's point of view is exactly that of the lexicographer.

The second feature, bi-planarity, is also a basic characteristic of lexicographical presentation. Each dictionary entry correlates just two components, lemma and interpretation. Each word in the lan-guage is thus identified as a bi-partite combination of form plus meaning. Saussure assumes this to be characteristic of the structure of all linguistic signs, whatever their function or grammatical status. For him, anything which does not have this bi-planar structure is simply not a linguistic sign, whatever else it may be. The form of a sign is its *signifiant*, and the meaning its *signifié*. Saussure does not distinguish different kinds or categories of *signifiés*, any more than a dictionary marks out different kinds or categories of interpretation for its lemmata.

[1] In a sense, indeed, he was invented. For it is fairly clear that the materials posthu-mously gathered together in the *Cours de linguistique générale* did not at any one time form a coherent whole in the mind of their author. Had he lived to publish his own book, there can be no doubt that Saussure would have revised the theoretical basis in such a way as to eliminate at least some of the most awkward gaps, obscurities and incon-sistencies.

[2] At one point in the *Cours de linguistique générale* we appear to find an explicit denial that the sentence belongs to *la langue* (p. 172). Elsewhere (p. 148), the question to what extent the sentence may be considered as belonging to *la langue* is raised, only to be left unanswered.

The third feature, self-containment, is perhaps the most crucial, and insistence upon it distinguishes Saussure's approach most markedly from that of the nineteenth-century philologists. For Saussure, the whole language at any given time is not just a temporary concurrence of transitory developments, but a self-contained system in just the same way as, according to the monolingual dictionary, its vocabulary is. That is to say, it is the contrasts and correlations between the signs themselves which alone define the system. Nothing external belongs to it. In particular, it is not a system of correlations between sounds and things or states of affairs in the external world; even though it can be used to provide a classification of external reality, in just the same way as, if we wish, a dictionary can. Nor are the signs of one language equatable, *qua* signs, with those of any other language: for essentially the same reason that a monolingual dictionary is not translatable. Here the difference between a monolingual dictionary and a bilingual dictionary is vital. For it is to its own users that a language system is what it is, and not as seen through the eyes of a foreigner.

Fourthly, the signs of the language system are finite in number and each is uniquely identifiable. This again is a basic implication of lexicographical presentation. Two words may share the same form, and two words may share the same meaning. But two words cannot be identical both in respect of form and also in respect of meaning. Nor, unless the dictionary is deficient, are there words which it does not include; nor words whose inclusion is arbitrary, or undecidable. If the inventory of signs comprising a language system were in principle indeterminate, either by reason of its being indefinitely extendible, or else because of the co-existence of conflicting ways of itemising the inventory, it would have no structure in the Saussurean sense; i.e. criteria external to the system would have to be brought in at some point in order to define the signs. That is not, according to Saussure, what a language is. A language is something which exists in the community in one definite form, as a sum of impressions in the brains of all those concerned, 'as if identical copies of a dictionary had been issued to the individuals'.[1]

Fifthly, just as no use of words by any individual can affect the validity of what the dictionary says, so equally no part of the language system is affected by any individual linguistic act. The system

---

[1] Saussure, op. cit., p. 38.

itself (*la langue*) is supra-individual. The linguistic activity of the individual belongs only to *la parole*. In practice, no single person has a grasp of *la langue* in its entirety; just as, in practice, no single person knows all the words in the dictionary. The linguistic knowledge possessed by any given individual will be only an approximation to the language system: the system itself 'exists perfectly only in the mass'.[1]

No writer on language in the post-Renaissance period can be said to have anticipated Saussure; a fact all the more remarkable when one considers that the basic model for a Saussurean theory had been available ever since the rise of the European nation-state had called the national monolingual dictionaries into being. Not until a time when the European nation-state was itself in crisis as a viable social and political entity did European linguistics at last embrace a theory of languages which explicitly mirrored the ideally integrated, stable community which the nation-state would have liked to be.

The relevance of Saussurean doctrine to Europe's most critical social and political problems in the first half of the twentieth century is too striking to be ignored. Its quasi-mystic appeal to the absolute sovereignty of the community, its deliberate subordination of the linguistic role of the individual, and its presentation of *la langue* as a kind of psychological manifestation of collective uniformity can hardly have counted for nothing in its rapid and widespread acceptance; the more so as Saussure never seems to have offered any detailed argument concerning the problematic issues which these very points raise. They are not so much dismissed *ex cathedra* in Saussurean linguistics as not even recognised. Understandably; for to take them seriously is to question the foundations on which the monolithic idealisation of *la langue* rests.

*　　*　　*

The Achilles' heel of Saussurean linguistics first became exposed in the wake of a development which Saussure could hardly have foreseen; not as a result of any counter-attack by champions of the evolutionary approach to the study of languages, but because of a revolution in the neighbouring discipline of psychology.

[1] ibid., p. 30.

Saussure had hypothesised *la langue* to be an abstract psychological system which was the collective property of the whole community. The linguistic sign, he insisted, 'unites not a thing and a name, but a concept and an acoustic image.'[1] Both *signifiant* and *signifié* were thus psychological entities. The independence of synchronic linguistics within the domain of psychology was to be guaranteed in part by the fact that, in so far as the psychologist considered sign-using merely as a function of the individual, he would in any case be considering only *la parole*.[2] On the other hand, granted that the linguistic sign was a unique kind of psychological unit, neither concept nor acoustic image existing independently of each other, the psychologist would have no special authority to speak about either unless he turned himself into a linguist. Thus synchronic linguistics was to be established in an academic enclave where it would be safe from all intruders.

Unfortunately, the promised academic land turned out almost immediately to look less than promising, when psychology was taken over by the behaviourists. The blatant psychologism of Saussure's doctrine of the linguistic sign, which had looked safe enough in the early years of the century, began to seem very unsound as soon as all talk of concepts or mental events of any kind came to be branded as 'unscientific'. This was a charge which linguistics could hardly afford to ignore. Any claim to be a descriptive science lacks credibility when it is not clear whether what is supposed to be described in fact exists at all.

The consequences of this were first realised in the United States, where Bloomfield in the 1930s condemned 'mentalistic views of psychology' as a hindrance to descriptive accuracy, and claimed that only 'scientific materialism' could provide a sound basis for linguistics. Language, on this view, had to be approached from the outside, and not from the inside. The study of a language was to be founded, in Bloomfield's words, on the 'mass-observation . . . of the speech-habits of a community',[3] and not on unverifiable hypotheses about what goes on inside people's heads. As a result of this rejection of the entire psychological basis of Saussurean linguistics[4]

---

[1] Saussure, op. cit., p. 98. [2] ibid., p. 34. [3] *Language*, London 1935, p. 38.
[4] Saussure is mentioned only once in Bloomfield's *Language* (p. 19), where his teaching concerning the difference between descriptive and historical linguistics is briefly approved. No explicit reference is made to Saussure's views on the theoretical basis of that distinction.

the initiative in linguistic theory passed for the first time from Europe to America.

Since European linguists were rather slow to become aware of the implications of behaviourism, the rift between European and American linguistics might have grown even wider, but for the fact that Bloomfield had no wish to see the synchronic baby thrown out with the psychological bath water. Like Saussure, he rejected the predominant nineteenth-century view which equated the scientific study of languages with the study of their historical evolution. Like Saussure, he accepted the individual sign rather than the sentence as the central unit of linguistic structure, and treated it as a bi-planar unit. He was, in effect, prepared to accept almost exactly the same set of assumptions about a language as Saussure, except for those which depended crucially on the Saussurean psychological doctrine of *signifiant* and *signifié*. In other words, he had to find an alternative account of the correlations which underlay the regular 'speech-habits' observable in the linguistic community at large.

To supply this missing keystone for his own version of synchronic structuralism, Bloomfield had recourse to one of the oldest options available in the Western tradition, and reinstated a crude reocentric surrogationalism of the kind to which Saussure had been utterly opposed. In Bloomfieldian theory, languages thus became again what Saussure had denied they were: nomenclatures. Words were merely vocal substitutes for non-vocal things and events in the external world. To the question of how words came to function as substitutes for things, behaviourism supplied an answer in terms of conditioned responses, and thus no necessity arose for any mysterious entity such as the Saussurean *signifié*.

From the standpoint of behaviourism, to appeal to thought processes to elucidate certain aspects of speech would be rather like a householder trying to augment his income by paying himself rent. For thinking was simply silent speech: 'language habits ... exercised implicitly behind the closed doors of the lips.'[1] Thought was 'nothing but talking to ourselves.'[2] If so, manifestly it would be absurd to try to describe observable phenomena of speech by reference to unobservable versions of the same phenomena.

Behaviourist psychologists of Bloomfield's day held quite expli-

---

[1] J. B. Watson, *Behaviorism*, 2nd ed., London 1931, p. 225.   [2] ibid., p. 238.

citly that 'words are but substitutes for objects and situations'.[1] A language provides the user with 'a verbal substitute within himself theoretically for every object in the world'.[2] Once he has mastered the language, 'he carries the world around with him by means of this organisation'.[3] But how he learns to do this is quite different from the way imagined by Augustine, in which the infant is already envisaged as 'thinking' before he has acquired any verbal habits at all.

If we compare Augustine's account of language-learning with Bloomfield's, it is clear that Wittgenstein could have picked a better example of pure surrogationalism without going outside the present century. Bloomfield's account[4] starts by positing that the tendency to utter and repeat vocal noises is an inherited trait in the human child.[5] Having once uttered, e.g., the sound *da*, and having heard himself do so, the child will attempt to duplicate that performance by a process of self-imitation. He thus acquires a habit in which certain mouth movements are correlated with certain patterns of sound which he can hear. What happens next is that the mother utters in the child's presence a sound which resembles one of the child's babbling syllables; for instance, she says the word *doll*. The child hears this, equates it with his sound *da*, and accordingly says *da*. His mother interprets this as an attempt to imitate the word *doll*. Since the mother will normally utter the word *doll* when she is showing or giving the infant his doll, the child learns to associate his syllable *da* with the sight and handling of the doll. Thus he forms a new habit, for the sight and feel of the doll are sufficient to evoke the response of saying *da*. When this habit is formed, according to Bloomfield the child has the use of a word. On the basis of this habit, further habits are then acquired. Suppose that regularly the child is given his doll to play with, and thus articulates *da*, immediately after having his bath. He thus acquires the habit of uttering *da* when he has had a bath. So if one day the mother does not produce the doll, the child will say *da*, and his mother will interpret this as the

---

[1] ibid., p. 230.   [2] ibid., p. 234.

[3] ibid., p. 234. Ironically, Watson at one point (op. cit., p. 233) supports this view by reference to the large bundles of things which Swift's sages of Lagado have to carry around with them for purposes of communication. Were it not for languages, says Watson, 'the world would be in this situation today', evidently failing to recall the satirical thrust of Swift's description.

[4] Bloomfield, op. cit., p. 29.   [5] Cf. Watson, op. cit., p. 226.

child's asking for his doll. This is not, according to Bloomfield, a case of the mother foisting an inappropriate analysis upon the situation. She is right to say that the child is asking for his doll, because when we say that an adult asks for something, the situation involved, although more complex, is basically no different. From this stage, the child's efforts at using words are perfected by their results. If he says *da* well enough, his elders understand him: that is, they give him his doll. Whereas if his utterances depart too far from the usual adult pronunciation *doll*, he will not get his doll. Thus success is encouraged by reward, and failure is discouraged by lack of reward. At the same time as learning how to be an effective speaker, the child is also learning to act the part of the hearer. When he is handling his doll, he hears himself saying *da* and his mother saying *doll*. Thus after a time, the sound will suffice as a stimulus for the child to handle the doll.

The essential difference between Augustine's account and Bloomfield's is that the notion of using language to achieve practical ends does not enter into the Bloomfieldian child's world until the correlation between sound and object is already habitually established. The prior phase is acquiring the use of the word. Using the word as a means of bringing about certain results is grafted on to this basic habit at a subsequent stage. This is a typically surrogationalist analysis, in that the connexion between sound and thing is treated as fundamental, and the use of the word for communicational purposes treated as an added behavioural superstructure which is based on this connexion.

Augustine's instrumentalist account reverses this priority. He depicts the puzzled child as first working on the problem of how to achieve a certain result by means of vocalisation, and then hitting upon the correlation between sound and thing as a solution. Farfetched as that may seem as an account of the earliest phase of language-learning, its plausibility is not our present concern. The relevant point is that it reflects a view of language in which effectiveness in bringing about certain practical results is seen as making the word what it is. Whereas for Bloomfield that effectiveness merely acts as a reinforcement of a word-use already established.

The most profound effect of Bloomfield's espousal of behaviourism concerned semantics. Bloomfield criticises[1] the view of meaning

[1] Bloomfield, op. cit., p. 142.

held by those 'adherents of mentalistic psychology' who believe that prior to the act of speech there occurs within the speaker a non-physical process, involving a 'thought, concept, image, feeling, act of will or the like', and that an equivalent or corresponding mental process is triggered in the hearer when he hears the utterance. (Again, Saussure is not mentioned specifically, although this description fits very well Saussure's account of the *circuit de la parole*.)[1] The mentalist, according to Bloomfield, is thus mistakenly led to identify the meanings of linguistic forms with certain unobservable mental events accompanying speech. Bloomfield proposes to do away with all this, by defining the meaning of a linguistic form as 'the situation in which the speaker utters it and the response which it calls forth in the hearer'.[2]

By putting forward this pivotal definition, Bloomfield unhesitatingly took surrogationalism to an extreme which the Western linguistic tradition had not previously seen. That is, he proposed that as far as the linguist was concerned everything in the universe should be divided into just two categories: speech events on the one hand, and the corresponding speakers' situations and hearers' responses on the other. Linguistics, ideally, would consist of phonetics, which studied speech events without reference to situations or responses; and semantics, which studied the regular correlations between speech events, situations and responses. He did not shrink from the conclusion that therefore semantics, ideally, required the linguist to be 'little short of omniscient': it would call upon 'the sum total of human knowledge'.[3]

It is relevant to remark that implicit in this dramatic expansion of the boundaries of linguistics—an expansion far surpassing anything that Saussure or his predecessors had envisaged—is the idea that ultimately linguistics could dispense with the concept of a language altogether. Different linguistic communities would, as it

[1] Saussure, op. cit., p. 28. According to Saussure, the 'speech circuit' begins with a psychological event in the speaker, which occurs when a particular concept triggers the corresponding acoustic image. This in turn triggers a physiological event, which is the transmission to the organs of phonation of an impulse corresponding to the acoustic image. Thus speech occurs. Phonation sets in motion a train of physical events, in which sound waves are transmitted to the ear of the hearer. An impulse then travels from the hearer's ear to his brain, where the appropriate acoustic image triggers the corresponding concept. Understanding what has been said is thus not complete without a matching of the speaker's original concept with the hearer's.

[2] Bloomfield, op. cit., p. 139. [3] ibid., p. 74.

were, stand revealed on a space-time map of the universe as fluc-
tuations in the density of correlations between types of speech
event and types of situation and response. Talk of 'languages'
would thus be seen as a grossly oversimplified way of referring to
certain prominent configurations in the collective history of human
behaviour.

In practice, however, Bloomfieldian surrogationalism meant not
only surrendering the academic independence of synchronic linguistics, which had been part of the Saussurean ideal, but also cur-
tailing the scope of its descriptions. This followed from the fact that
science was simply not in a position to give the descriptive linguist
all the information he needed. Some features of the human situation
had been carefully studied, but vast areas of ignorance remained.
'We can define the meaning of a speech-form accurately,' said
Bloomfield,[1] 'when this meaning has to do with some matter of
which we possess scientific knowledge.' However: 'In order to give
a scientifically accurate definition of meaning for every form of a
language, we should have to have a scientifically accurate knowledge of everything in the speakers' world. The actual extent of
human knowledge is very small compared to this.' Thus although it
was possible to define the meaning of the English word *salt*, since
science knows that salt is sodium chloride (NaCl), it was not possible to define the meanings of words such as *love* and *hate*, since
science had not yet discovered what love and hate were. Bloomfield
was forced to the conclusion that 'the statement of meanings is therefore the weak point in language-study, and will remain so until
human knowledge advances very far beyond its present state'.[2]
Since, however, the very identification of linguistic units presumably depended on the accuracy of correlating forms and meanings,
this was bound to leave linguistics at best as a science of the partly
possible, a kind of parson's egg among the academic disciplines.

The post-Bloomfieldian phase of American linguistics saw an
attempt to develop a methodology of descriptive analysis which
would improve this position by dispensing with the unsatisfactory
appeal to meaning entirely. Thus emerged distributionalism, which
treated the formal structure of languages as sets of units and relations determined simply by the patterns of substitution and combination observable among overt elements in speech. The distribution

[1] ibid., p. 139.   [2] ibid., p. 140.

of an element was defined as 'the sum of all its environments'.[1] Distributionalism in practice reduced descriptive linguistics to phonology, morphology and syntax, with predominant attention paid to the first two, since at these levels the number of elements and classes involved were small enough to make them manageable.

In support of the distributionalist's antipathy to semantics, examples were offered to demonstrate that distributional criteria were more reliable for purposes of descriptive analysis than taking meaning into account. Thus, whether the words *persist* and *person* contain one morpheme each or two was said to be unresolvable by analysis of the meanings involved. Distributional criteria, on the other hand, revealed that the structure of *persist* was bimorphemic (since it was comparable with *consist, resist, pertain, contain, retain*), whereas *person* was monomorphemic (there being no comparable series for the distribution of *per-* and *-son*).[2]

What such examples often showed rather more convincingly than the superiority of distributional criteria was the element of circularity which automatically infiltrates any attempt to provide a strictly monoplanar analysis of linguistic form. The circularity emerges if, for instance, we ask with respect to the above example what the conclusion that *persist* comprises two morphemes means. All that it means is stated once reference is made to the 'evidence' on which it is based: namely, comparison with the set of forms *consist, resist*, etc. But if we then ask why that comparison should be treated as particularly significant, there is no answer. It is certainly difficult to think of any prediction about English speakers' use of the word *persist*, or of any other words, which could be tested either to confirm the conclusion that *persist* is bimorphemic or to refute it.

The result of reliance on such analytic procedures was a much narrower concept of what a language was than Bloomfield's. Speech was considered apart from the linguistic community and the associated patterns of communicational behaviour. What the linguist was concerned with was said to be not even 'the whole of speech activities' available to observation, but merely 'distributional relations among the features of speech' which he had selected for observation: that is to say, 'the occurrence of these features relatively to each other within utterances'.[3]

[1] Z. S. Harris, 'Distributional structure', *Word*, vol. 10, 1954, pp. 146–62.
[2] ibid., §4.   [3] Z. S. Harris, *Methods in Structural Linguistics*, Chicago 1951, §2.1.

In brief, the reaction against Bloomfield's wholehearted surrogationalism led American linguistics to the somewhat drastic alternative of attempting to consider vocal utterance as an entirely autonomous activity, isolated from any context except itself. Instead of treating languages in the Bloomfieldian manner as bi-planar systems with one plane partly missing (that plane not being entirely amenable to 'scientific' description), the distributionalists sought to find some self-contained structure in the externally observable features of utterance, existing quite independently of anything else. Whether the units or relations discovered in this monoplanar system had any semantic functions just did not matter.

The theoretical commitment to the feasibility of monoplanar analysis survived unchanged from distributionalism into the earliest phase of transformationalism.[1] It was not until the behaviourist tenets which Bloomfield had originally espoused came under attack in linguistics[2] that at long last, in the early 1960s, semantics acquired a new academic respectability in the United States, and a 'semantic component' was rather grudgingly added to the equipment of transformational grammar.

What is significant is that when semantics at last gained readmission to American linguistics, there was no reversion to the old Bloomfieldian surrogationalism. Semantics was not seen as making a comprehensive attempt to correlate utterances with situations in the real world and hearers' responses. On the contrary, the feasibility of 'systematising all the knowledge about the world that speakers share' was explicitly denied.[3] Instead, linguists were invited to make a Saussurean act of faith in the existence of stable meanings as psychological entities independent of 'real world' knowledge. How the distinction was to be drawn between semantic knowledge and 'real world' knowledge was never explained. Hence, how the descriptive linguist was expected to compile his dictionary

---

[1] For example, in N. Chomsky, *Syntactic Structures* (1957), a whole chapter is devoted to arguing that grammar can be, and must be, analysed independently of considerations of meaning.

[2] In 1959, an influential review of B. F. Skinner's *Verbal Behavior* by N. Chomsky criticised the behaviourist account of language-learning, and questioned in particular the utility of behaviourist notions such as 'stimulus', 'response' and 'reinforcement' as applied to speech (*Language*, vol. 35, pp. 26–58).

[3] J. J. Katz and J. A. Fodor, 'The structure of a semantic theory', in Fodor & Katz, op. cit., p. 491.

entries remained just as mysterious as how the founders of monolingual lexicography had compiled theirs.

Having thus, half a century behind the times, got back to roughly
the position Saussure had originally started out from, American
linguistics then embarked upon a long debate about the problems of
bi-planar analysis. This was complicated in the first place by the
fact that transformationalism, taking the sentence and not the individual linguistic sign as its basic unit, had somehow to integrate
semantics systematically with a grammar for generating sentences.
It was further complicated by the fact that transformationalists
failed to see the virtues of Saussure's insistence on making bi-planar
correlation definitional for linguistic signs. So, in accordance with
the recent history of their own transatlantic tradition, they treated
the plane of meaning as something which in fact existed separately
in its own right, but now had to be brought into some kind of juxta-
position with the plane of linguistic form. Hence arose arguments
about the 'priority' or 'centrality' of semantic structure and grammatical structure, and the nature of the relationship between
the two.

From a strictly Saussurean viewpoint, nothing could have been
more futile than the ensuing theoretical struggles between rival
transformationalist schools, which came down in the final analysis
to disagreements about competing systems of rules for the same linguistic facts. None the less, by the early 1970s it was possible to claim
that transformationalism provided in no sense a radical alternative
to Saussurean linguistics, but a development and amplification of
it. The transformationalists, like Saussure, accepted a fundamental difference between synchronic and diachronic linguistics.
Like Saussure, they treated languages as bi-planar systems, pairing
forms with meanings. The Saussurean distinction between *langue*
and *parole* could be equated with the transformationalist's distinction between 'competence' and 'performance'. By developing sen-
tential syntax, the transformationalists could be said to have added
depth to Saussure's bare schematisation of surface-structure relations. By regarding linguistic knowledge as represented in the
individual in the form of 'internalised' language rules, transformationalism confirmed the Saussurean view that each speaker carries
a set of bi-planar correlations in his head, which he puts to use in
engaging in speech activity. Finally, by claiming a linguistic descrip-

tion to be in the last resort a description of the competence of an 'ideal speaker-hearer', transformationalism turned its back on the cautious empiricism of the post-Bloomfieldian period, and endorsed the Saussurean postulation of a single supra-individual system uniting the collectivity of language-users.

By this circuitous route, the orthological dogma of Renaissance nationalism was finally reinstated as the official doctrine of twentieth-century linguistics. What had started out as a patriotic aspiration was eventually given the solemn blessing of modern science.

8

Speech is then the joint Energie of our best and noblest Faculties (that is to say, of our Reason and our social Affection) being withal our peculiar Ornament and Distinction, as Men.

From the beginning of the Western tradition, debate on linguistic topics, however fundamental the disagreement between those involved, was always conducted within a framework of assumptions defining what may be called the 'ethological' concept of a language. These assumptions have to do with man's place in nature, and they are perhaps most clearly stated in a well-known passage from Isocrates:

> In most of our abilities we differ not at all from the animals; we are in fact behind many in swiftness and strength and other resources. But because there is born in us the power to persuade each other and to show ourselves whatever we wish, we not only have escaped from living as brutes, but also by coming together have founded cities and set up laws and invented arts, and speech has helped us attain practically all of the things we have devised. For it is speech that has made laws about justice and injustice and honor and disgrace, without which provisions we should not be able to live together. By speech we refute the wicked and praise the good. By speech we educate the ignorant and inform the wise. We regard the ability to speak properly as the best sign of intelligence, and truthful, legal and just speech is the reflection of a good and trustworthy soul . . .[1]

Claims that it is the capacity for language-using which ultimately distinguishes man from brute are repeated endlessly from one

[1] Tr. G. Kennedy, *The Art of Persuasion in Greece*, Princeton 1963, pp. 8–9.

century to the next, and become virtually a rhetorical *locus communis* for any writer touching on the subject of speech. The further idea that this distinguishing mark is of divine origin appears independently in Graeco-Roman and Judaeo-Christian sources. Quintilian says: 'That god, who was in the beginning, the father of all things and the architect of the universe, distinguished man from all other living creatures that are subject to death, by nothing more than this, that he gave him the gift of speech.'[1] It is an idea which has the backing of Biblical authority for all of Christian Europe. Even when, during the eighteenth century, freethinkers begin deliberately to take issue with the Biblical account of the origin of languages, they do not question the uniqueness of man's linguistic capacity, but are concerned rather to show that he could have developed it without divine assistance.

The first signs of any serious challenge to the ethological concept of a language coincide, as might be expected, with the first serious challenge to previous assumptions about man's relationship to other species of living creatures. Darwin, in *The Descent of Man*, argues at length that the intellectual powers which man possesses are not in themselves unique in the animal kingdom, and that there is no fundamental difference between man and the higher animals in their mental faculties. Such differences as he observed were differences of degree rather than of kind, and he saw nothing in the evidence pertaining to what *homo sapiens* could do with words which would contradict this view. For many of Darwin's contemporaries, this apparent devaluation of the significance of language-using was not to be heeded, since it was all part of the scandalous thesis that 'men are descended from monkeys'.

It must be admitted that Darwin's interest in the subject was mainly a negative one. He wished simply to show on the one hand that the difference between animal communication systems and human communication systems was not such as to require for the latter 'a special act of creation'; and, on the other, that 'the faculty of articulate speech in itself' did not offer 'any insuperable objection to the belief that man has been developed from some lower form'.[2] However, his contribution to the topic cannot be ignored, for two reasons which have a relevance to its subsequent history. First, he

[1] *Institutio Oratoria* II. xvi. 12 et seq., tr. H. E. Butler (Loeb Classical Library edition).
[2] *The Descent of Man*, London 1871, p. 62.

spoke as a biologist, and not as a 'language expert'; and secondly the kind of argument he adopted set an unfortunate stamp on the ensuing course of the debate, which can be traced in its twentieth-century prolongations.

Darwin's contention was in direct conflict with the opinion held by most nineteenth-century philologists, who were anxious to insist that the study of language had now become a 'science'. It is understandable that they should not have taken kindly to pronouncements about the subject of their science by one who, not being a philologist, *ex hypothesi* knew nothing about it. Much the same antagonism of professional stances was to emerge a hundred years later in a similar debate on the same topic. In 1861, Max Müller had summarised what was probably the view of the majority of his philological colleagues when he said: 'The one great barrier between the brute and man is *Language*. Man speaks, and no brute has ever uttered a word. Language is our Rubicon, and no brute will dare to cross it.'[1] The metaphor reveals more than perhaps Müller realised about the psychology behind much of the opposition (both then and now) to the suggestion that man's language-using is not quite as unique as he might like to think. In what sounds like a direct rebuttal of Darwinian views, Müller adds: 'No process of natural selection will ever distill significant words out of the notes of birds or the cries of beasts'.[2]

Darwin and Müller were both in agreement, unfortunately, that it was not for any physiological reason that other animals lacked speech. Both conceded that the difference lay in the mental faculties. But whereas Müller concluded that the absence of language in animals was simply the outward sign of their lack of reason, and that since they lacked reason they could never either be or become language-users, Darwin pointed out that other than 'rational' communicational purposes were also served by words and by animal cries as well. Consequently it seemed by no means impossible to Darwin that a progressive development from certain primitive communicational uses had gradually taken place. Müller's claim that 'natural selection' could never bring about such a development must have seemed to Darwin rather like denying that fins used for swimming could ever become limbs used for walking.

It throws an interesting light on modern intellectual history that

[1] *Lectures on the Science of Language*, London 1861, p. 340.   [2] ibid., p. 340.

whereas Darwin's views about evolution as a whole triumphed, it was Müller's views about the uniqueness of language which survived. There is too much of a *quid pro quo* about this result for it to be entirely coincidental. It is as if *homo sapiens*, unexpectedly demoted from the privileged position he had for centuries believed himself to occupy in Creation, at least insisted on public recognition that there was one thing he could do which was forever beyond the capabilities of other creatures.

*   *   *

The twentieth century's best-known book on animal behaviour has a chapter entitled 'The Language of Animals', which opens with the bald assertion: 'Animals do not possess a language in the true sense of the word'.[1] Lorenz's statement formulates with uncanny accuracy the central issue of subsequent debate, since it is precisely 'the true sense of the word' which has been fought over, i.e. the concept of a language, rather than the evidence concerning the abilities of animals. For many, the term *language* is abused by those who apply it to animal communication, while the expression *human language* is regarded as redundant 'on the grounds that the capacity for language, properly so called, is unique to man'.[2] To say that *human language* is a redundant expression is another way of claiming that the ethological concept of a language is actually enshrined in our use—or at least in correct use—of the very word *language*; for that makes the exclusion of non-human communication a matter of definition. If it is true, as has been proposed,[3] that such a view is probably taken by the majority of contemporary linguists, this suggests that one of the present functions of the ethological concept of a language is to provide a 'strong classification' (in the Bernsteinian sense) which will demarcate the academic boundaries of linguistics. We are dealing, consequently, not merely with a thesis about the nature of languages, but with the structure of an educational system and its related attitudes. This is confirmed by the fact that linguists often seem surprised if asked to give specific reasons for accepting Lorenz's proposition: its acceptance has become for them part of the social role of 'being a linguist'.

[1] Konrad Lorenz, *King Solomon's Ring*, tr. M. K. Wilson, London 1961, p. 76.
[2] J. Lyons, 'Human language', in *Non-Verbal Communication*, ed. R. A. Hinde, Cambridge 1972, p. 49.
[3] Lyons, loc. cit.

Lorenz, however, does give reasons for his view, and these are of considerable interest. He discounts a whole range of signals, visual and auditory, by which the higher vertebrates and insects express feelings, on the ground that such signals are innate: as are also, he claims, the reactions to them on the part of fellow members of the same species. But it is, Lorenz says, the perfect co-ordination of social behaviour brought about by these innate signals and reactions which conveys to a human observer that he is witnessing a language in operation.

The explanation is not without its paradoxical aspect. It reminds one of Johnson's remark about claret: 'It would be port if it could.' In other words, the recognisable aim of a language is taken to be the achievement of co-ordination in social behaviour by means of a signalling system. A perfect language would presumably achieve perfect co-ordination. Yet when perfect co-ordination is achieved by means of innate signalling, far from being acclaimed as a linguistic achievement, the system by which this is brought about is denied the status of a language altogether. Just as a claret which actually tasted like port would very likely be decried as not a genuine claret.

However, the distinction Lorenz draws between innate animal signalling systems and languages, 'every word of which must be learnt laboriously by the human child',[1] is open to challenge. One form of challenge comes from detailed studies of the emergence of species-specific behavioural patterns in animals, leading to the conclusion that, in some cases at least, 'behaviour cannot meaningfully be separated into learned and unlearned components'.[2] If this is so, it seems that species-specific signalling behaviour may be subject to the same uncertainty. Darwin did not accept that bird song was entirely innate,[3] and the work of modern ornithologists has confirmed this. For example, experiments show that when chaffinches are reared in isolation, they fail to develop the normal song of their species, but can achieve only a distorted version.[4]

[1] Lorenz, op. cit., p. 76.

[2] J. P. Hailman reaches this conclusion from a detailed analysis of feeding movements of the newly hatched young of the laughing gull. ('How an instinct is learned', in *Animal Behavior*, ed. T. Eisner & E. O. Wilson, San Francisco 1975, pp. 241–9).

[3] *The Descent of Man*, London 1871, p. 55.

[4] The first part is not divided into phrases in the normal way, and it lacks the elaborate concluding flourish 'which is one of the most striking characteristics of the chaffinch song in the wild' (W. H. Thorpe, 'The language of birds': in *Animal Behavior*, ed. T. Eisner & E. O. Wilson, San Francisco 1975, pp. 273–7).

A complementary challenge is represented by the so-called 'innateness hypothesis' championed by some transformationalists, which claims that although particular languages are not innate, the general form of a species-specific language is part of the information genetically transmitted in human beings from parent to offspring.

Thus it turns out that to differentiate languages from animal signalling systems on the basis of a simple dichotomy between innate and learned behaviour is, to say the least, by no means as uncontroversial a matter as was at one time widely supposed.

However, whether or not that distinction can be made to hold, its use as a criterion prompts two general comments. The first is the observation that, even granted the possibility of distinguishing clearly between innately based and non-innately based communication, that distinction relates to the organism rather than to the system of behaviour. Its basis is an assumption which is biologically rather than communicationally oriented. Secondly, it may be thought to be unclear why in principle it should matter, as regards distinguishing between languages and non-languages, how the organism acquires the system. To take an analogy, if an individual manifested a capacity to play chess brilliantly without ever having learned the game, it would be extremely curious to argue that the mere fact of his having beaten several grand masters did not prove that he could play chess, because in order to play chess in the proper sense of the term, a programme of previous training is necessary. Whether or not one is playing chess depends on what one does at the chessboard, not on how one found out what to do at the chessboard. Or if, miraculously, a child was born who, instead of going through the babbling stage, began straight away to produce sentences like 'Thank you, madam, the agony is abated', it would be very odd to claim that it was not speaking English simply on the ground that it had had no opportunity to learn the language.

The second reason Lorenz gives for distinguishing between languages and animal signalling systems is that in animal signalling systems there are no 'dialects'. Jackdaws in Northern Russia, he claims, 'talk' no differently from jackdaws in Altenberg. The difficulty here is that it is doubtful whether this holds good for non-human communication systems in general. Bird song, according to Darwin, exhibits local variations comparable to 'provincial dialects'.[1]

[1] *The Descent of Man*, London 1871, p. 55.

Again, this is confirmed by more recent investigations.[1] The chaffinch does not develop the full details of its song until it sings in a territory in competition with neighbouring birds of the same species, and when it does so there is evidence that it may learn slightly different songs from different neighbours. In a paper entitled 'Dialects in the language of the bees',[2] Karl von Frisch showed that there are distinct versions of the honeybee's nectar dance which are not mutually intelligible as between, e.g., Austrian honeybees and Italian honeybees. As these are different varieties of bee, even though they can interbreed, we do not have here a local variation of the same kind as in the case of bird song. However, even as regards human languages, it is an open question to what extent there may be some genetic basis for certain kinds of dialect feature. The fact of dialectal variation is one thing: how it is to be explained is another.

The third reason Lorenz adduces is that the sounds and movements made by animals to express their emotions are not made with the conscious intention of influencing a fellow member of their species. 'This is proved,' argues Lorenz, 'by the fact that even geese or jackdaws reared and kept singly make all these signals as soon as the corresponding mood overtakes them. Under these circumstances the automatic and even mechanical character of these signals becomes strikingly apparent and reveals them as entirely different from human words.'[3]

This third reason is thus based on the contention not that animals do not have communicationally viable signals at their disposal, but that they do not use them intentionally. There is perhaps an element of circularity in this line of thinking, inasmuch as the notion of 'intention' is so bound up with human beings' use of words and human rationality that it is quite unclear in what sense it could be applied to animals so as to allow even the possibility that animals might use communicational signals intentionally. If there is no such possibility, then this reason, like the first, merely asserts an irreducible difference between animal nature and human nature.

Lorenz's reasons for denying that animals have a language provide a particularly clear illustration of how adopting an ethological approach to communication already prejudges what will count as

---

[1] W. H. Thorpe, loc. cit.　　[2] Eisner & Wilson, op. cit., pp. 303–7.
[3] Lorenz, op. cit., p. 72.

deciding between languages and non-languages. Once attention is focused upon the ways in which patterns of behaviour characterise the organism and its place in nature, on an equal footing with its physiological characteristics, then what is envisaged as rendering human communication different from animal communication will be the ways in which that communicational behaviour manifests the characteristic differences between man and other species. Priority will automatically be given to man's infinitely greater capacity for learning, and his correspondingly diminished reliance on innately programmed forms of action. If one is committed to the ethological standpoint and the question arises whether the communication systems of other species count as languages, it almost suffices to point out that such resemblances as there are between human and non-human communication are biologically accidental. That, indeed, is what would be meant by saying that such resemblances are 'superficial'. This is how Lorenz deals with the question. It is no surprise, therefore, to find that his three reasons for denying that animals have a language—lack of learning, lack of variation and lack of intention—in the end reduce to one. The absence of a need to learn the system, the absence of local variation, and the absence of voluntary control of the use of the system are all predictable if it is assumed that man is the only species with sufficient intelligence to be able to use a communication system which is not the direct endowment of genetic programming.

However, the most influential and controversial interpretation of the ethological concept of a language in recent years has taken the form of a claim which, in one major respect, is diametrically opposed to that put forward by Lorenz. It is what came to be known as the 'innateness hypothesis', or 'linguistic nativism', according to which, although particular languages are not innate in man, the general form of a species-specific language is part of the equipment genetically transmitted to human beings.

The development of this hypothesis may be dated from consideration in the late 1950s of the problem of inferring a grammar of a language from a finite set of observations of instances of language use. The problem can be viewed as that of constructing a device such that, from an input of utterances in the language, a formalised grammar of the language is generated as output. It was subsequently claimed that a description of such a device could be viewed as representing a hypothesis about 'the innate intellectual equipment that a child brings to bear in language learning'.[1]

In support of this approach, Lenneberg[2] argued that it was possible that human beings were equipped with 'highly specialised, biological propensities' that favoured and shaped the development of speech in children. He contrasted this possibility with the view which assumed that language was 'a wholly learned and cultural phenomenon, purposefully introduced to subserve social functions, the artificial shaping of an amorphous, general capacity called *intelligence*'.[3] He pointed out that innate behaviour may be dependent on the organism's interaction with its environment, even though the relevant programme of action is 'innately given'; and cited as an example the fact that female rats do not attempt to build nests for their young if reared in conditions where no suitable nest-building materials are available, yet invariably do so when such materials are present. Lenneberg proposed four criteria for distinguishing activities which are 'biologically given' from those which are the result of cultural achievement. The first was whether or not there were intraspecies variations; the second, whether or not there was evidence of an evolution of the behaviour within the species; the third whether or not there was evidence for an inherited predisposition favouring the behaviour; and the fourth, whether or not there were specific organic correlates corresponding to the behaviour.

On the basis of the first criterion, Lenneberg developed an argument from linguistic universals. That is to say, the fact that all known languages exhibited certain features, including phonematisation, concatenation and syntactic structure, which were not logically necessary for a communication system pointed, in his view, to the likelihood that these universals reflect some trait related to the genetic mutation which constituted *homo sapiens* as a species.

He further pointed out that evidence from historical and comparative linguistics shows no reason to postulate that languages developed from some primitive aphonemic or agrammatical type of communication system. There was a strong indication of inherited predisposition in the fact that language-like behaviour develops in

[1] N. Chomsky, 'Explanatory models in linguistics', in *Logic, Methodology and Philosophy of Science*, ed. E. Nagel, P. Suppes & A. Tarski, Stanford 1962.
[2] E. H. Lenneberg, 'The capacity for language acquisition', in Fodor & Katz, op. cit., pp. 579–603.
[3] ibid., p. 579.

human beings even under the most unfavourable conditions of impairment of the nervous system. Finally, he claimed that the evidence from language acquisition in children showed a progress through identical phases, irrespective of the particular circumstances in which the child is exposed to language.

To explain these facts, Lenneberg appealed to the theory of 'innate releasing mechanisms' developed by ethologists to explain the ability of animals to produce appropriate behaviour in reaction to certain stimuli, even though the stimuli in question had never been previously encountered in the life history of the individual animal. Analogously, according to Lenneberg, the emergence of language may be considered due to 'an innately mapped-in *program* for behavior, the exact realisation of the program being dependent upon the peculiarities of the (speech) environment'.[1]

In 1965, the notion of an innate 'language-acquisition device' was incorporated into a revised theory of transformational grammar.[2] The theory now explicitly assimilated the task facing the child acquiring his native language to the task facing the linguist attempting to write a descriptive grammar of that language. Specifically, it attributed to the child an initial delimitation of a class of possible hypotheses about language structure, a method of determining what each such hypothesis implies with respect to each sentence, and a method of selecting one of the infinitely many hypotheses about language structure that are compatible with 'the given primary linguistic data'.[3] The language-acquisition device thus constructs a theory of the language from a sample presented to it, and the theory thus constructed and internally represented specifies the knowledge of the language acquired. Hence the child's knowledge of the language, as determined by this internalisation, 'goes far beyond' the primary linguistic data available to him. According to Chomsky, exposure to certain kinds of data and experience 'may be required to set the language-acquisition device into operation',[4] although without affecting the manner in which the device functions. As a parallel, Chomsky cites the fact that although depth perception in lambs appears to be facilitated by contact between the newborn lamb and its mother, there is no reason to suppose 'that the nature

[1] ibid., p. 600.
[2] N. Chomsky, *Aspects of the Theory of Syntax*, Cambridge, Mass. 1965.
[3] ibid., p. 30.   [4] ibid., p. 33.

of the lamb's "theory of visual space" depends on this contact'.[1] In a later paper,[2] Chomsky likened the problem of characterising the structure of a language-acquisition device to that of studying the 'innate principles' that make it possible for a bird to acquire the knowledge that finds expression in nest building or bird song. Like Lenneberg, he emphasised the importance of linguistic universals as evidence for innate features; but, more specifically, identified some of the theoretical constructs of the revised theory of trans-formational grammar, namely deep structures and transformational rules, as exhibiting a type of organisation present in all languages but significantly inexplicable in terms of *a priori* necessity. He pointed out the 'meagre evidence' available to the child in its lan-guage-acquisition task, and the 'degenerate' nature of that evidence. The child, according to Chomsky, learns the principles of sentence formation and interpretation on the basis of 'a corpus of data that consists, in large measure, of sentences that deviate in form from the idealised structures defined by the grammar that he develops'. By stressing the paucity and poor quality of the child's early experi-ence of his native language, Chomsky sought presumably to make the postulation of innate mechanisms appear necessary for explain-ing how the child could ever achieve success in the well nigh impos-sible task of becoming a fluent speaker.

This empirical assumption about the kind of primary linguistic data available to the child later proved, however, to be a serious weakness of the language-acquisition device theory. When detailed studies were carried out on the language samples available to young children,[3] it emerged indisputably that adults on the whole take great care over how they address the very young, using short, simple sentences, well formed grammatically, with clear intonation, and sentence boundaries well marked. As the child progresses in acquir-ing the language, the adult gradually uses syntactically more com-plex speech. Furthermore, the adult monitors the child's progress by means of frequent questions, and familiarises the child with con-versational patterns by slow and careful training in them. In short, the learning situation provides almost exactly the opposite of the

---

[1] ibid., p. 34.

[2] 'Recent contributions to the theory of innate ideas', reprinted in *The Philosophy of Language*, ed. J. R. Searle, Oxford 1971, pp. 121–9.

[3] A survey of the impact of this work is presented in W. J. M. Levelt, *What Became of LAD?*, Lisse 1975.

chaotic and fragmentary 'primary linguistic data' assumed by Chomsky's version of the child's task. Furthermore, once it becomes evident that the child progresses from exposure to what is in effect a very limited sublanguage, gradually enlarged over a period of time, the need to postulate initial possession of some very powerful device for analysing the complexities of adult speech dwindles.

The postulation of an innate language-acquisition device could also be used to explain why language is specific to *homo sapiens* and does not correlate either within the species or across species with other forms of apparently 'intelligent' behaviour. In a paper of 1963, Chomsky and Miller remark: 'After all, stupid people learn to talk, but even the brightest apes do not.'[1]

This observation aptly sums up an attitude from which the ethological concept of a language has derived a great deal of tacit support for a long time. Man's nearest evolutionary neighbours apparently did not have communication systems which at all approximated to languages. Any account such as that of Garner[2] who, in the late nineteenth century, claimed to have discovered that monkeys have a vocabulary of some forty words, was dismissed as unscientific. Furthermore, apes could not apparently be taught even the rudiments of a language. Attempts to teach non-human primates to talk had been made at various times throughout the twentieth century by reliable investigators, and all had failed more or less completely. In 1916, Furness reported having taught a young orangutan to say the two words *papa* and *cup*.[3] Yerkes and Learned[4] in 1925 reported failure in attempts to teach an ape to use an articulate syllable in order to ask for a banana. Gua, a female chimpanzee, was brought up for nine months by the Kelloggs in company with their own child, but uttered only two recognisably distinct types of noise, to express assent and fear respectively, by the time the experiment ended.[5] Eventually, in the early 1950s, Vicki, a chimpanzee brought up by the Hayes, managed to outstrip all her simian

[1] 'Finitary models of language users', *Handbook of Mathematical Psychology*, ed. R. D. Luce, R. R. Bush & E. Galanter, vol. 3, New York 1963.
[2] R. L. Garner, *The Speech of Monkeys*, 1892.
[3] W. H. Furness, 'Observations on the mentality of chimpanzees and orang-utans', *Proceedings of the American Philosophical Society*, LV, 1916, pp. 281–90.
[4] R. M. Yerkes and B. Learned, *Chimpanzee Intelligence and its Vocal Expression*, Baltimore 1925.
[5] W. N. & L. A. Kellogg, *The Ape and the Child*, New York 1933.

predecessors by mastering a vocabulary of some half a dozen words.[1]

The apparent implications of the inability of non-human primates to acquire a language were reinforced by their experimentally demonstrated aptitude in acquiring non-linguistic skills, particularly of a problem-solving character. The contrast between the respective ability and lack of ability was one which would be readily explained if apes, unlike human beings, possessed for purely genetic reasons no innate language-acquisition device. This might even have seemed at one time the only really plausible explanation for the failure of creatures so closely related to man to develop some rudimentary prototype of a language.

If so, it began to look like a much less plausible explanation during the late 1960s, when experiments were first begun by R. A. and B. T. Gardner to teach Ameslan, the American deaf-and-dumb sign language, to a young female chimpanzee called Washoe.[2] The progress made in these experiments soon confirmed that a principal factor in the previous failures of attempts to teach apes to talk lay in the physiological limitations of motor control over the primate's vocal apparatus, since by contrast the use of a gestural system proved to be very readily acquired.

More significantly, Washoe used the signs she had been taught in such a way as to suggest that they were not for her mere mimicry routines or circus tricks. In various respects, she operated with signs in ways quite analogous to a child's early use of words. She used signs in connexion with objects not only (i) when she wanted the object in question, but also (ii) in response to her trainer's signing 'What's that?', and (iii) spontaneously on seeing the object. She would also practise new or favourite signs on her own, in the absence of any corresponding stimulus.

Whereas the orang-utan trained by Furness to say *papa* and *cup* may well have used these words as indicators akin to proper names, Washoe showed an ability to distinguish signs functioning as proper

[1] K. J. Hayes & C. H. Nilson, 'Higher mental functions of a home-raised chimpanzee', in A. M. Schrier & F. Stollnitz (eds.), *Behavior of Nonhuman Primates*, vol. 4, New York 1971.

[2] B. T. & R. A. Gardner, 'Teaching sign language to a chimpanzee', *Science*, 1969, pp. 664–72; 'Two-way communication with an infant chimpanzee', in *Behavior of Nonhuman Primates*, ed. A. M. Schrier & F. Stollnitz, vol. 4, New York 1971, pp. 117–84; 'Early signs of language in child and chimpanzee', *Science*, 1975, pp. 752–3; 'Evidence for sentence constituents in the early utterances of child and chimpanzee', *Journal of Experimental Psychology: General*, 1975, pp. 244–67.

names, in the sense of being correlated with one particular object or person, and signs functioning as general words for a class. Thus she would apply the sign for *dog* to any dog, whether or not she had encountered that particular dog before. She could also spontaneously transfer the sign for an object to a picture of the object. In short, she soon mastered what had long been regarded in the Western intellectual tradition as the very foundation of man's expression of rational judgments, namely the distinction between particulars and universals. Moreover, she would use the sign for *open* in the presence of doors or boxes or taps that she wanted open for her, even though the physical process of 'opening' was quite different in the various cases, thus showing also an ability to conceptualise classes of action as well as classes of object.

Washoe began combining signs in sequences from the time when she had a repertoire of only eight or ten signs. She made very extensive use of combinations of the type 'More X', 'Gimmee X' and 'Go X', and the combinations did not have to be taught separately, but occurred freely as the appropriate occasion for them arose. In other words, she showed an ability to generate new combinations from a fixed stock of components. All her combinations 'made sense'. She showed no inclination to try out 'senseless' combinations of signs at random.

She designated new objects by using combinations of familiar signs, sometimes independently of teaching, and sometimes preferring a name of her own to the one she had been taught. Her own combination names were invariably 'sensible' choices. Finally, she also invented not merely her own sign combinations but her own basic signs, and used them consistently. By the age of 5 years, when she was cutting her milk teeth, Washoe had a basic vocabulary of 130 signs.

Subsequently to the Gardners' pioneering experiment with Washoe, other programmes using different training methods and different types of communication system, notably those of the Premacks[1]

[1] D. Premack, 'A functional analysis of language', *Journal of the Experimental Analysis of Behavior*, vol. 14, 1970, pp. 107–25; 'The education of Sarah', *Psychology Today*, vol. 4, 1970, pp. 55–8; 'On the assessment of language competence in the chimpanzee', in *Behavior of Non-human Primates*, ed. A. M. Schrier & F. Stollnitz, vol. 4, New York 1971; 'Language in the chimpanzee?', *Science*, 1971, pp. 808–22; D. & A. J. Premack, 'Teaching language to an ape', *Scientific American*, vol. 227, 1972, pp. 92–9; 'Teaching visual language to apes and language deficient persons', in *Language Perspectives: Acquisition, Retardation and Intervention*, ed. R. Schiefelbusch & L. L. Lloyd, Baltimore 1974.

and of the Yerkes Primate Research Centre,[1] have shown that the original achievements of Washoe were undoubtedly only a small sample of the potential range of communicational ability with signs which apes evidently share in common with *homo sapiens*. From an evolutionary perspective, this can hardly be said to be surprising, granted a broadly Darwinian view of evolution. What is of more immediate concern here is the academic impact of these experiments, and the role of the ethological concept of a language in the ensuing debates.

In view of these very remarkable achievements (remarkable by comparison with all previous experiments concerned with the linguistic capacities of non-human primates), what is all the more remarkable is the academic scepticism and even denigration which greeted Washoe's performance. It is significant that this scepticism came principally from scholars working in theoretical linguistics and in psycholinguistics—precisely those fields which might be said to have a vested professional interest in maintaining the credibility of the ethological concept of a language. Thus it was claimed, for example, that Washoe had not even achieved what was rather arbitrarily called 'Level I' in the human child's progress in language acquisition,[2] even though a comparison of the chimpanzee's performance in sign combination with a child's at this level showed that the chimpanzee achieved a higher score. It is also significant that Washoe's evident ability to achieve relevant conceptualisation on the basis of signs learned was discounted, and emphasis placed instead on whether or not she had acquired a grasp of abstract rules of syntax. For Chomsky's language-acquisition device was a mechanism which essentially ignored the content of linguistic signs and merely concentrated on the problem of producing them in the grammatically correct combinations. Thus from the start, the mysterious 'internal structure' of the language-acquisition device had been warped by a singularly narrow-minded view of linguistic skills projected into it from linguistic theory outside. This view insisted on the primacy and autonomy of purely syntactic knowledge, a bias particularly marked in the formative period of transformational grammar.

---

[1] Bibliography in *Language Learning by a Chimpanzee: the Lana Project*, ed. D. M. Rumbaugh, New York 1977.

[2] R. Brown, 'The first sentences of child and chimpanzee', *Psycholinguistics: Selected Papers*, New York 1970.

It has been argued¹ that the controversy over the language abilities of non-human primates bears witness to the belated realisation of the full implications of Darwinism in the behavioural sciences, reinforced by the rejection of an attitude towards nature which gives man a moral right to plunder natural resources, including other species, in the way which modern civilisation has come to take for granted. It is difficult not to believe that there is an important element of truth in this analysis. The ultimate dethroning of *homo sapiens* as the uniquely gifted living creature, supreme in virtue of his mastery of language and hence of reason, is evidently too far-reaching a scientific event not to be traumatic. It represents the latest of a long series of milestones set up by Copernicus, Galileo, Darwin, Freud, and others, marking stages in the progressive collapse of an entirely anthropocentric universe where man held a specially privileged position.

But once that has been said, a number of significant features in this particular chapter of intellectual history remain to be accounted for.

In the first place, recent nativism has found itself in conflict with at least two older versions of the ethological concept of a language. One of these provided a historical explanation for the fact that the languages of man are all alike in certain respects, by hypothesising that all are ultimately derived from the same primitive system. This originated at a point which, although remote in human cultural pre-history, was subsequent to the evolutionary divergence of *homo sapiens* from other primates.

Another version supposed that, even though there might not have been a common origin for the languages of man, they had evolved to fulfil essentially the same communicational functions for different human communities; and since the basic communicational requirements depend on man's general mental and physical capacities, which do not vary significantly as between one community and another, it is hardly surprising that language should, by responding to those needs, have evolved basically similar structures.

Nativists rejected these alternative explanations of the resemblances between languages as communication systems. What is interesting is not the arguments that were used, so much as the very spectacle of three equally unprovable theses competing as

¹ E. Linden, *Apes, Men and Language*, Harmondsworth 1976.

allegedly empirical explanations of the facts. That circumstance in
itself is more eloquent as to the nature of what was really at issue
than anything that was claimed on behalf of one side or another.
For it was apparent throughout that man's present state of knowledge, genetic, neurological and evolutionary, was simply not adequate to resolve the question with anything approaching certainty.
What was at issue was how best to provide psychological comfort
and intellectual justification for those defending certain attitudes
and positions which were becoming increasingly awkward to maintain as time went on.

The attractiveness of nativism was, on one level, that it provided
an ultimate reply to questions about the status of linguistics as a
science. If correct, it settled the issue which had been a constant
worry in modern linguistics since Saussure: namely, what linguistics
was, what defined its subject matter, and how it was demarcated
academically from neighbouring disciplines. For if mankind was
endowed with a genetically determinate language-acquisition
device, linguistics was ultimately studying an unquestionable reality,
a fact of nature. The theoretical linguist thereby became a scientist
ranking with the biologist, the physiologist, the biochemist and the
geneticist. He was at last free of the stigma of inventing his subject,
the stigma associated with Saussure's dismaying remark that in
linguistics it is the point of view that creates the object.[1] He could
claim to be engaged in something more fundamental than the mere
manipulation of mathematical systems for accommodating arbitrarily different types of language description. Nativism thus
offered an assurance which none of its rivals could match, since
they could not forge the vital link between languages and man's
physiological nature.

But, on a different level, it can be seen that what masqueraded as
linguistic nativism was ultimately something else. When the osten-
sible intellectual content of the nativist position is subjected to analysis what happens, as certain of its critics have pointed out,[2] is that
it gradually disappears in much the same way as an onion disappears
when subjected to peeling.

For example, nativists reacted with exaggerated suspicion and

---

[1] *Cours de linguistique générale*, 2nd ed., p. 23.
[2] E.g. M. Atherton & R. Schwartz, 'Linguistic innateness and its evidence', in *Innate
Ideas*, ed. S. P. Stich, Berkeley 1975, pp. 203–18.

even contempt to the achievements of Washoe and her peers; and this is curious on at least two counts. First of all, whether or not apes could master a language is, strictly speaking, irrelevant to the nativist thesis; or at least no more relevant than whether a language can be taught to a goldfish or a hedgehog. Talking hedgehogs would not invalidate nativism: all the nativist would need to do is promote the hedgehog to the rank of creature genetically endowed with a capacity for languages. Secondly, a demonstration that apes shared with man at least a partial capacity for languages ought, logically, to be welcomed with some eagerness by the nativist as collateral support, granted acceptance of the evolutionary affinity between *homo sapiens* and the other primates. This makes it all the more puzzling why 'the nativist response typically has been to deny that what the animal communicates with is really a language'.[1]

These are features which makes the debate so manifestly bizarre as to call for an explanation, in just the same way as the debate between Cratylus and Hermogenes, which opens the first chapter in European linguistics, is so manifestly bizarre as to call for an explanation. Both debates are explicable only in the light of their immediate political, social and academic background.

Part of that background in the more recent case involves a significant change in the position which language-using occupies in the human communicational spectrum. As a result of the 'communications revolution' of the twentieth century, the skills of reading and writing no longer have the special prestige in Western culture which they did a hundred years ago.[2] The printed word has lost its old power. In the end, it took less than a generation to destroy the influence of the newspaper as a social and political institution of modern society. Among the mass media, radio briefly resurrected the spoken word, only for television to reduce it to a selective accompaniment for information presented primarily in non-verbal form. For the first time in the history of literate societies, verbal encoding of information is itself challenged by the technical superiority of new audio-visual forms of transmission.

In the new communications age, speed of transmission alone

[1] ibid., p. 204.
[2] Himmelweit's 'principle of functional equivalence', which predicts that an established activity will tend to be replaced by a newer form which serves the same needs, but does so more cheaply or conveniently, has an application which ranges across the communicational spectrum (*Television and the Child*, pp. 35-6.)

renders the kind of linguistic patchwork presented by the map of Europe already an anachronism; just as its jigsaw of political frontiers is already outdated by the long-range missile. Linguistic divisions correspond less and less to divisions that are militarily or economically meaningful in the modern world.

Both the ancient debate over natural nomenclaturism and the modern debate over linguistic innateness were simultaneously product and symptom of Western man's involvement in an unprecedented complex of responsibilities. In ancient Greece, the responsibilities were those attendant upon a new form of social organisation: democracy. Today, the responsibilities are also those conferred by the potentialities of power. But the power in question is no longer confined within the political framework of the community.

If we wish to understand why belief in man's monopoly of language, having survived the Darwinian revolution, eventually came under attack when it did, the answer must be sought in the social, political and intellectual climate that has developed in the West since 1945.

In terms of politics, the period has been overshadowed by a struggle for supremacy between superpowers, which threatened at various moments to provoke a third world war. In terms of technology, it has been dominated by the increasing availability of weapons of such destructive power as to pose a substantive threat to the future of *homo sapiens* if they were ever used. The same technology, on the other hand, has also opened up the possibility of ending at last the long age of man's confinement to his native planet. At the same time, it has been a period of serious social tension and questioning, not only as regards the ethical basis of social divisions and institutions, and the morality of wielding world power, but more fundamentally as regards the rights and duties of civilised man in relation to his natural environment.

This quite unparalleled concomitance of potential mass self-destruction, potential conquest of space, pervasive moral doubts, and awareness of social failures could hardly fail to foster a deepening intellectual malaise, of which the controversy over language can be seen to provide a direct reflexion.

For what was needed was seemingly an impossibility, a simultaneous reassurance on quite divergent points. First, reassurance that language provided the means of making a mere agglomeration of individuals into a society in the fullest sense: a fellowship in which all shared a common understanding through participating in a common means of communication. Secondly, reassurance that language was not in the final analysis a barrier which must inevitably divide nation from nation and people from people, but a bond which afforded the basis for a potential brotherhood of man. Thirdly, reassurance that *homo sapiens* was not a lonely Caliban-figure, isolated in an otherwise languageless universe, alienated by the mysterious gift of tongues from all other living creatures.

The more modern analysis of man's linguistic abilities could provide one of those reassurances, the less it seemed able simultaneously to provide the others. How the concept of a language can fulfil a role consistent with these conflicting demands upon it remains the underlying dilemma of contemporary linguistics.

Bibliography

M. Atherton & R. Schwartz, 'Linguistic innateness and its evidence', *Innate Ideas*, ed. S. P. Stich, Berkeley 1975.

J. L. Austin, *How to do things with words*, ed. J. O. Urmson, Oxford 1962.

C. E. Bazell, 'The grapheme', *Litera*, no. 3, 1956.

B. B. Bernstein, 'Linguistic codes, hesitation phenomena and intelligence', *Language and Speech*, vol. 5, 1962.
'Social class, linguistic codes and grammatical elements', *Language and Speech*, vol. 5, 1962.
'A critique of compensatory education', *Education for Democracy*, ed. D. Rubinstein & C. Stoneman, Harmondsworth 1970.
'A brief account of the theory of codes', *Social Relationships and Language: Some Aspects of the Work of Basil Bernstein*, ed. V. Lee, Milton Keynes 1973.

M. Black, *The Labyrinth of Language*, Harmondsworth 1972.

L. Bloomfield, 'A set of postulates for the science of language', *Language*, vol. 2, 1926.
Language, London 1935.

R. Brown, 'The first sentences of child and chimpanzee', *Psycholinguistics: Selected Papers*, New York 1970.

T. Burrow, *The Sanskrit Language*, 2nd ed., London 1965.

G. L. Bursill-Hall, *Thomas of Erfurt: Grammatica Speculativa*, London 1972.

J. B. Bury, 'The age of illumination', *Cambridge Ancient History*, vol. v, 4th impr., Cambridge 1953.

Y. R. Chao, 'The non-uniqueness of phonemic solutions of phonetic systems', *Bulletin of the Institute of History and Philology, Academia Sinica*, vol. iv, part 4, 1934.

N. Chomsky, *Syntactic Structures*, The Hague 1957.
'A review of B. F. Skinner's *Verbal Behavior*', *Language*, vol. 35, 1959.
'Explanatory models in linguistics', *Logic, Methodology and Philosophy of Science*, ed. E. Nagel, P. Suppes & A. Tarski, Stanford 1962.

Aspects of the Theory of Syntax, Cambridge, Mass. 1965.

'Recent contributions to the theory of innate ideas', *The Philosophy of Language*, ed. J. R. Searle, Oxford 1971.

N. Chomsky & G. A. Miller, 'Finitary models of language users', *Handbook of Mathematical Psychology*, ed. R. D. Luce, R. R. Bush & E. Galanter, vol. 3, New York 1963.

L. J. Cohen, 'Do illocutionary forces exist?', *Symposium on J. L. Austin*, ed. K. T. Fann, London 1969.

H. B. Corstius (ed.), *Grammars for Number Names*, Dordrecht 1968.

C. Darwin, *The Descent of Man*, London 1871.

R. Etiemble, *Parles-vous franglais?*, Paris 1964.

G. Evans & J. McDowell (eds.), *Truth and Meaning*, Oxford 1976.

B. Farrington, *Greek Science*, vol. I, Harmondsworth 1944.

J. A. Fodor, *The Language of Thought*, Hassocks 1976.

K. Freeman, *Companion to the Pre-Socratic Philosophers*, 2nd ed., Oxford 1966.

G. Frege, *Logical Investigations*, ed. P. T. Geach, Oxford 1977.

K. von Frisch, 'Dialects in the language of the bees', *Animal Behavior*, ed. T. Eisner & E. O. Wilson, San Francisco 1975.

Y. L. Fung, *A History of Chinese Philosophy*, tr. D. Bodde, 2nd ed., Princeton 1952–3.

W. H. Furness, 'Observations on the mentality of chimpanzees and orang-utans', *Proceedings of the American Philosophical Society*, vol. LV, 1916.

B. T. & R. A. Gardner, 'Teaching sign language to a chimpanzee', *Science*, 1969.

'Two-way communication with an infant chimpanzee', *Behavior of Nonhuman Primates*, ed. A. M. Schrier & F. Stollnitz, vol. 4, New York 1971.

'Early signs of language in child and chimpanzee', *Science*, 1975.

'Evidence for sentence constituents in the early utterances of child and chimpanzee', *Journal of Experimental Psychology: General*, 1975.

H. Garfinkel, *Studies in Ethnomethodology*, Englewood Cliffs 1967.

R. L. Garner, *The Speech of Monkeys*, London 1892.

H. A. Gleason, *An Introduction to Descriptive Linguistics*, rev. ed., New York 1961.

J. P. Hailman, 'How an instinct is learned', *Animal Behavior*, ed. T. Eisner & E. O. Wilson, San Francisco 1975.

R. A. Hall, 'Linguistic theory in the Italian Renaissance', *Language*, vol. 13, 1936.

R. Harris, 'The Strasburg oaths: a problem of orthographic interpretation', *Revue de linguistique romane*, vol. XXXIV, 1970.

Z. S. Harris, *Methods in Structural Linguistics*, Chicago 1951.
'Distributional structure', *Word*, vol. 10, 1954.
K. J. Hayes & C. H. Nilson, 'Higher mental functions of a home-raised chimpanzee', *Behavior of Nonhuman Primates*, ed. A. M. Schrier & F. Stollnitz, vol. 4, New York 1971.
H. T. Himmelweit, A. N. Oppenheim & P. Vince, *Television and the Child*, Oxford 1958.
C. F. Hockett, 'Two models of grammatical description', *Word*, vol. 10, 1954.
A Course in Modern Linguistics, New York 1958.
J. R. Hurford, *The Linguistic Theory of Numerals*, Cambridge 1975.
L. H. Jeffery, *Archaic Greece*, London 1976.
O. Jespersen, *Language, its Nature, Development and Origin*, London 1922.
The Philosophy of Grammar, London 1924.
P. Juliard, *Philosophies of Language in Eighteenth-Century France*, The Hague 1970.
J. J. Katz, 'Analyticity and contradiction in natural language', *The Structure of Language*, ed. J. A. Fodor & J. J. Katz, Englewood Cliffs 1964.
J. J. Katz & J. A. Fodor, 'The structure of a semantic theory', *The Structure of Language*, ed. J. A. Fodor & J. J. Katz, Englewood Cliffs 1964.
H. Keil (ed.), *Grammatici Latini*, Leipzig 1855–1923.
W. N. & L. A. Kellogg, *The Ape and the Child*, New York 1933.
B. H. Kennedy, *The Shorter Latin Primer*, ed. Sir James Mountford, 3rd impr., London 1966.
G. Kennedy, *The Art of Persuasion in Greece*, Princeton 1963.
A. Kenny, *Wittgenstein*, London 1973.
N. Kretzmann, 'The main thesis of Locke's semantic theory', *History of Linguistic Thought and Contemporary Linguistics*, ed. H. Parret, Berlin/New York 1976.
D. Lawton, *Social Class, Language and Education*, London 1968.
V. Lee (ed.), *Social Relationships and Language: Some Aspects of the Work of Basil Bernstein*, Milton Keynes 1973.
W. R. Lee, *Language-Teaching Games and Contests*, Oxford 1965.
E. H. Lenneberg, 'The capacity for language acquisition', *The Structure of Language*, ed. J. A. Fodor & J. J. Katz, Englewood Cliffs 1964.
W. J. M. Levelt, *What Became of LAD?*, Lisse 1975.
C. I. Lewis, 'The modes of meaning', *Philosophy and Phenomenological Research*, vol. 4, 1944.
E. Linden, *Apes, Men and Language*, Harmondsworth 1976.
G. E. R. Lloyd, *Early Greek Science: Thales to Aristotle*, London 1970.

K. Lorenz, *King Solomon's Ring*, tr. M. K. Wilson, London 1961.

J. Lyons, *Introduction to Theoretical Linguistics*, Cambridge 1968.
'Human language', *Non-Verbal Communication*, ed. R. A. Hinde, Cambridge 1972.
Semantics, Cambridge 1977.

H. I. Marrou, *A History of Education in Antiquity*, tr. G. Lamb, London 1956.

J. S. Mill, *A System of Logic*, London 1843.

V. N. Misra, *The Descriptive Technique of Pāṇini*, The Hague 1966.

F. M. Müller, *Lectures on the Science of Language*, London 1861.

J. J. Murphy, *Rhetoric in the Middle Ages*, Berkeley 1974.

J. C. Nesfield, *Manual of English Grammar and Composition*, London 1898.

A. Ninio & J. Bruner, 'The achievement and antecedents of labelling', *Journal of Child Language*, vol. 5, 1978.

C. K. Ogden & I. A. Richards, *The Meaning of Meaning*, London 1923.

D. Parisi & C. Castelfranchi, *The Discourse as a Hierarchy of Goals*, Urbino 1976.

C. S. Peirce, *Collected Papers*, ed. C. Hartshorne & P. Weiss, Harvard 1931–5.

J. Piaget, *Le Structuralisme*, Paris 1968.

R. J. D. Power & H. C. Longuet-Higgins, 'Learning to count: a computational model of language acquisition', *Proceedings of the Royal Society*, 1978.

D. Premack, 'A functional analysis of language', *Journal of the Experimental Analysis of Behavior*, vol. 14, 1970.
'The education of Sarah', *Psychology Today*, vol. 4, 1970.
'On the assessment of language competence in the chimpanzee', *Behavior of Nonhuman Primates*, ed. A. M. Schrier & F. Stollnitz, vol. 4, New York 1971.
'Language in the chimpanzee?', *Science*, 1971.

D. & A. J. Premack, 'Teaching visual language to apes and language deficient persons', *Language Perspectives: Acquisition, Retardation and Intervention*, ed. R. Schiefelbusch & L. L. Lloyd, Baltimore 1974.

W. V. O. Quine, *From a Logical Point of View*, rev. ed., Cambridge, Mass. 1961.

L. D. Reynolds & N. G. Wilson, *Scribes and Scholars*, 2nd ed., Oxford, 1974.

M. Riffaterre, *Essais de stylistique structurale*, Paris 1971.

R. H. Robins, *A Short History of Linguistics*, London 1967.

R. Robinson, *Definition*, Oxford 1954.

W. D. Ross, *Plato's Theory of Ideas*, Oxford 1951.

D. M. Rumbaugh (ed.), *Language Learning by a Chimpanzee: the Lana Project*, New York 1977.

B. Russell, *An Inquiry into Meaning and Truth*, London 1940.

H. Sacks, 'Sociological description', *Berkeley Journal of Sociology*, no. 8, 1963.

J. E. Sandys, *History of Classical Scholarship*, 3rd ed., Cambridge 1921.

F. de Saussure, *Cours de linguistique générale*, 2nd ed., Paris 1922.

J. R. Searle, 'What is a speech act?', *The Philosophy of Language*, ed. J. R. Searle, Oxford 1971.

R. Simone, 'Sperone Speroni et l'idée de diachronie dans la linguistique de la Renaissance italienne', *History of Linguistic Thought and Contemporary Linguistics*, ed. H. Parret, Berlin/New York 1976.

J. F. Staal, 'The origin and development of linguistics in India', *Studies in the History of Linguistics*, ed. D. Hymes, Bloomington 1974.

D. Stampe, 'Cardinal number systems', *Proceedings of the 12th Annual Conference of the Chicago Linguistics Society*, 1976.

E. Stengel, 'Die ältesten Anleitungsschriften zur Erlernung der französischen Sprache', *Zeitschrift für neufranzösische Sprache und Literatur*, vol. I, 1879.

B. Stross, 'Speaking of speaking: Tenejapa Tzeltal metalinguistics', *Explorations in the Ethnography of Speaking*, ed. R. Bauman & J. Sherzer, Cambridge 1974.

W. H. Thorpe, 'The language of birds', *Animal Behavior*, ed. T. Eisner & E. O. Wilson, San Francisco 1975.

G. J. Warnock, *Berkeley*, Harmondsworth 1953.

J. B. Watson, *Behaviorism*, 2nd ed., London 1931.

H. G. Wells, *A Short History of the World*, rev. ed., Harmondsworth 1946.

A. N. Whitehead & B. Russell, *Principia Mathematica*, Cambridge 1910.

L. Wittgenstein, *Tractatus Logica-Philosophicus*, tr. D. F. Pears & B. F. McGuinness, 2nd ed., London 1971.

Philosophische Untersuchungen, tr. G. E. M. Anscombe, 2nd ed., Oxford 1958.

Notebooks 1914–1916, ed. G. H. von Wright & G. E. M. Anscombe, tr. G. E. M. Anscombe, Oxford 1961.

R. M. Yerkes & B. Learned, *Chimpanzee Intelligence and its Vocal Expression*, Baltimore 1925.

Index